# Confronting
# the Holocaust

Elie Wiesel

# Confronting the Holocaust

## The Impact of Elie Wiesel

Edited by Alvin H. Rosenfeld
and Irving Greenberg

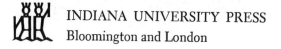

INDIANA UNIVERSITY PRESS
Bloomington and London

Library of Congress Cataloging in Publication Data
Main entry under title:
Confronting the Holocaust.

    Bibliography
    1. Wiesel, Elie, 1928–   —Religion and ethic—
Addresses, essays, lectures.  2. Wiesel, Elie,
1928–   —Knowledge—History—Addresses, essays,
lectures.  3. Holocaust, Jewish (1939–1945), in
literature—Addresses, essays, lectures.  4. Holocaust,
Jewish (1939–1945)—Moral and religions aspects—
Judaism—Addresses, essays, lectures.  I. Rosenfeld,
Alvin, 1938–  II. Greenberg, Irving, 1901–
PQ2683.I32Z65    813'.5'4    78-15821
ISBN 0-253-11290-7    1  2  3  4  5  82  81  80  79  78

# Contents

# The Contributors

Irving Abrahamson, *Kennedy-King College*
Michael Berenbaum, *Wesleyan University*
Terrence Des Pres, *Colgate University*
A. Roy Eckardt, *Lehigh University*
L. Eitinger, *Psykiatrisk Institutt, Universitet I Oslo*
Sidra Ezrahi, *Jerusalem, Israel*
Emil L. Fackenheim, *University of Toronto*
Irving Greenberg, *City College of New York*
Rosette Lamont, *Graduate School, City University of New York*
Lawrence L. Langer, *Simmons College*
André Neher, *Jerusalem, Israel*
Alvin H. Rosenfeld, *Indiana University*
John K. Roth, *Claremont Men's College*
Byron L. Sherwin, *Spertus College*

# Acknowledgments

We gratefully acknowledge the encouragement and support of the following, whose dedication to serious study of the Holocaust made possible the conference "The Work of Elie Wiesel and the Holocaust Universe":

Sigmund Strochlitz, *New London, Connecticut*

Joseph Feiner, *Tulsa, Oklahoma*

Irvin Frank, *Tulsa, Oklahoma*

Eugene Grant, *Mamaroneck, New York*

Simon Konover, *Hartford, Connecticut*

Stephen Muss, *Miami Beach, Florida*

Charles Rutenberg, *Belleair Bluffs, Florida*

Raphael Recanati, *New York, New York*

Sol Seltzer, *New York, New York*

Eli Zborowski, *Forest Hills, New York*

We also wish to thank Sara Suleri, for assistance in reading and helping to edit the manuscripts, and Susan Stryker, for typing them.

# Introduction

The Holocaust is an event of such magnitude that it creates an historical force-field of its own. Like other singular and transforming events, it has changed our way of being in the world and looking at it. The Holocaust shatters the ruling paradigm of modernity, forcing us to extend the limits of human nature to lower depths and greater heights. No other experience has so created, simultaneously, the sense of a radical absence of God and a breaking of the bands of self-sufficient secularity, thus opening the world to the possibility of divine presence.

The Holocaust Universe is so weighty that it forces light back on itself. It provokes expression only to reveal the poverty of our powers of articulation. This is so much the case that we are finally forced to ask: is it one of those giant red stars whose gravity distorts the light of perception or is it a black hole into which all matter is swallowed into oblivion and from which no light can escape?

Without exception, those of us who bring ourselves to reflect on the Holocaust are met by the most wrenching of paradoxes: the events must be recorded and remembered, yet language, our primary medium for such tasks, fails us when we most need it. In the words of Elie

Wiesel, who has struggled with this ambiguously revelatory nature of the Holocaust for more than a quarter of a century now, "How can we speak of it . . . how can we not speak of it?" There are no easy answers to this question, as any reader of Holocaust literature knows. Such readers know as well that these questions, while they present writers with the most formidable of obstacles, have not prevented the emergence of a considerable body of writing of the most compelling kind.

Within the precincts of this literature, Elie Wiesel occupies a position of preeminence, both for the sustained nature of his oeuvre and for its profundity. From the time of the publication of the autobiographical memoir *Night* (1958) to the latest collection of essays and short fictions, *A Jew Today* (1978), Wiesel has wrestled with the most disturbing and recalcitrant of historical, moral, and theological problems. In doing so he has, more than any other single writer of the postwar years, educated this generation to the absolute need not only to remember but continually to confront the anguish and mystery of the Holocaust. His writings have come to embody the witness and the crisis of facing this event.

The present book is a long-overdue attempt to extend this confrontation by addressing Wiesel's works themselves and the manifold issues that arise out of them and the Holocaust Universe at large. Since it is by now clear that no single "approach" to this subject will carry inquiry far enough, the editors have attempted to assemble studies of a variety of kinds—philosophical, theological, literary, and psychiatric. These several disciplines begin to show us the presence in Wiesel's work of both a remarkable phenomenology of the event and, at the same time, an unsettling and evocative commentary on its implications. Wiesel's own contribution to this volume, "Why I Write," adds what none of the other contributors could have provided—the most personal kind of reflection on what it means to be a writer after Auschwitz.

The growing interest in Elie Wiesel's writings came to expression first in a conference on "The Work of Elie Wiesel and the Holocaust Universe," convened by the National Jewish Conference Center in New York in September 1976. This conference brought together three generations of writers and scholars from all over the world and made manifest Wiesel's far-reaching influence as an author whose sustained literary encounter with the Holocaust carries implications for every field of scholarly work. The present volume seeks to extend and deepen the exploration of Wiesel's corpus and the problematics of Holocaust literature. Through it, we hope to encourage others to enter into a similar engagement even at the risk of disturbing long-held beliefs, attitudes, and methods. As Wiesel has taught us, anything less will be an inadequate response to living after this event.

# Confronting
# the Holocaust

Alvin H. Rosenfeld

# The Problematics of
# Holocaust Literature

Is there such a thing as Holocaust literature? By that I mean a literature that is more than topical, as, say, a literature of the sea or a literature of warfare might be considered merely topical. For if by Holocaust literature all we have in mind is a large but loosely arranged collection of novels, poems, essays, and plays about a *subject*, even one so enormous and unnerving as the Nazi genocide against the Jews, then our concerns, while interesting and legitimate enough, are not truly compelling. Topical studies of all kinds—of the family, of slavery, of the environment, of World War I or World War II—abound today, and while they can be individually engaging, their value does not and cannot transcend the limitations inherent in their definitions *as* topical literatures.

By contrast—and the contrast must be conceived of as being one of the first degree—Holocaust literature occupies another sphere of study, one that is not only topical in interest but that extends so far as to force us to contemplate what may be fundamental changes in our modes of perception and expression, our altered way of being-in-the-world. What needs to be stressed is this: the nature and magnitude

1

of the Holocaust were such as to mark, almost certainly, the end of one era of consciousness and the beginning of another. And just as we designate and give validity to such concepts as "the Renaissance mind" and "romantic sensibility" and "the Victorian temper" to indicate earlier shifts in awareness and expression, so, too, should we begin to see that Holocaust literature is a striving to express a new order of consciousness, a recognizable shift in being. The human imagination after Auschwitz is simply not the same as it was before. Put another way, the addition to our vocabulary of the very word Auschwitz means that today we *know* things that before could not even be imagined. How we are to live with such knowledge is another matter, but there is no denying that possessed with it or by it, we are, in some basic ways, *different* from what we might have been before. Different because we have been compelled to occupy a realm of experience—acknowledge a realism—that previously was understood as that of private invention alone, a realm conceived of as being entirely separate from and of another kind than that which might ever cross with historical event. With the advent of Auschwitz, the necessary distance that once prevailed between even the most extreme imaginings and human occurrence closes. Following upon that closure, the eye opens to gaze unbelievingly on scenes of life-and-death, death-and-life, which the mind cannot rationally accept or the imagination take in and adequately record. Stunned by the awesomeness and pressure of event, the imagination comes to one of its periodic endings; undoubtedly, it also stands at the threshold of new and more difficult beginnings. Holocaust literature, situated at this point of threshold, is a chronicle of the human spirit's most turbulent strivings with an immense historical and metaphysical weight.

I use the term "human spirit" quite deliberately here, acknowledging in full the awkwardness and imprecision inherent in the term, because I cannot but conceive of Holocaust literature, when taken in its most encompassing definition, except as an attempt to retrieve some ongoing life—posit a future tense—for whatever it is of human definition that remains to us. The bodies—that is to say, the people—are gone and cannot be rescued back to life; neither can meaning in the old sense, nor absolute faith, nor old-fashioned humanism, nor even the senses intact; yet the writers we are concerned with have argued in their writings—*by writing*—that an articulate life must be preserved. Writing itself, as we know from such a strongly determined work as Chaim Kaplan's diary, could be an effective counterforce to nihilism, not so much an answer to death as an answer to barbarism, a last-ditch means of approximating and preserving the human in the face of a viciousness poised to destroy it. As a result, the vicious and the barbarous could win only partial victories, destroy the living but not altogether submerge life. What remains is less than what perished but more than that which wanted to conquer and prevail. We do have the books while the night has nothing but itself.

Given these considerations, what can we say about the attitude that denies the validity or even the possibility of a literature of the Holocaust? In one of its earliest and by now most famous formulations, that of the eminent critic T. W. Adorno, this position states that it is not only impossible but perhaps even immoral to attempt to write about the Holocaust.[1] Adorno had poetry specifically in mind, moreover—perhaps just a single poem, the *"Todesfuge"* of Paul Celan, which struck him as being incongruously, and perhaps even obscenely, lyrical. As it happens, this poem is one of the great documents of Holocaust literature, but to Adorno it was hopelessly out of touch with its subject, as, he surmised, all such literature seemed destined to be. That judgment is re-echoed by the German critic Reinhard Baumgart, who objects to Holocaust literature on the grounds that it imposes artificial meaning on mass suffering, and, "by removing some of the horror, commits a grave injustice against the victims."[2] The point has also been reaffirmed in a recent pronouncement of denunciation by Michael Wyschogrod:

> I firmly believe that art is not appropriate to the holocaust. Art takes the sting out of suffering. . . . It is therefore forbidden to make fiction of the holocaust. . . . Any attempt to transform the holocaust into art demeans the holocaust and must result in poor art.[3]

Those who would know and could best judge the truth of this

assertion—the artists themselves—have on occasion spoken similarly, even if out of a different ground and for different reasons. Thus Elie Wiesel, whose writings perhaps more than any other's attest to the continuing possibility of Holocaust literature, has newly and pointedly spoke of its utter *impossibility*:

> One generation later, it can still be said and must now be affirmed: There is no such thing as a literature of the Holocaust, nor can there be. The very expression is a contradiction in terms. Auschwitz negates any form of literature, as it defies all systems, all doctrines. . . . A novel about Auschwitz is not a novel, or else it is not about Auschwitz. The very attempt to write such a novel is blasphemy. . . .[4]

The fact that such a view is put before us by an Elie Wiesel—and only that fact—renders it understandable and respectable, even if not acceptable. We know, for a dozen books by Elie Wiesel alone have now told us, that the Holocaust demands speech even as it threatens to impose silence. The speech may be flawed, stuttering, and inadequate, as it must be given the sources out of which it originates, *but it is still speech*. Silence has not prevailed—to let it do so would be tantamount to granting Hitler one more posthumous victory—just as night has been refused its dominion. If it is a blasphemy, then, to attempt to write about the Holocaust, and an injustice against the victims, how much greater the injustice and more terrible the blasphemy to remain silent.

What really is involved here is the deep anguish and immense frustration of the writer who confronts a subject that belittles and threatens to overwhelm the resources of his language. The writer's position is, in this respect, analogous to that of the man of faith, who is likewise beset by frustration and anguish and, in just those moments when his spirit may yearn for the fullness of Presence, is forced to acknowledge the emptiness and silence of an imposed Absence. The life centers of the self—intelligence, imagination, assertiveness—undergo paralysis in such moments, which, if prolonged, have the almost autistic effect of a total detachment or the profoundest despair. If it is out of or about such negative and all but totally silencing experience that proclamations are made about the disappearance of God or, its close corollary, the collapse of language, then of course one is moved to sympathize. Yet it is simply not possible to sympathize by indulging in silence, for to do so is to court madness or death. At just those points where, through some abiding and still operative reflex of language, silence converts once more into words—even into words *about* silence— Holocaust literature is born. Its birth, a testament to more than silence, more than madness, more even than language itself, must be seen as a miracle of some sort, not only an overcoming of mute despair but an assertion and affirmation of faith.

Faith in what? In some cases, perhaps in nothing more than human tenacity, the sheer standing fast of life in the face of a brutal death; in other cases, faith in the will to reject a final and wicked obliteration; in still others, faith in the persistent and all but uncanny strength of character to search out and find new beginnings. Given these dimensions of its existence and power, Holocaust literature, with all its acknowledged difficulties and imperfections, can be seen as occupying not only a legitimate place in modern letters but a central place. Long after much else in contemporary literature is forgotten, future generations of readers will continue to answer—by their very presence *as* readers—the question that ends Chaim Kaplan's diary: "If my life ends—what will become of my diary?"[5] It will stand to the ages—and not by itself but with other accounts of what happened to man in the ghettos and camps of Europe—as a testament of our times.

If it is possible to reply to the view that would deny the existence or validity of Holocaust literature, it is much harder to know how to read confidently or assess adequately such literature. The problems are many and, in some cases, hardly manageable at all. For instance, one begins by recognizing that the diaries, notebooks, memoirs, sketches, stories, novels, essays, poems, and plays that comprise Holocaust literature have been written in virtually all the languages of Europe, including, of course, Yiddish and Hebrew, the specifically Jewish languages. Holocaust literature is, in short, an international literature, and it would be the rare scholar indeed who could command all the tools necessary to investigate it in its fullest sweep. Literary scholarship in this area is unusually demanding, for the linguistic and cross-cultural requirements that are wanted far exceed those normally called into play for literary studies. As a result, most scholars will have to limit themselves, of necessity, to only some of the material they might want to read and, in addition, will have to rely to an unusual degree on translation. Obviously these are handicaps, and while they need not be ultimately discouraging, they are limiting.

Then there is the question of knowing *how* to read, respond to, and comprehend the kinds of material that come before us. The stress here must fall on "kinds" because it is almost certain that we confront the works of survivors in markedly different ways than we do the works of those who perished, just as we assume still another reading stance for writings about the Holocaust by those who were not there. Knowing what we do know—but what the authors themselves could not when they wrote—about the ultimate fates of a Chaim Kaplan or an Emmanuel Ringelblum or a Moshe Flinker, we do not take up their books with the same expectations and read them with the same kinds of responses as we do, say, the books of a Primo Levi or an Alexander Donat or an Elie Wiesel. The difference is not reducible solely to the dimension of tragic irony implicit in the writings of the first group but absent from those of the second; nor is it just that we read, react to, and interpret the dead with a greater deference or solemnity than the living, for within the context of Holocaust literature the living often carry a knowledge of death more terrible in its intimacy than that ever recorded in the writings of the victims. Who, in fact, *are* the real victims here, the dead or those cursed back into life again, guilt-ridden and condemned by a fate that would not take them?

Is it not the case that the most lacerating writings often belong to those who survived, not perished in, the Holocaust? The concern here is with the problem of survivorship and with trying to determine the reader's role in Holocaust literature, a role that seems more difficult and anguished when confronting the living than the dead. When, for instance, we read the diary of young Moshe Finker or Ringelblum's notebooks, we inevitably "complete" the narrative by bringing to the text material that it itself does not contain; we do that almost by reflex, filling in and interpreting with knowledge gained through biographical or historical notes. That is a wrenching but still possible act for the sympathetic imagination to perform. Oddly enough, the fact that it is *we* who are asked to perform it, and not the authors themselves, makes reading them somewhat more bearable, somewhat more possible. When, however, the task of not only recording but also interpreting, judging, and ever again suffering through the agony falls to a living writer—as it clearly does in the works of Elie Wiesel—then we are no longer talking about acts of sympathetic imagination but about something else, something that we do not have a name for and hardly know how to grasp. The nightmare, in a word, is never-ending, and repeats itself over and over again.

It is not for nothing that the Holocaust seems to expel certain writers from its provenance after a single book, that they are, from this standpoint, one-book authors. Did the curse of obsessive recurrence lift from them (consider, for example, the writing careers of André Schwarz-Bart or Jerzy Kosinski) or merely change its terms? If they have found their way to new fictional territory, what was the purchase price for their release? Why can an Elie Wiesel or a Ka-Tzetnik not pay it? These are problems—among other things, reader's problems—that we do not understand and have hardly even begun to take note of.

Here is a simple test: read Anne Frank's diary—one of the best-known but, as such things go, one of the "easiest" and most antiseptic works of Holocaust literature—and then read Ernst Schnabel's *Anne Frank: A Profile in Courage,*[6] which "completes" the work by supplying the details of the young girl's ending in Auschwitz and Bergen-Belsen. You will never again be able to rid your understanding of the original text of dimensions of terror, degradation, and despair *that it itself does not contain.* We need, but do not have, a suitable hermeneutics to explain that phenomenon and render it intelligible, just as we need, but do not have, a working theory of the miraculous to explain the mere existence of other texts. That certain books have come down to us at all is nothing short of astonishing, and we can never distance ourselves from an accompanying and transfiguring sense of awe as we encounter them. A manuscript written secretly and at the daily risk of life in the Warsaw ghetto, buried in milk tins or transmitted through the ghetto walls at the last moment, finally transmitted to *us*—such a manuscript begins to carry with it the aura of a holy text. Surely we do not take it in our hands and read it as we do those books that reach us through the normal channels of composition and publication. But how *do* we read it? At this point in the study of Holocaust literature, the question remains open-ended.

Other examples might be brought forth and additional problems raised, all with the aim of intentionally complicating our task. For if we do not make the effort to read Holocaust literature seriously, within the extraordinary precincts of its uncanny origins and problematic nature, we simply will never understand it. For instance, Emil Fackenheim not long ago suggested that eyewitness accounts of events may at times be less credible than studies made after the fact and by people at some distance from it. Although Fackenheim was incarcerated briefly at Sachsenhausen and thus was given first-hand knowledge of that camp, it was not until he read a study of Sachsenhausen years later, he admits, that he felt he truly understood what had taken place there and what he himself had experienced.[7]

The issue in this case is not analogous to the one that always obtains when a personal and perhaps "emotionally colored" account of experience is weighed against the "cooler" and more objective kinds of information gathered after the fact by the working historian. For, as Fackenheim came to understand only much later, a built-in feature of the Nazi camp system was deception of the victims, rendering accounts of the eyewitness in many cases less than reliable. The fictitious element of camp life—its pervasive irreality—was calculated to confuse and disarm the rational faculties, making the camp prisoners more pliable to their masters and hence more vulnerable to the diabolical system in which they were entrapped.

What does Fackenheim's case suggest about the relationship between proximity and authority in writings about the Holocaust? Normally we are willing to grant a greater validity to the accounts of those who were there, and to withhold it from—or grant it only reluctantly to—the writings of those who were not. Fackenheim's questions may bring us to revise these notions and to understand newly our measures not only of historical truth but of imaginative penetration and narrative effect as well. Within the contexts of Holocaust literature, in fact, the question of what constitutes *legitimacy* promises to become even more important as the years pass and direct access to events becomes impossible. But, as Fackenheim's statement already shows, even such direct access may not always reliably render up the truth.

And what about the truth of endings—writers' endings? Because Paul Celan and Tadeusz Borowski terminated their lives as they did, is it not the case that we are almost forced into a reader's stance vis-à-vis their stories and poems that we otherwise would not have and indeed do not want? Was suicide in each case an inevitable outcome of their work, a final and desperate conclusion to it, ultimately even a bitter evaluation of it? Was the self-destructive act of the man only and not of the writer? That such questions raise themselves at all means that we read these writers under a shadow of some kind—a different kind, incidentally, than the one that now hangs over the work of a Sylvia Plath or a John Berryman. (While their suicides also mediate between us and their books, one senses no historical determinism behind the personal anguish that must have led them to take their lives; the pressure to which they succumbed seems to have been biographically generated, its pain not larger than that of the single life.)

Kafka said that we are usually too easy on ourselves as readers, that we should choose books that ask more of us than we normally are willing to give. "We must have those books," he wrote, "which come upon us like ill-fortune, and distress us deeply, like the death of one we love better than ourselves, like suicide. A book must be an ice-axe to break the sea frozen inside us."[8] To make that formulation, Kafka must have been a great reader, as well as a great hungerer (in his case the two are really one), and yet, despite all his intense suffering and estrangement, he was spared the worst that the twentieth century was to bring upon writers such as Celan and Borowski. Had Kafka known them, could he still have spoken in the terms just cited above? When, in a writer's life, suicide becomes not a metaphor for something but the thing itself, we grow more cautious and defensive as readers and do not so readily welcome the kinds of hard blows that Kafka exhorts upon us. Better to read warily and keep the seas of empathy inside us safely frozen awhile longer.

By now the point should be clear: we lack a phenomenology of reading Holocaust literature, a series of maps that would guide us on our way as we picked up and variously tried to comprehend the writings of the victims, the survivors, the survivors-who-become-victims, and the kinds-of-survivors, those who were never there but know more than the outlines of the place. Until we devise such maps, our understanding of Holocaust literature will be only partial, well below that which belongs to full knowledge.

One conclusion to these questions is that we are yet to develop the kind of practical criticism that will allow us to read, interpret, and evaluate Holocaust literature with any precision or confidence.[9] Older criticisms of whatever orientation or variety—Freudian, Marxist, formalist, structuralist, or linguistic—will not do here for any number of reasons. The largest is that the conception of man, or world view, embodied in psychoanalysis or dialectical theory or theories of aesthetic autonomy had almost no place in the ghettos and camps, which were governed by forces of an altogether different and far less refined nature. As a result, it would seem a radical misapplication of method and intentions to search through literary accounts of Auschwitz or the Warsaw ghetto for covert Oedipal symbols, class struggle, revealing patterns of imagery and symbolism, mythic analogies, or deep grammatical structures. Auschwitz no more readily reduces to these considerations than death itself does.

Nor will it do to confine understanding within a framework of literary history that would tend to see Holocaust literature as part of the literature of warfare-in-general or even of World War II. There are novels eligible for such study, including certain novels by Jewish writers, such as Irwin Shaw's *The Young Lions*, Norman Mailer's *The Naked and the Dead*, or Herman Wouk's *The Caine Mutiny*. Each of these books will be of interest to students of the Second World War, but the interest will be the topical one that I referred to earlier and not that which belongs to our subject.

The distinction—a hard one that needs to be held firmly in mind— has an illuminating parallel within historical writings about the period. In a newly published history of the Second World War written by A. J. P. Taylor, for instance, I find a total of two pages out of two hundred and thirty-five devoted to the Holocaust, this despite the fact that the author concludes his four-paragraph summary by stating that "the memory of Oswiecim and the other murder camps will remain when all the other achievements of the Nazi Empire are forgotten."[10] Given that view—a correct one—it seems shocking at first that Taylor would mention the Holocaust only, as it were, in passing. And yet he is not entirely wrong to do so, for to do otherwise would be to see the war against the Jews as an integral part of World War II. More and more it seems that it was not, neither in intention, nor in kind, nor in outcome. The war against the Jews may have occupied some of the same dimensions of time and space as World War II, but it was not fought as a logical part of that war, nor can the literature it generated be compared to or profitably studied with the topical literature of the Second World War. Holocaust literature is simply and complexly something else, as the cataclysm that triggered it was something else, and not part of the general storm that swept over Europe four decades ago.

In referring to such extreme cases we tend to use the language of weather, but the analogy with earthquakes and storms will finally not hold; nor will most other analogies. That precisely is part of the problem. It supports the view that we must make distinctions between the literature of the Holocaust and the literature of general warfare, including that of World War II. This is not to belittle those books that belong to this other literature or to suggest that the Great Wars of our century did not pose their own problems for writers. Clearly they did. The First World War in particular came with an enormous jolt and hardly presented itself to the grasping intelligence in neatly formed and easily apprehensible ways. Hemingway wrote that among the casualties of that war were "the words 'sacred,' 'glorious,' and 'sacrifice' and the expression 'in vain,'" that these were words he "could not stand to hear," and that "finally only the names of places had dignity."

Hemingway's loss was huge, the collapse of a whole idealistic code that once sustained life by giving it a measure of purpose and honor. In reading his fiction of the Great War, it does not take much to realize that Hemingway was saying farewell to far more than arms.

To what, though, was the young Elie Wiesel saying farewell when, in an often quoted and by now famous passage from *Night*, he wrote that he will never forget the flames that turned the bodies of children "into wreaths of smoke beneath a silent blue sky," the flames that consumed his faith forever?[11] What was his loss when, in turning the pages of an album of Holocaust photographs, he made this monstrous discovery:

> At every page, in front of every image, I stop to catch my breath. And I tell myself: This is the end, they have reached the last limit; what follows can only be less horrible; surely it is impossible to invent suffering more naked, cruelty more refined. Moments later I admit my error: I underestimated the assassin's ingenuity. The progression into the inhuman transcends the exploration of the human. Evil, more than good, suggests infinity.[12]

For that plunge to the bottom of a final knowledge, that fall into a wicked and savage clarity, we simply have no analogy, except perhaps to hell—a possibility that we shall have occasion to pursue a little later. For now, though, I think we must accept as a given the proposition that the Holocaust was something new in the world, without likeness or kind, a truth that was set forth years ago in a forceful and memorable poem by Uri Zvi Greenberg:

> Are there other analogies to this, our disaster that came to us at their
>     hands?
> There are no other analogies (all words are shades of shadow)—
> Therein lies the horrifying phrase: No other analogies!
> For every cruel torture that man may yet do to man in a Gentile
>     country—
> He who comes to compare will state: He was tortured like a Jew.
> Every fright, every terror, every loneliness, every chagrin,
> Every murmuring, weeping in the world
> He who compares will say: This analogy is of the Jewish kind.[13]

There have been attempts to find analogies—with Job, with the destruction of the Second Temple, with the *Akeda*, with the concepts of *Kiddush ha-Shem* or the Thirty-Six Righteous Men who uphold the world—and, to the extent that such allusions and antecedents have allowed certain writers at least a partial grasp of the tragedy, it would seem that we must qualify the notion that the Holocaust was altogether without parallels. On closer examination, however, it becomes clear in almost all cases that the gains in perspective are only temporary and provisional, for what inevitably emerges in Holocaust literature is that such analogies are introduced only to reveal their inadequacy, and they are in turn either refuted or rejected as being unworkable. Schwartz-Bart, for instance, ultimately shows us the *exhaustion* of the tradition of the *Lamed Vov* rather than its continuing usefulness, just as Elie Wiesel will time and again adopt the stance of a Job only to find that it will not serve. In the end he will have to stand alone, rooted in the solitary ground that became his the moment he was struck by the isolating knowledge that "the Holocaust defies reference, analogy."[14] It must have been this realization more than any other that led Wiesel to remark that "by its nature, the Holocaust defies literature,"[15] an incapacitating insight that a writer *as* writer simply cannot tolerate and that this writer has been struggling against in book after book, sometimes winning his way through, at other times all but succumbing.

As Wiesel's case shows, the implications of a literature without antecedents or analogy are frightening in the extreme, for our whole conception of literature insists on recognizing its traditional base, and, as such, affirms that writing grows as much from within as from without. A poem or a novel, that is to say, is not a new and wholly undetermined thing—a sudden and unprecedented appearance in the world —but bears some necessary relationship to other poems and novels that have gone before and, in some sense, have sired it. While every good piece of writing must be, in its way, an original act of creation, all literature is formed as much from reactions to an antecedent literature as from more direct or unmediated reactions to life. A poem descends from other poems, a novel from other novels, a play from other plays.

Whether we know it or not, we read and understand literature exactly in this way, with implicit reference to and analogy with prior texts. Indeed, we could not begin to read at all, nor could writers write, if that were not so. Our whole fund of literacy, in short, comes into play in reading.

Yet when we confront those texts that are our concern here, we sooner or later find ourselves without the expected and necessary moorings in a familiar literary landscape, and, as a result, it is sometimes hardly possible to know how to proceed. Lost in a place whose dimensions we cannot easily recognize, let alone acknowledge as our own, we strive for orientation through intimacy with the common and familiar things of the world, but grasp only fog. The object in our hands looks like a book but seems to have turned into something else.

Some contrasting examples from past literature can be instructive here. Even a casual reader of Edgar Allan Poe or Franz Kafka, for instance, knows that a literature of terror and radical estrangement is not exclusively a product of the post–World War II decades. Read Poe's "The Pit and the Pendulum" or Kafka's "In the Penal Colony" and you will have all the terror you might want. Poe, in particular, relished macabre sensations and "the exquisite terror of the soul," and was gifted at finding precise literary correlatives for them. That is why to this day the best of his stories possess the power to "thrill" and "haunt" us with simulations of extreme psychic torment. It was his subject, and he went about developing it with all the props and atmospherics of the Gothic romance or early symbolist fiction—a whole catalogue of literary horrors that will please and stimulate the imagination with fright. Yet at no time in reading Poe do we ever come to believe that the fantasy world we are invited to enter—his "dream kingdom"—is the "real" world, the phenomenal world of our day-to-day existence. We know that Poe is inventing, that at his best he is a gifted inventor, that his literary inventions possess a stark psychological power and can grip us, at times, mightily. In short, we pretty well know how to read him.

Kafka is a deeper and more complicated writer, one who is still far enough ahead of us to render his works less accessible to full and confident understanding. In his case, we may recognize affinities with an antecedent literature of the grotesque or absurd, but to read him in these terms does not carry us very far, just as it finally will not do to reduce his more enigmatic parables and stories to the critical categories of symbolism or expressionism or surrealism. While Kafka seems to embody elements of all of these, he simultaneously transcends them, so that in the end he is only what we have come to call, inadequately and at the risk of tautology, "Kafkaesque." Let us admit that we have not yet entirely caught up with him and, as a result, he is a far more dangerous writer for us than Poe.

Nevertheless, even in Kafka's case—as, say, in "In the Penal Colony" or "The Metamorphosis"—we are never led to abandon altogether our hold on a normative, stabilizing sense of things, on the saving power of the mundane. We may be released by his fiction into a universe of absurd and frightening proportions, but it is a highly *composed* universe, and while few would welcome a prolonged residence there, it is not a totally alien place. Kafka possessed the power, in fact, to domesticate us rather easily to his strange but familiar world, and we can cross back and forth between it and what we perhaps too comfortably call "reality" without paying an ultimate price in credulity. In its depictions of a mechanized or technological terror, of a reigning injustice, of brutal and systematic and causeless punishment, of an accepted guilt and passivity before annihilation, "In the Penal Colony" is an uncanny prefiguration of Holocaust literature, a premonitory text. Nevertheless, in reading it we are still a step or two away from a direct knowledge of *history* as Holocaust, and no reader of the novella would confuse the infernal torture machine that is its elaborate centerpiece with the actual machinery of Auschwitz or Treblinka, just as no reader of "The Metamorphosis" would accept Gregor Samsa's transformation into a giant insect as a change that could ever actually overtake him. We accept these intricate literary devices as complex acts of initiation—a series of bridges that we must cross to enter the Kafkaesque world—and once we acknowledge them as such, we are usually content to let the stories take over and develop in their own terms. Since we do not read Kafka within predominantly realistic or naturalistic frameworks, credulity is not unduly strained by these inventions, which we recognize as the components of a profoundly disturbing but nevertheless fictional universe.

What happens, though, when we enter *l'univers concentrationnaire* and come upon the kind of metamorphosis cited earlier, one in which living children are suddenly tranformed into wreaths of smoke? What is our interpretive frame of reference for *that*? One finds nothing like it in Poe or Kafka or any other literary precursor I know, including the Marquis de Sade. Since it is altogether too disorienting to acknowledge such writing as a piece of realism, one perhaps tries initially to shift the terms into the language of dreams—of some inverted symbolism or dark allegory. Yet these are evasive gestures, strategies of defense, and ultimately they must be abandoned in order to perform a reluctant and all but impossible act—*reading*—which in this case means acknowledging a truth that we do not want to be true. How, after all, can we accept a realism more extreme than any surrealism yet invented? It is one thing to grant Kafka the artistic liberty he needs to write "The Metamorphosis," changing a man into a bug, but it is something else again entirely—and altogether too much for rational belief—when Elie Wiesel writes of children being metamorphosed into smoke. Yet that is what is presented to us in *Night*, presented moreover in such a way as to permit us to read it on one level only—the literal one—the level of plainly declared, unencumbered truth. This, we are told, is what happened. It has no symbolic dimensions, carries no allegorical weight, possesses no apparent or covert meaning. Do not think about it in terms of Ovid or Poe or Kafka, for the mythical or metaphorical aspects of their writings do not  come into play here; nor does anything else you have ever read before. Know only one thing—the truth of what happened—which sounds like this:

> Not far from us, flames were leaping up from a ditch, gigantic flames. They were burning something. A lorry drew up at the pit and delivered its load—little children. Babies! Yes, I saw it—saw it with my own eyes . . . those children in the flames.[16]

Has there ever before been a literature more dispiriting and forlorn, more scandalous than this? Who would not erase it at once from memory? Yet we must stay with these words, or with others like them, in an effort to determine one of the distinguishing characteristics of Holocaust literature.

In order to do that, I turn briefly from prose to poetry and offer two short poems. The first was written in the nineteenth century by Henry David Thoreau; the second, written closer to our own day, is by the Yiddish poet Jacob Glatstein. The poems carry the same title: "Smoke." Here is Thoreau's:

> Light-winged Smoke, Icarian bird,
> Melting thy pinions in thy upward flight,
> Lark without song, and messenger of dawn,
> Circling above the hamlets as thy nest;
> Or else, departing dream, and shadowy form
> Of midnight vision, gathering up thy skirts;
> By night star-veiling, and by day
> Darkening the light and blotting out the sun;
> Go thou my incense upward from this hearth,
> And ask the gods to pardon this clear flame.

Among the first observations one makes about this poem is that, in writing it, Thoreau had little interest in smoke *as* smoke but rather was attracted to it as the base for his transfiguring imagination, which loved to dissolve phenomena into fanciful patterns of thought. The poem, that is to say, employs its central figure in a clearly metaphorical sense, likening the smoke to other things—to birds, to the mythical Icarus, to dreams and clouds, finally to incense. Through this series of delicate imagistic changes, the poem develops the author's sense of the fugitive and transient quality of life. It is a finely wrought if uncomplicated poem, one that holds closely to classical patterns of poetic rhetoric, and therefore presents no particular problems to interpretation.

Compare it to Glatstein's "Smoke" (in the original Yiddish title, "*Roikh*"), which I quote now in an English translation:

> From the crematory flue
> A Jew aspires to the Holy One.
> And when the smoke of him is gone,
> His wife and children filter through.
>
> Above us, in the height of sky,
> Saintly billows weep and wait.
> God, wherever you may be,
> There all of us are also not.[17]

This, too, is a fine poem, but what is it saying? In the opening
lines it describes a Jew ascending to his God through a chimney, followed soon after by his wife and children passing upward in the same
way. The poem says that they do so by turning into smoke; moreover,
it says so with a certain jauntiness of rhythm—the hippety-hop of
nursery school jingles—and the playfulness of rhyme. Is it a children's
poem of some kind? It is not inconceivable that a reader who chances
upon this poem a hundred years from now might ask such questions,
for there are elements here that call them forth. They do so, however,
only to disabuse us rather quickly of our innocence, for before very
long we will see that the sprightliness of rhythm and rhyme serves as
a trap, the apparent lightheartedness only a lure to draw us forward into
the poem's deadly center.

In searching to locate this center, we are soon brought to see that
the entire poem is predicated upon the author's certain knowledge
that we will recognize and be able to name the crime that resides behind or before words, in the silence that the poem was written to break.
The unspoken but unmistakable ground of this poem, that is to say,
is the Holocaust—our impoverished term for the cruelty that overtook
the Jew and turned him into smoke.

Now we have just looked at a poem about smoke and recognized
that it served as a source of considerable metaphorical richness and
variety. Thoreau changed the smoke into birds and clouds and religious incense, into a whole flock of wafting and melting and dissolv-
ing images. Glatstein, far from doing that, does the opposite: he
changes the Jew into smoke. Worse yet—and at this point the poem
turns into something else, something new in the history of poetry—he

does so in a way that has *nothing at all to do with metaphor*, a dis-abling fact that he forces upon us from the start. To read this poem at all, we must disown the figurative use of language, then, and interpret literally: the Jew has become smoke, and a similar fate will overtake his wife and children. Thereafter Glatstein will add a religious dimension to his poem, at which point we recognize play of another kind, that of Jewish speculative theology. The poem ends, in fact, on a note of theological paradox: the destroyed Jews will become absent company for an Absent God. Their "aspiration," or ascent, however, must not be understood in the first place in terms of paradox or fantasy or anything else that would detract from the brutal literalness of their end. For an exact parallel to their fate, remind yourselves of that casual but unforgettable moment in Hochhuth's *The Deputy* when the Doctor remarks, quite matter-of-factly, that "On Tuesday I piped the sister of Sigmund Freud up the chimney."[18]

It is all too strange but, at the same time, it is powerfully affecting. The poem, as we come to realize, is an assertion about a negation, a *double* negation: that of man and that of God. Both in this poem *are not*. Is there also a triple negation implied, the third loss being that of poetry itself? For what kind of poetry can we have that eschews the metaphorical use of language? The answer to this question compels us to recognize one of the deepest and most distinguishing characteristics of Holocaust literature and to state what may be one of its abiding laws: *there are no metaphors for Auschwitz, just as Auschwitz is not a metaphor for anything else*. Why is that the case? Because the flames were real flames, the ashes only ashes, the smoke always and only smoke. If one wants "meaning" out of that, it can only be this: at Auschwitz humanity incinerated its own heart.[19] Otherwise the burnings do not lend themselves to metaphor, simile, or symbol—to likeness or association with anything else. They can only "be" or "mean" what they in fact were: the death of the Jews.

The only knowledge we are left with, then, is this: in our own day, annihilation overleapt the bounds of metaphor and was *enacted* on earth. Is it possible to make poetry out of that? Insofar as it is a poem that has led us to this question, the answer, clearly, must be yes.

Poetry—in this instance, a something about nothing, an assertion about a negation—survives to remind us of all that has been destroyed. And also to remind us of what has not been destroyed, for while it is true that Holocaust literature is nothing if not language in a condition of severe diminishment and decline, it is still capable of articulating powerful truths—if none other, then those that reflect life in its diminishment and decline. We have lost so much, but not yet the power to register what it is that has been taken from us.

Surely that is one of the major functions of Holocaust literature, to register and record the enormity of human loss. "For me," as Elie Wiesel once stated, "writing is a *matzeva*, an invisible tombstone, erected to the memory of the dead unburied."[20] There is no denying the nobility of that conception of art nor the importance of its execution. Yet a tombstone is not a literary genre, and part of Wiesel's problem as a writer, as of all writers of the Holocaust, is to discover the literary forms most appropriate to representing the extremities of dehumanization and heroism that together begin to define what the Holocaust was.

In this connection, we must begin by recognizing that even before the advent of a literature of the Holocaust, the major literary genres were in a weakened state of flux and great uncertainty. Holocaust literature, which places its own heavy burdens on literary forms of all kinds, arrived, in fact, at a time when considerable doubt was already being raised about the ongoing viability of the narrative, dramatic, and lyrical modes. While it is not possible here to rehearse adequately the troubled state of modern fiction, drama, and poetry, it can be stated that a large part of the trouble derives from an increasingly felt imbalance between what the world daily offers us as raw data and the mind's ability to make sense of it through its own conceptual and inventive capacities. This imbalance reached its most extreme point in Nazism's campaign of terror and destruction against the Jews. In the ghettos and camps of Europe "reality" underwent so radical a distortion as to disarm and render no longer trustworthy the normal cognitive and expressive powers. As a result, reason seemed to give way to madness, as language did time and again to silence. When those thresholds dissolve, literature—a product of the composed mind and senses—is reduced to screams and whimpers: *it decomposes*. And there is no escaping the fact that, in part, Holocaust literature is a literature of decomposition. "No, this is not life!" runs the familiar refrain in Chaim Kaplan's diary. Although Kaplan had lived in Warsaw for forty years and must have come to know it well, the city's transformation under Nazi rule into a place of madness and slaughter disoriented him almost totally. "At times," he wrote, "it seems to me that I am in an alien land, entirely unknown to me." At other times his sense of displacement exceeded anything even resembling the terrestrial, so that it appeared "the ghetto was suspended over nothingness."[21]

That strain of irreality runs throughout Holocaust literature and continually undermines it. "Today at this very moment as I sit writing at a table, I am not convinced that these things really happened."[22] The confession in this instance is Primo Levi's, but it speaks a common truth, one known to all writers of the Holocaust and one as well that quite obviously subverts the writer's enterprise. For what literary means—what mere words—could possibly compete with the extravagant inventiveness of Nazism? In that time when day was ruled over by the twisted sun of the swastika and night by the dominant black of the Death's Head, life itself became a kind of macabre theatre. Nazism was far more than that, of course, was nothing less than an unrestrained plague of steel and flame, but it also worked in more subtle ways, preparing its ultimate terror by intermediary steps of manipulative distortion and deception. In this respect it might legitimately be grasped within the terms of literary fabrication, terms that a Joseph Goebbels or a Leni Riefenstahl was intimate with. Moreover, it is not difficult to locate the imaginative sources of this aspect of its genius. George Steiner pointed to them quite specifically and also quite accurately, I think, when he argued that Nazism was a literal staging of hell on earth, a perception confirmed by virtually all writers of Holocaust literature.[23] Hell as a prototype of the ghettos and death camps—that, it seems, was Christianity's distinctive contribution to the Final Solution, although one would hope to understand it as a Christianity turned against itself, in rebellion against itself and its own deepest principles.

In this paradigm of ethical and religious subversion, we may be able to discover a literary paradigm as well, one that is constant enough in Holocaust literature to constitute another of its governing laws. To grasp it, we must understand the revisionary and essentially antithetical nature of so much of Holocaust writing, which not only mimics and parodies but finally refutes and rejects its direct literary antecedents. The *Bildungsroman*, as Lawrence Langer has demonstrated, is one of these.[24] In such a book as *Night*, the traditional pattern of successfully initiating a young boy into social life and his own maturity is altogether reversed. Primo Levi's *Survival in Auschwitz*, which chronicles the devolution of a man, is a more complicated instance of the same thing. In both cases one sees not only the reversal of a familiar literary pattern but also a repudiation of the philosophical basis on which it rests. Wiesel defined that for us precisely when he concluded that "at Auschwitz, not only man died, but also the idea of man."[25] With the crumbling of that idea, all narrative forms that posit the reality of *persons*—rational, educable, morally responsible beings—are undermined and perhaps even invalidated. Yet such personal narratives of the Holocaust as the two just mentioned necessarily depend upon the traditional means of memoir, autobiography, and *Bildungsroman*, even though the stories they relate rewind the progress of growth *backwards*—from life toward death. I do not know that Wiesel and Levi consciously chose to counterpose their terrifying accounts of dehumanization against forms that are essentially civilized and humane, but the effects of such a jarring contrast are unmistakable and strongly felt in their books.

In the case of Paul Celan, it is clear that an attitude of repudiation was not only consciously held but specifically developed as a technique for writing post-Holocaust poetry. The evidence, as Jerry Glenn has shown,[26] is everywhere—in the ironically destructive allusions to the Songs of Songs and Goethe's Faust in *"Todesfuge"*; in the radical undoing of Hölderlin's famous hymn "Patmos" in *"Tenebrae"*; in the denial of the Genesis account of God's creation of man in *"Psalm."* In each of these cases (and many similar ones could be brought forward), Celan employs a technique of literary subversion that the German critic Götz Wienold has called a *"Widerruf."*[27] We have no precise English equivalent for the term—"repudiation" comes closest —but it is not difficult to explain through an illustrating example.

Consider, for instance, this line from Chaim Kaplan's diary: "The enemy of Israel neither sleeps nor slumbers."[28] Kaplan wrote that, almost certainly, not out of a mood of blasphemy but as an expression of genuine religious despair. It appears in his pages in an entry dated "October 12, 1940/End of Yom Kippur, 5701." On that very day the edict to establish the ghetto went into effect. The year before, at the end of Yom Kippur 5700, Kaplan noted in his diary that "on the Day of Atonement the enemy displayed even greater might than usual," employing its artillery to destroy and kill at random. In the intervening year the bombardments only got worse, and it became clear to Kaplan that Warsaw Jewry was to face complete destruction. "Is this the way the Almighty looks after His dear ones?" he asks. "Has Israel no God?" He could not admit that, so on Yom Kippur 5701 he gathered with his fellow Jews, "like Marranos in the fifteenth century," to pray secretly and illegally for God's forgiveness and mercy. What Jewish Warsaw received, however, was not the protection of the Guardian of Israel but the ghetto edict, which then and there effectively sealed the fate of hundreds of thousands of Polish Jews. Kaplan's profound shock at this reversal registers in that terrible line—"The enemy of Israel neither sleeps nor slumbers"—a few words only but enough to show a whole sustaining faith come crashing down. The entry for "October 24, 1940/ The night of Simhat Torah, 5701" brings the matter to its bitter conclusion: "But he who sits in Heaven laughs."[29]

In Kaplan's case, it would make no sense to identify such expressions of forlornness and raw pain as examples of "technique," if by that we imply a conscious literary method. Kaplan, a highly literate Jew, composed his diary in Hebrew and quite naturally thought in a language pervaded by biblical and Talmudic passages. These influences never drop from his prose, but, as he witnessed the level of Nazi barbarism rise in the ghetto, they undergo inversion, substitution, and reversals. In brief, they are demoralized, destabilized, subverted. Writing under this kind of pressure becomes countercommentary.

Celan, uneducated to Talmud but a sophisticated modern poet, adopted these changes deliberately and developed them technically in his poems. The Yiddish poet Jacob Glatstein frequently did the same. I suspect that André Schwarz-Bart worked somewhat similarly in writing *The Last of the Just,* a novel that should be understood, I believe, not only as an exhaustion of the Jewish tradition of the *Lamed-Vov* but of the Christian traditions of the saint's life and the *imitatio Christi* as well. In *The Painted Bird* Jerzy Kosinski will appropriate some of the language of the New Testament and Christian liturgy only to undermine it and invalidate its claims to permanent religious truth. Rolf Hochhuth will do the same in his highly charged and controversial play, which, among other things, offers itself as a contemporary rewriting of the lives of the popes.

The common element in all these examples is the employment of the literary text as refutation and repudiation, a denial not only of an antecedent literary assertion but also of its implicit premises and explicit affirmations. If the camps had lasted longer, Primo Levi speculated, "a new, harsh language would have been born,"[30] an argot sufficiently wasted in spirit and befouled by crime to express the demolition of man that took place in the Holocaust universe. Such a new language in fact did begin to emerge, but in the main Holocaust literature relies for its expression on the received languages and the established literary forms. It does so, however, in the profoundly revisionary way that we have been noticing, turning earlier literary models against themselves and, in the process, overturning the reigning conceptions of man and his world that speak in and through the major writings of our literary traditions.

In part, the result is a literature of dystopia, a winding down of human actions and expectations, a severe record of life "on the bottom." Recording as it does the unprecedented fate of innocent people sealed into the living hell of boxcars, penned into filth and terror by ghetto walls and electrified barbed wires, how could it be anything but constricted, despairing, and dystopic?

And yet, for the greater part it *is* otherwise, for while Holocaust literature offers no new affirmations, the very fact that it exists is proof that its writers have not opted for the ultimate negation: *silence*. The struggle into words may appear an impossibility to some and a madness to others, but the story will be told, again and again and again, even if there is little confidence that it will be listened to and heeded.

What kind of story is it? Who is its rightful teller? And how much should we trust him? Among other questions about the nature of Holocaust literature, these three are particularly pressing. For if we do not recognize the story for what it is, or the storyteller for who he is, it becomes impossible to give credence to his tale.

The first of these questions is best answered by another question— this one, posed by Primo Levi: "Our stories, . . . all different and all full of a tragic, disturbing necessity, . . . are they not themselves stories of a new Bible?"[31] I think we must agree that they are, that Holocaust literature at its heart of hearts is revelatory in some new way, although of what we do not yet know. We must acknowledge, however, that it returns us to biblical revelation in newly compelling and urgently critical ways, which force us to rethink all received truths about God and man and world under the pressure of history's worst crime.

There is something preposterous and even obscene about the notion of gross evil being inspiring, yet more than anything else, it is this crime, simultaneously searing and illuminating, that has inflicted the writer's vocation on the novelists and poets of the Holocaust. That it *is* an infliction is no longer open to doubt, for all survivors of this catastrophe who venture to write about it confess a disfiguration or impairment of one kind or another—a lapse in vision, a muteness of voice, other vaguer disturbances of the sensorium. Think of how badly mutilated Ernie Levy is, how some of Celan's poems break down into stammering, how pervasive the fear of blinding is in Kosinski's writings, how often Elie Wiesel's survivors seem to be struck dumb. For a summarizing example, think most of all of that frightening line in one of Nelly Sachs's late poems—the most costly *ars poetica* I know—"This can be put on paper only / with one eye ripped out."[32] No one touched by the Holocaust is ever whole again—that much this literature makes clear.

Yet that is not the whole truth, for while crime is impairing, it is also powerfully vivifying, exposing the world as never before in all its most frightful detail. The Holocaust has worked on its authors in a double way, then, simultaneously disabling them and enlarging their vision. If you would know the type, think of Bellow's Artur Sammler, whose left eye, crushed by the blow of a gun butt, "distinguished only light and shade," but whose right eye, "dark-bright," was full of the keenest observations.[33] Sammler, I believe, is our prototype of the Holocaust writer, a man so wounded by his past as to suffer a detached and admittedly distorted sense of the present but also so thoroughly chastened by experience as to see with an almost prophetic exactness, farther and deeper than ordinary insight allows. *Holocaust writers, in short, are one-eyed seers, men possessed of a double knowledge: cursed into knowing how perverse the human being can be to create such barbarism and blessed by knowing how strong he can be to survive it.*

How, though, can we put our trust in one-eyed seers, men of impaired and only partial vision? How can we *not* trust them, for they are the prophets of our time—maimed into truth by the crack of the gun butt. To see with them may indeed mean to risk seeing under the handicap of a shattered vision, but to foreswear what they have seen is to court blindness altogether.

If all Holocaust writers are in some sense one-eyed seers, what is the extent and what are the forms of impairment in the writings of Elie Wiesel? And how well does he cope with it? The first of these questions is answered readily enough: virtually all of Wiesel's writings are shadowed by silence and madness, the twin terrors of a childhood experience so monstrous as to be hardly accessible to language or to reason. Read almost anywhere in the succession of books from *Night* to *Zalmen* and you will find words struggling to express a pain that, the author insistently believes, may best be indicated by acts of deliberate silence. Yet speechlessness does not give us a dozen books—*writing* does—and Wiesel is a prolific, even a driven, writer. How, then, does one reconcile this extreme tension between the claims of silence and the claims of the word? That is one of the most persistent and least resolved questions that one asks in reading through the canon of this author's work.

As to madness, it is a fearsome thing, although some readers have preferred to see elements of sanctity in it and to interpret it in "positive" terms, as a necessary part of some kind of religious mystique. Wiesel himself has encouraged this kind of thinking by reiterating a theme of "holy madness" in many of his books. Consider, for instance, how Zalmen pushes the rabbi to the limits of his spiritual and imaginative powers—"Be mad, Rabbi, be mad!" he urges, for "one has to be mad today to believe in God and man."[34] We try to understand the experience that moves Wiesel in that direction, and to understand as well the urgency behind it, but nonetheless it is wiser to distrust the impulse to have imagination go mad. For most, it is far better to resist rather than provoke such feelings.

As outsiders, though, we have to acknowledge that Wiesel must follow his own compulsions, wherever they might lead him. Is it not the case, however, that in *Zalmen* they lead him to contemplate the end of his strength as a writer? For this is, among other things, a play about the futility of gesture, the emptiness of language, the uselessness of Jewish protest. Ultimately, and in the most highly personal terms, it is also a play in which Wiesel reflects despairingly on his whole career as one of futile gesture, impotent and empty words, an unlistened to and unheeded story.[35] Hence the madness that haunts so much of his writing, which increasingly has become the compelling *subject* of that writing.

Yet just as there are no literary forms that encompass silence, there are none that accommodate madness. There is a kind of prose that approximates hallucination, and Wiesel has written in it, at times with great success. He has also taken frequent recourse to parables, paradoxes, riddles, dreams, and reverie—once more, apparently, in an attempt to discover some adequate form to express the extreme *gnosis* that stands at the heart of his vision. The aim seems to be to descend

deeper into madness, there to confront and even perhaps to heal the
fearful madness of God himself. Such a prospect takes the breath
away; it also reduces words to what they were at Babel. Does the rabbi
in *Zalmen* not state the case revealingly for the author himself when
he cries, in utter frustration, "My strength is gone. Sentences tear
apart inside me. Words are drained of meaning, they fly away, disperse
and fall on me like enemies. They strangle me."[36] There is nothing
liberating or illuminating about that kind of wildness, which, if too
long encouraged, carries us beyond literature into a silence that has
nothing holy or otherwise "positive" about it. It is a side to Wiesel's
writing that badly needs to be tamed or transcended. To plunge further into it, though, is to enter a madness from which there is no assured return. It is, in fact, to join the Kotzker rebbe behind a locked
and never-to-be-opened door.[37]

   These, we might say, are the maimings that Wiesel has suffered
as a writer. There is no question but that he is aware of them, is alert
to their dangers, and has taken steps to defend against and grow
beyond them. One such step is to adopt a style of discursive prose that
permits a far greater control of ideas than is possible in the trancelike
prose-poetry of some of his fiction. Wiesel has written with great sensitivity and a notable persuasiveness in the essay form, which seems on
occasion the most appropriate for some of the problems he addresses.
Actually, he has been laboring to create a literary form situated somewhere *between* fiction and the essay, a kind of writing that will allow
him to utilize the dramatic elements of dialogue and character, which
we normally associate with fiction, together with the more rational
elements of discourse and coherent argument, which belong more
typically to exposition. He has already achieved some memorable
successes in this mixed mode—as many of the pieces in *Legends of
Our Time* and *One Generation After* show—and one expects that he
will go on to refine and further develop a significant strain of his writing along these lines.

   His turn to Midrash, or neo-Midrash, represents another movement away from silence and madness, and one which twice now in
recent years has shown itself to be especially fruitful. Both *Souls on*

*Fire* and *Messengers of God* are strong books—works of original commentary and synoptic insight—that demonstrate an ability to exercise imagination and intellect without driving either mad. In giving us these portraits and legends, it is clear that Wiesel has returned to one of the specifically Jewish sources of his literary and spiritual sensibility, and one expects that this rediscovery of a native strain will be sustaining and not quickly played out.

Fiction, though—and, more than anything else, Wiesel has been seen as a fiction writer—presents problems that are not so easily solved. A fiction writer responds in the first place to the texture of experience— to *this* particular place, and how it looked and smelled and sounded; to *these* particular people, and how they dressed and talked and ran about; to specific seasons of the year, and their special fruitfulness or desolateness; to a landscape seen once and never forgotten, against which a life played itself out in a way that had an inevitability and a consequence all its own. Sighet, Wiesel's particular place, was torn away from him too violently and too soon, one imagines, for it to return in his fiction in this closely felt and completely rounded way. It does return, to be sure, but more as *idea* than as place; perhaps it would be more accurate to say that he returns in idea to *it*, but to it as it existed for him in potential, not as densely lived and concretely realized fact. This loss of surfaces is, to a novelist, a deprivation that no amount of ideas can make up for. And while Wiesel has worked admirably to relocate himself in the town of his birth, to resettle its streets and repopulate its houses, one feels that his is a homecoming that will remain forever incomplete and unfulfilled.

As it must be unfulfilled, given the fate of Sighet and of the young boy hurled so brutally out of that place into a realm of unreality. What exists between the two—between home and hell—is a space that fiction is hard put to occupy. Ideas can flow into that kind of existential vacuum, but the senses cannot. As a result, in most of his books *nothing palpable comes to replace place*. Wiesel's fiction, rich in reflection, meditation, and the accents of a sustained spiritual striving, does not shape itself easily around a phenomenal world. *Things* are lacking, and it is through things that a novelist makes his progress into thought.

After *Night*, though, the pattern in Wiesel's writings largely seems to run the other way: thought *precedes* and is looking to find its way back into things. But for the most part this is a searching without finding, a return to a place that is no longer there; hence the abstract, somewhat disembodied quality of experience in much of the fiction, its frequent disconnections, and its heavy reliance on a world made up of words alone. Wiesel's French masters—especially Camus and Sartre—seem to have been able to manage better in that mode, but they were writing by and large about a merely theoretical or philosophical *Angst*, an anguish and fear several steps removed from the pit of flames that the young Elie Wiesel almost was forced into at Auschwitz. For that tragically Jewish experience, French thought and French literary forms seem inadequate. Whether there *is* an adequate fictional form for it at all is a question that still remains to be answered. It would seem that Wiesel is at a stage in his career where he is striving to reach an accommodation between what the French writers taught him fiction might be able to do and what his Jewish masters tell him must be done. In this respect, the recent turn to Midrash seems especially promising.

Lawrence L. Langer

# The Divided Voice:
# Elie Wiesel and the
# Challenge of the Holocaust

Through a cruel contemporary paradox that has made atrocity an *expression* rather than a violation of history, the writer who confronts the ordeal of atrocity is compelled to redefine the idea of humanity and to ask how that ordeal has tarnished the image of man. Albert Camus, who represents one of the important influences on the thought of Elie Wiesel (see Lamont, this volume), expresses the challenge precisely: "slave camps under the flag of freedom, massacres justified by philanthropy or by a taste for the superhuman, in one sense cripple judgment. On the day when crime dons the apparel of innocence—through a curious transposition peculiar to our times—it is innocence that is called upon to justify itself."[1] What an inversion of values: that the survivor should be burdened with guilt for being alive, and that we should still have to proclaim the innocence of the dead by reminding ourselves almost daily of their existence! Somehow our diminished humanity is related to those victims, its survival contingent on our finding a way to acknowledge their meaningless deaths. The dialogue between language and history, which is at the heart of Wiesel's work, forestalls the advent of the crippled judgment. As time passes and memory fades, the imagination will be the only bulwark between silence and the extermination of an entire people.

But let us remember at the outset not to expect the impossible from only one man. We err if we hope to find the essence of the Holocaust in a single voice. The most we can wish from one writer is a partial point of view, an attitude, an access to that elusive experience that almost annihilated a people and became the prologue to later atrocities perhaps unthinkable if Auschwitz had not come first.

In confronting so complex an issue, we should be prepared for contradictions and unusually wary of generalizations. There is no doubt that, as Alvin Rosenfeld has claimed, some Holocaust literature "posits a future tense" and attempts "to retrieve some ongoing life"; but I have difficulty fitting the sardonic tones of Jakov Lind into this category, or even the more compassionate portrait of *l'univers concentrationnaire* by Charlotte Delbo, who posits a *past* tense in her effort to retrieve some ongoing memory of the *dead*. The compelling fact is that the millions of people are *not* gone, they haunt the writer with a ghostly persistence that casts a shadow on the imagination and leaves a disfiguring scar on the characters who populate his literary world. The imagination contending with the Holocaust is never free to create an independent reality; it is circumscribed by the literal event, by the history of the horror, by the sheer mass of anonymous dead who impose a special responsibility on the writer's talent. That burden is one feature of the altered consciousness that our age requires of us. The spirit of tragedy cannot absorb these dead; neither time nor history will silence their wail. They bestow on us a heritage that brings us to what Rosenfeld has properly called "the threshold of new and more difficult beginnings." They present us with the dismal image of men dying for nothing.

This is a bizarre challenge for a reader nurtured on life, hope, and the future. "*Sterbespieler sind wir,*" says Nelly Sachs in a moving poem. "Those who had no papers entitling them to live lined up to die," begins "Soul of Wood," Jakov Lind's most famous short story. "Dead though they be, the dead do not immediately become ageless," begins Pierre Gascar's "Season of the Dead." And we all know the final lines from Elie Wiesel's first, and still one of his finest works, *Night*: "From the depths of the mirror, a corpse gazed back at me. The look in his eyes, as they stared back into mine, has never left me." Multiply that corpse a hundred, a thousand, a millionfold, and we will understand more clearly what is implied when we are told that because of the Holocaust, "the imagination has come to one of its periodic endings and stands at the threshold of new and more difficult beginnings."

The burden of the dead, of *such* dead, which the Holocaust has bequeathed to us and which is present on nearly every page Elie Wiesel has written, was anticipated before the invention of the extermination camp. In an essay unpretentiously called "Thoughts for the Times on War and Death," published in 1915 shortly after the outbreak of World War I, Sigmund Freud recognized how a conflict of such dimensions would disfigure conventional assumptions about dying. We "cannot maintain our former attitude towards death," Freud insisted, "and we have not yet discovered a new one."[2] Thirty years later the Holocaust confirmed Freud's intuition, for he had also argued that until men found a way of absorbing into their cultural assumptions the phenomenon of mass dying for no justifiable reason, they would continue to live psychologically beyond their means. One of the main problems of the Holocaust writer is to find a secure place, somewhere between memory and imagination, for all those corpses who, like the ghost of Hamlet's father, cry out against the injustice of their end, but for whom no act of vengeance or ritual of remembrance exists sufficient to bring them to a peaceful place of rest.

So their chorus of voices continues to haunt Wiesel's pages, from *Night* to *Ani Maamin*, and thus the minds of his readers. "Our dead take with them to the hereafter not only clothes and food," says the narrator in *The Accident*, "but also the future of their descendants. Nothing remains below."[3] "In their frozen world the dead have nothing to do but judge," says the narrator in *Dawn*, "and because they have no sense of past or future they judge without pity. They condemn not with words or gestures but with their very existence."[4] "Each of us has a ghost that follows him everywhere in this life," says Michael in *The Town Beyond the Wall*, adding later. "It's very heavy work

carrying the dead on your back."[5] "To live is to betray the dead," thinks
Gregor in *The Gates of the Forest*, expressing one of Wiesel's favorite
themes. "We hasten to bury and forget them because we are ashamed;
we feel guilty towards them."[6] All those "who entered, by night, the
crucible of death," says Wiesel in his own voice, after meeting an apparent reincarnation of Moshe the Madman, "emerged from it by day
more healthy and more pure than the others who had not followed
him."[7] Again in his own voice, in *One Generation After*: we need to
face the dead to appease them, "perhaps even to seek among them,
beyond all contradiction and absurdity, a symbol, a beginning of promise."[8] And in *A Beggar in Jerusalem* Katriel brings the narrator to a
sudden moment of insight: " 'I' had remained over there, in the kingdom of night, a prisoner of the dead. The living person I was, the one
I thought myself to be, had been living a lie; I was nothing more than
an echo of voices long since extinguished. . . . I thought I was living
my own life, I was only inventing it. I thought I had escaped the ghosts,
I was only extending their power."[9]

The kingdom of night, like Wiesel's own first volume, thus casts
its shadow over everything he has written. It causes the foundations of
our civilization to totter, but provides little light to illuminate the path
toward a rehabilitated future. Tragedy as a literary form offered carthar-
sis to men contemplating with pity and terror the image of their own
mortality; but we have not yet discovered a form to fuse six million
deaths into a reflection of our destiny in the modern era. In his own
quest for insight, a way of managing the unmanageable and the un-
imaginable, Wiesel himself is capable of the following dubious reasoning: "To die struggling would have meant a betrayal of those who
had gone to their death submissive and silent. The only way was to
follow in their footsteps, die their kind of death—only then could the
living make their kind of peace with those who had already gone." The
sentiment—which I do not find convincing—is less important than the
need that gave rise to it, a desperate desire to discover some alliance
between the living and the dead that permits a feeling of continuity
between survivor and victim. We cannot accustom ourselves to the
fact that during the Holocaust, in the absence of a tragic atmosphere

(and hence of the possibility of moral and physical heroism), men were made to meet their death "submissive and silent," through no fault of their own. We cannot imagine a reality so fraught with terror and confusion that victims could be made to feel, in Wiesel's own words, "that they were neither worthy nor capable of honor."[10] Among his most striking achievements is his ability to crystallize this dilemma, still unresolved, of what to do with the meaningless deaths of our ancestors. The fate of the Jews is a persistent irritant to those who still echo Enlightenment rhetoric about progress and culture.

Wiesel hurls at his readers some unpalatable truths, which a world raised on a different diet has difficulty digesting:

> Auschwitz signifies not only the failure of two thousand years of Christian civilization, but also the defeat of the intellect that wants to find a Meaning—with a capital M—in history. What Auschwitz embodied has none. The executioner killed for nothing, the victim died for nothing. No God ordered the one to prepare the stake, nor the other to mount it. During the Middle Ages, the Jews, when they chose death, were convinced that by their sacrifice they were glorifying and sanctifying God's name. At Auschwitz the sacrifices were without point, without faith, without divine inspiration. If the suffering of one human being has any meaning, that of six million has none. . . .

If this is literally true, if it was all for nothing, if the effect had no morally distinguishable cause, if the episode is merely an excrescence on the flesh of history—then what is there to discuss? We discuss the experience of atrocity itself, the reality that divides men into victims and executioners, and the qualities inherent in us that make us capable of being both. To clarify the relationship, Wiesel invents a third category, the spectator, but his analysis of the triumvirate warns us to regard even so reliable a witness as himself with caution, for he suddenly drifts into a sentimentality that one can only regard as the momentary lapse of a stubbornly clear-sighted intelligence. "At the risk of offending," begins Wiesel, as if to forestall criticism, "it must be emphasized that the victims suffered more, and more profoundly, from the indifference of the onlookers than from the brutality of the executioner. The cruelty of the enemy would have been incapable of breaking the prisoner; it was the silence of those he believed to be his friends—cruelty more cowardly, more subtle—which broke his heart." More subtle than selection for the gas chamber? Such a comment seems to fall under Wiesel's own charge in another context that to "find one answer or another, nothing is easier; language can mend anything."[11] For who among us, after Auschwitz, fears a broken heart more than a mutilated body? What victim of physical torture suffered more from the indifference of his torturers than from the pain inflicted by their cunning devices? *Retrospectively* the survivor may suffer more from the indifference of the world (which he only came to understand fully after his return) than from his remembered pain; but who will ever be convinced that the immediate threat of physical extinction was not the greatest source of terror for the potential victim? One is tempted to conclude that Wiesel wishes to transfer to the rest of the world the mantle of guilt that, by his own confession, still weighs heavily on the shoulders of so many survivors. But the price is too high if it requires us to shift the ordeal of atrocity from the locus of the body to the palpitating regions of the heart.

Perhaps behind this exaggeration lies Wiesel's own understandable need to lay sufficient blame on the world of the living, as a kind of penance for the dead, a world that then as now never acknowledged its portion of responsibility. Looking backward, six million dead is also too high a price to have paid to support the indifference of the world: "the further I go," writes Wiesel, "the more I learn of the scope of the betrayal by the world of the living against the world of the dead. I take my head in my hands and I think: it is insanity, that is the explanation, the only conceivable one."[12] Closer to the truth is that the broken heart *follows* rather than precedes the broken body. Having survived, one learns that one's fate might have been prevented by the outrage and protest of others; and it is to an understanding of these "others" that Wiesel directs our attention and so much of his imaginative energy. One studies the Holocaust less to explain the murder of six million than to comprehend the six hundred million who permitted or encouraged it. We learn less from how men die than from why others let—or cause them—to die so.

Hence one focus of Wiesel's art is to distinguish between what we need to understand and what we should not attempt to. "Not to understand the dead," he observes in one of his subtlest commentaries on the subject, "is a way of asking their pardon." For where does it lead us to ask how so many victims "permitted" themselves to be murdered, as if they had any real choice in the matter once their deaths had been determined and they had been deprived of means of physical defense? That unfortunate and inappropriate expression "like sheep to the slaughter" distorts the truth of extermination in innumerable ways. It deflects our concern from the "slaughter," too terrible for most readers to confront, to the "sheep," as if the impotence of human fear is in any way comparable to the mindless confusion of animal innocence. "The lesson of the Holocaust," says Wiesel, "—if there is any—is that our strength is only illusory, and that in each of us is a victim who is afraid, who is cold, who is hungry. Who is also ashamed."[13] "How could they let themselves be killed?" is an obvious evasion of the more significant question, "How could the rest of the world let them be killed?" Despite his unusual conclusion that victim and survivor suffered more from this question than from the threat of extinction, Wiesel sees clearly that many roads diverge in the yellow wood of the Holocaust, that some are safer than others, and that only our willingness to risk following the most menacing ones will lead us up the paths to significant insight.

One ventures along such a path when one fuses Wiesel's injunctions to "know thyself" and to "know others" into a new moral imperative, consonant with the history of atrocity in our time. For if each of us contains the seeds of a victim, are we not also inhabited by an executioner who scorns the human image and wills its humiliation? How else can we explain the indifference of the world, not only to Auschwitz, but to all its successors? Wiesel has argued cogently that all the post-Auschwitz atrocities we have lived through have their roots in the Holocaust: we tolerate each one more easily than the one before. Our waning *reverence* for the image of man, diluted by the slaughters of our century—does this not also make us contemptuous of that image, at least in some of its forms, and does not this contempt war constantly with our sense of shame at what men have done to men in our time? As victim, our strength may be illusory, as Wiesel argues, but as executioner, it is vindicated; and perhaps we need to fear such vindication even more than the loss of illusion that weakens our dignity and encourages future executioners.

Much of what I have just said is based on an interpretation of Wiesel's essays, not his fiction, and we must distinguish between the two. Although he alters his opinion from essay to essay, when he speaks with his own voice we are not faced with the ambiguity of his art—or at least, it is much less evident. In his essays he offers conclusions, if not answers; but in his fiction he introduces attitudes that represent points of view, not conclusions, and though they may be consistent with the feelings of a particular character, we identify them with Wiesel's own beliefs at our peril. "Where are questions allowed to remain unanswered?" he asks in the chapter on Cain and Abel in *Messengers of God*. "In art, particularly in literature,"[14] he replies, and this is an axiom we must keep in mind as we consider some of the paradoxes that infuse his work. His fiction dramatizes that need to confront the past which afflicts any serious student of the Holocaust, but he also cautions humility to anyone undertaking that task: "everything depends on the inner attitude of whoever looks back to the beginning: if he does so purely out of intellectual curiosity, his vision will make of him a statue in some salon."[15]

Because in the beginning there were *many voices*, not only *one word*: this is a major clue to Wiesel's literary strategy. He is determined to complicate the reality of that past by multiplying the tongues that speak of it. It is an art of chorus, of dialogue, of language in quest of conscience. Words are more fluid than characters, who become fixed in time. Perhaps this is why his characters are less memorable than what they say: a voice must flow into the present, not echo with regular vibrations from the past. Oddly enough, in his tales based on legend and history, where his art is less visible, his figures are more vivid than the words they speak: Rebbe Nahman of Bratzlav, Menahem-Mendl of Kotsk, Abraham and Moses, are more fully realized than Michael and Pedro in *The Town Beyond the Wall* and Gavriel in *The Gates of the Forest*. The latter are more disembodied voices than men, perhaps because they are wrestling with post-Holocaust problems that the rebbes and patriarchs did not have to confront. In those days the world was not yet a slaughterhouse, so that men still had time to be themselves and affirm the human in the face of injustice. For Wiesel, as for the authors in the tradition, the Holocaust has split all human reality and shattered the durability of time: "Man can't afford to wait for God's decision to send the Messiah," says one of the voices from *The Gates of the Forest*, "because his life hangs in the balance."[16]

It is as if Wiesel were saying, over and over again, "If you cannot see, at least you can hear—or overhear." And part of what we hear is the silence—the silence of God in Auschwitz, the silence of the world as it turned deaf ears on atrocity, the silence of the victims as they recognized their awful fate. But the silence does not issue from a void; it surges around the words that conceal it. One hears it between the sounds of language: if we did not speak of the Holocaust, we would not be able to hear its silences. How else are we to explain Wiesel's periodic insistence that it is impossible to create literature about Auschwitz, while in volume after volume he does precisely that himself? All those who decry the writer's efforts to evoke atrocity through language, who fear that words may desanctify the suffering of the victims, who continue to insist that atrocity is an uncanny experience, a perversion rather than an expression of human impulse, who argue that literature about Auschwitz is impossible despite the shelf of complex, sensitive, and challenging books on the subject—these skeptics reflect not the recalcitrance of the phenomenon, but their own difficulty in coming to terms with how Auschwitz has diminshed the image of man, to say nothing of the image of God. For to admit that the experience has inspired a "literature of decomposition"—as it has indeed—is to confess that suffering can soil as well as purify the soul. And the decay of humanist doctrine implicit in this conclusion does not flatter our hopes for a saner future.

We need to listen with both ears, therefore, not only the one that favors what we want to hear. Every question about the Holocaust contains the seeds of its own contradiction. How can one speak about anything so inexpressibly terrible? How can one not?

How can one believe in God after Auschwitz? How can one *not* believe in God after Auschwitz? Did some survive through an inner social impulse, a desire to share in a collective effort to retain dignity? Others survived by preying on the impotence of the weak. From one point of view, Wiesel's literary work is a sustained dramatization of counterpositions, a long monologue disguised as a series of dialogues, revealing his own divided self. His inconsistency is both real and imagined, the reflection of a writer who feels trapped by two necessities— to speak and to hold his tongue—and who incorporates this very tension into the substance of his vision. Even in one of his most recent works, the text of *Ani Maamin*, the complaints of the patriarchs are opposed by God's silence—for in Wiesel, silence too is a feature of dialogue. Patriarchs and God—the two are tenuously joined by a few divine tears and an intermediate Voice, which consoles but does not— cannot—establish a final reconciliation to banish the tension in the dialogue between man and transcendence, hope and despair, speech and silence. That dialogue is a heritage of Auschwitz, and Wiesel offers no reassurance that a new Voice from the Whirlwind will emerge to satisfy the spiritual needs of Job's descendants. In the balance between the human and the divine, the dead still weigh too heavily on the scale.

As a messenger from those dead, Wiesel's task has been to explore how men respond when the line "between humanity and inhumanity becomes blurred." If on the one hand he affirms that a literature of the Holocaust is a contradiction in terms, on the other he is dedicated to helping men discover "the link between words and the ashes they cover."[17] The image is central to our theme and illuminates some of the objections to it. For to uncover ashes is to unbury the past; most human beings would prefer to celebrate the phoenix that rises from them. The literature of the Holocaust is not a literature of hope, though Wiesel's personal mood has veered away from the opposite pole of despair more so than some others in the tradition. His strategy has been to pour hope and despair into the crucible of experience, without losing sight of the event that inspires and modifies them both, and to permit his voices to work out the implications on the stage of their lives. If the results are not harmonious, they are nonetheless faithful to his vision of the night: his shifting positions are themselves an imaginative statement of the futility of seeking to escape its eternal shadows.

From the victims' son who reluctantly becomes an executioner in *Dawn* to the futile sacrifice of that ancestor and contemporary of victims, Moshe the Madman in *The Oath*, men seek a gesture to affirm the human in the midst of threatened chaos—but who among them has succeeded? They only confirm the contradictions implicit in the attempt. The quest is Wiesel's theme, not the arrival, and a quest is literally the beginning of a question. His work is one entry into the labyrinth of the Holocaust, but he has not yet discovered an Ariadne who possesses the secret of the way out. One of the darker twists in this labyrinth is illuminated by the narrator of *Dawn*, who wrestles with the paradox that he must be an agent of the very violence that destroyed his own past, and seeks a principle to bolster his waning courage:

> Why do I try to hate you, John Dawson? Because my people have never known how to hate. Their tragedy, throughout the centuries, has stemmed from their inability to hate those who have humiliated and from time to time exterminated them. Now our only chance lies in hating you, in learning the necessity and the art of hate.[18]

Scarcely a humanist position, this attitude solves nothing, as Wiesel understands, since the victim is an innocent hostage, not an enemy executioner, a scapegoat who must die as an example, and not an agent of evil. The Holocaust itself was full of such wanton executions; this one lays no ghosts but only creates one more to haunt the imagination of the survivor.

Yet the voice defending this position in *Dawn* is a vigorous one. In most tragic art, evil finally exhausts itself and society regains equilibrium as justice restores order among men. But Wiesel perceives that an age of atrocity disclaims the spirit of tragedy and the redeeming moral dignity of which it was the supreme expression. The voice of the warrior Gad in *Dawn* (he returns in *A Beggar in Jerusalem*) proclaims the harsher morality: "We can rely only on ourselves. If we must become more unjust and inhuman than those who have become unjust and inhuman to us, then we shall do so. We don't like to be bearers of death; heretofore we've chosen to be victims rather than execution-ers."[19] But when the executioner arrives before the Messiah, as Wiesel elsewhere suggests, then hope withers and the sense of the future shrivels: we are left facing the impossibility of finding a position com-mensurate with both Jewish destiny and a reality mutilated by atrocity. Hence we should not be surprised to find Wiesel, in another of his voices, in his letter "To a Young German on the New Left," contra-dicting the earlier attitude: "No, I shall never hate you. Not for yester-day and not even for today. It is something else: for yesterday you have my pity; for today, my contempt."[20] Which position insures survival: the shocking one of turning executioner in self-defense or the conven-tional one of meeting hostility with pity and contempt, but not the aggressive posture of hatred? Or is there a middle ground? We begin to understand what Wiesel means when he says that to be a Jew is to ask a thousand questions—about surviving in a hostile universe, about reason and unreason in history, about meaningless suffering, about God's silence.

The problem then, for Wiesel at any rate, is not the nature of the Holocaust itself, which may indeed be indescribable in its essence (though not in its consequence), but how to respond to it. In his use of dialogue, in the diversity of his voices, he confirms a principle we need to remember: "every witness expresses only his own truth, in his own name."[21] In addition to the burden of the dead and the multiple points of view, both of which as literary themes and strategies reinforce the elusive quality of Holocaust reality, the idea that silence must be integrated into the vision of this reality is one for which he has become a leading spokesman. The dilemma is most clearly stated by Azriel in *The Oath*:

> "The story that is mine, I have been forbidden to tell. And so, what am I expected to do? I should like to be able to speak without betray-ing myself, without lying. I should like to be able to live without self-reproach. I should like to remain silent without turning my very silence into a lie or a betrayal."[22]

Although Azriel spends much time telling why he cannot narrate the story of the destruction of Kollvillàg, he eventually finds a reason for drowning his protest: his tale enters into legend as he speaks. Though we are often told that there are no metaphors for the Holocaust, which resists analogy, Wiesel develops one in the novel: the destruction of the Jewish community in Kollvillàg through an anachronous pogrom. I find this twentieth-century pogrom artistically unconvincing, chiefly because it is meant to anticipate an event whose systematic plan of extermination was far more sinister than a spontaneous outbreak of popular hatred. In *The Oath* Wiesel talks around the event, not about it.

Nevertheless, it is a crucial novel because it contains one of the most important and effective pieces of sustained writing in his corpus—the sermon of Moshe the Madman. It offers the most cogent argument to date for the counterposition to Wiesel's own earlier conviction that to "be a Jew today . . . is to testify."[23] Moshe's action—his willingness to sacrifice himself in order to save the town—is a gesture of martyrdom in an age that no longer supports such heroism. His deed prevents nothing because the morality of atrocity—or its amorality—recognizes none of the conduct that once lent credence and meaning to martyrdom. Moshe's act begets nothing, but his words survive him through the medium of Wiesel's art.

Moshe illustrates the monologue behind the dialogue, which is a characteristic of Wiesel's literary manner. He speaks eloquently for both sides, and if he finally chooses one, its opposite lingers in our memory, absorbed but not rejected by the "victorious" position. From Job to the present, the need to bear witness to suffering has been a major impetus to survival: "And I only am escaped alone to tell thee." Moshe sums up that view, before repudiating it: "Since the executioner seemed to be immortal, the survivor-storyteller would be immortal too. Jews felt that to forget constituted a crime against memory as well as against justice: whoever forgets becomes the executioner's accomplice." But when a holy responsibility is transformed by events, by the empirical consequences of the act of testifying, into a platitude, then it is time to reexamine the adequacy of that responsibility. "Words

have been our weapon, our shield," says Moshe; "the tale, our lifeboat.
. . . Since, in the end, someone would be left to describe our death, then
death would be defeated; such was our deep, unshakable conviction."[24]
He himself pierces the façade of this rhetoric and leaves a gaping
wound in its logic. For history, as one more extermination threatens
his people, has finally convinced him that this attitude represents an
exhausted faith, adherence to a belief that an age of atrocity no longer
supports. Several of Wiesel's literary themes coalesce at this moment,
as a voice proclaims death's triumph, not defeat—and then suggests
silence as the only remaining strategy to arrest its further victories.

To propose the abdication of the word, the *refusal* to testify, as
a sacred alternative to the legendary obligation of bearing witness is
indeed a unique approach to the ordeal of extermination. Moshe's
argument forces the imagination to face new frontiers of possibility.
Wiesel himself has contended that the publicity accorded the Holocaust made later atrocities easier to commit and easier to absorb into
the sponge of history. From this point of view, Moshe's logic, though
unconventional, is irreproachable: "If suffering and the history of
suffering were intrinsically linked, then the one could be abolished by
attacking the other; by ceasing to refer to the events of the present,
we would forestall ordeals in the future."[25] Is he correct? Such a question is itself incorrect. At this moment, fiction has little to do with
literal truth. It is imagined reality, a voice from the depths of art, adding a new plateau of possibility to the riddle of meaningless death.
Obsession with the history of suffering, instead of relieving suffering,
ironically sanctions some men to accelerate its growth. For the first
time in Wiesel's work, the cry for silence is furnished with an elaborate
rationale. The fact that this rationale falls from the lips of a fanatic, a
man called Moshe the Madman, only intensifies its ambiguous appeal.
And Wiesel's epitaph to him—"last prophet and first Messiah to a
mankind that is no more"—further complicates the validity of Moshe's
entreaty. For the reader is left with a twin heritage—the voice of Moshe
and a city reduced to ashes; a vow of silence and the concrete images
of charred dwellings, charred corpses, charred dreams and prayers and
songs.

But a rationale for silence does not satisfy the other dilemmas generated by the Holocaust. Not talking about it is one thing; not knowing about it is another. In one sense, all writing about the Holocaust represents a retrospective effort to give meaningless history a context of meaning, to provide the mind with a framework for insight without mitigating the sorrow of the event itself. *Knowledge* of this past cannot be exorcised: Wiesel discovered this melancholy truth when he tried to visit Germany after the war, and when he returned briefly to his native town of Sighet. Both journeys were in vain—what should he have expected to accomplish? Perhaps the failure to exorcise the past in life impels him to recreate crucial moments from it in his art—though aesthetically he achieves no more resolution there than he did in life. The theme of the "return" does not lead to renewal, but only to a greater sense of frustration and a fresh encounter with grief. The ruthlessness of the executioners, the impotence of the victims, the indifference of the spectators, float in bewildering suspension; the need to understand meets stubborn resistance from recalcitrant facts that defy the mind's urge to interpret. The events run in advance of critical attitudes that may one day unlock their mystery.

But awe in their presence will not do. The decision to speak or remain silent lies with those who have returned from the heart of darkness, but we do not ease their task by regarding them as sacred beings, transfigured by suffering, rather than as men. Similarly, the obligation to *know* remains with us, for in the end awareness is our only means of touching the Holocaust. But we do not simplify the challenge of interpretation, which is difficult enough, by seeing around the books we read the aura of a holy text. Why should we be astonished that men have wanted to transmit to us accounts of their suffering, especially when its dimensions are so unbelievable? An unapproachable book would be as unworthy of our attention as an unapproachable God. The literature of the Holocaust is neither awesome nor holy, only painful, and if a distance remains between us and this literature, the fault is ours. Such books are saturated in blood and they speak of death; or more precisely, they speak of atrocity, the modern term for meaningless death. "The subject matter to be studied," says

Wiesel in an essay fittingly called "A Plea for the Dead," "is made up of death and mystery, it slips away between our fingers, it runs faster than our perception: it is everywhere and nowhere. Answers only intensify the question: ideas and words must finally come up against a wall higher than the sky, a wall of human bodies extending to infinity."[26]

As the mind gropes for an image to contain this endless wall of human bodies, it is natural and almost inevitable to cling to George Steiner's suggestion that Holocaust literature, like the event on which it is based, represents a literal staging of hell on earth. But this too is a misleading and perhaps a treacherous analogy, a bizarre attempt to find a place in the spiritual cosmology of chaos for an episode without parallel in history or eschatology. For is not hell crowded with the souls of the damned, wailing in pain, doomed for eternity to suffer the fruits of their sins? But the landscape of Auschwitz is strewn with the mute ashes of anonymity, and for this we need new analogies, since this hell is populated with ghosts who are innocent. If anyone ever *were* to write an unholy scripture recording man's extermination and God's absence in Auschwitz, it would bear no resemblance to any Bible we know of. Satan, that restless spirit, would finally get *his* turn to be an author. As if to confirm this, one survivor of Auschwitz called his memoir of the experience *Was Dante Nicht Sah*. "And who says the truth is made to be revealed," asks the irascible Menaham-Mendl of Kotzk. "It must be sought. That's all."[27]

And as we seek, let me suggest that we be wary of talking about "the" literature of the Holocaust, just as we should resist the temptation to speak of "the" survivor. The Holocaust experience has generated such a rich and varied literary response that one marvels at its diversity, not its unity. Unlike Ilse Aichinger, Jorge Semprun, and Jakov Lind, to cite only a few examples, Wiesel does not experiment with new styles to dissolve the contours of physical, psychological, and temporal reality. Nor does he, like Jerzy Kosinski, leave the reader wandering in an alien terrain, seeking landmarks to orient himself to the Bosch-like grotesqueness that surrounds him. He is a philosophical novelist, a moralist who uses the fictional form to explore a universal theme that has been complicated by the pressures of an unprecedented experience: "Man's ultimate confrontation with himself, and with his idea of God."[28] These words appear in his chapter on "Job: Our Contemporary" in *Messengers of God*. A major difference between Job and Wiesel is that Job demanded an answer, while Wiesel expects none: the setting of the debate has shrunk from heaven and earth to earth alone. Job at least received a response, if not an explanation. Wiesel himself, who would pray, in the words of *Ani Maamin, for* God and *against* God, as well as *to* Him, wrestles with His silence—a continuing source of anguish.

He shares with Katriel in *A Beggar in Jerusalem* a distrust of words, because "they destroy what they aim to describe, they alter what they try to emphasize. By enveloping the truth, they end up taking its place." And this is a central paradox of the literature of the Holocaust: it cannot embellish on history as, say, Tolstoy could in *War and Peace*. It sets limits on the power of imagination, since it prevents the reader's mind from straying too far up the path of invented reality.

At the very end of *A Beggar in Jerusalem*, Wiesel alludes to the famous photograph, collected as a souvenir by a German officer, of a "father and his son, in the middle of a human herd, moving toward the ditch where, a moment later, they will be shot. The father, his left hand on the boy's shoulder, speaks to him gently while his right hand points to the sky."[29] How *do* we interpret this visual image of atrocity, a faded and melancholy moment of silence that cries out for words to rescue its victims from oblivion? What does a father say to his son in the vestibule of eternity—or on the edge of nothing? Is there a reasonable explanation for such a fate, that will console a young boy about to surrender a life he has not yet lived—and under such circumstances? Fathers protect their sons, they do not invite them to accept annihilation with equanimity. Do we violate the sanctity of that moment by trying to endow it with verbal life? Do we violate it if we refuse to do so? This photograph stands as an emblem of the difficulty facing readers *and* writers of the Holocaust: its authentic truth we will never know, but it challenges the imagination to penetrate a history that greets us with silence, a past of committed and irreversible atrocities like this one. What but words can strike through this mask, even though they are decoys for the real ones, and we, imposters offering as truth a language that only approaches it, guessing at meanings that memory and research can no longer recover. The quintessential problem, as Wiesel repeats over and over again, is finding a way of relating to these unhallowed dead—unhallowed by time, by art, by tragedy, by divine spirit. Their fate is in the hands of other men only—in our hands.

Terrence Des Pres

# The Authority of Silence
# in Elie Wiesel's Art

Reading back through Elie Wiesel's work, I am reminded anew
how much and how diversely he has written. In addition to the novels
there are the essays, the dialogues, the pieces of personal testimony,
and, more recently, the finely crafted parables, portraits, and legends.
Wiesel's output, in other words, is considerable, yet from a critical
point of view he continues to occupy an odd position. As a survivor
and a witness he is accorded a respect bordering on reverence. But as
an artist Wiesel has received little recognition, especially when compared with contemporaries like Malamud and Bellow. Lack of critical
attention may be explained partly by the fact that, until recently, most
literary criticism operated on the principle that a novel or story should
be self-contained and self-sustaining, without extraliterary reference.
Neither the author's life nor the import of actual events, from this
point of view, should be allowed to matter when judging a work of
art. But of course, in Wiesel's case the separation of the man from the
artist, and even more, the separation of his work from events in the
world—one event most especially—would be senseless. On the contrary,

what makes Wiesel and his work outstanding has to do first with his unique position as a writer *and* a witness, and then with the fact that everything in his work relates directly or indirectly to that overwhelming event we call the Holocaust.

Wiesel's position is therefore paradoxical from the start. In the spring of 1977 he was asked how he could continue so stubbornly to write about the Holocaust. His reply was unexpected: "I do not write about it." Here is a man whose personal and artistic vision has been shaped indelibly by experience of the death camps; a man whose voice, for most of us, seems to issue from the inmost center of that darkness. Yet he can say that he does not write about the Holocaust. On one level, of course, he means that most of his books are fiction rather than accounts of fact. But that is hardly the point; for, except in *Night*, which is autobiographical, Wiesel does indeed avoid direct description of the Holocaust. He does not write novels like, say, Rawicz's *Blood from the Sky* or Ilona Karmel's *An Estate of Memory*. Even in a novel like *Beggar in Jerusalem*, which includes a massacre of Jews by Nazi soldiers, the direction of Wiesel's vision moves elsewhere—to Israel and, as in *Dawn*, the relation between the European catastrophe and the birth of the Jewish state.

Yet having said this I must immediately offer a correction. For certainly *Dawn* and *Beggar in Jerusalem* are "about" the Holocaust, so much so that without clear knowledge of the Holocaust, the reader will make little sense of either book. And this, I think, is one of the essential characteristics of Wiesel's writing: it is the product of an artist who is also present in his own work as a witness, and its power resides in the way, either by allusion or brief reference or strategic omission, Wiesel makes the sheer fact of the Holocaust the omnipresent—we might almost say omnipotent—background for everything else. The Holocaust, in Wiesel's work, is absolute and the point from which all else shall be measured. It is so absolute that, like God, it need not be mentioned. It is *there*, a monolithic presence against which all human endeavor—spiritual, historical, artistic—meets its boundary.

And that is why, if I select one single aspect of his writing that gets to the heart of the matter, I would say that silence, and the tension between silence and the need of the witness to speak, is the matrix of meaning on which Wiesel's accomplishment stands.

# I

Speaking of "the impact of the Holocaust" in his *Legends of Our Time*, Wiesel makes the following remarks:

> Those who lived through it lack objectivity; they will always take the side of man confronted with the Absolute. As for the scholars and philosophers of every genre who have had the opportunity to observe the tragedy, they will—if they are capable of sincerity and humility—withdraw without daring to enter into the heart of the matter; and if they are not, well, who cares about their grandiloquent conclusions? Auschwitz, by definition, is beyond their vocabulary. [1]

Wiesel means that in this special case, our traditional categories of value and interpretation have been demolished by the very event they would seek to explain. The negativity of the Holocaust was so total, the event so massive and complete in itself, that concepts drawn from tradition and civilized experience—in short, the key terms of *our* world—become, if not useless, then extremely problematic.

What, for example, can justice mean when genocide is the issue? As an act of bearing witness the Eichmann trial was effective, but as an act of justice it was farce. And what of forgiveness? Can the victims, or for that matter can we, forgive those hundreds of thousands of guards and informers and collaborators and bureaucrats and loyal members of the Reich for the death camps? If not, if these people are condemned and cast out, what has become of the ideal of human solidarity, of the human community as such? And what, again, of our "faith in humanity?" Over and over the survivors tell us that one reason they did not resist was that, until it was too late, their "faith in humanity" made the prospect of such monstrous inhumanity impossible to imagine. And evil? On the scale of the concentration camps it seems satanic, even cosmic, and yet it was the product of men and women no different from ourselves—people small, ambitious, afraid, or even, as Albert

Speer insists, idealistic and not without intelligence. Suffering?—all
the pain we justify by saying that it ennobles, that sorrow refines the
soul? In Auschwitz, suffering was as empty as the dead eyes of the
*Muselmänner.*

That kind of list is very long. Possibly it does not end. Think of
any key concept in the vocabulary of civilized discourse and immediately, if its sounding board is the Holocaust, you are in trouble. And
the problem is not with terminology alone, but likewise with traditional structures of narrative art. Such time-honored structures of
meaning as, for example, the quest, the tragic resolution, the significant
death, make no sense at all in the Holocaust Kingdom. Yet here we
are, men and women aware of our inadequate means, earnestly dedicated to a firmer understanding of Elie Wiesel, and through him, of
the Holocaust itself. The paradox—if not the downright contradiction—is obvious; and our situation is not unlike Wiesel's own predicament as writer and witness. What artistic apparatus can he possibly
employ, when by definition the function of cultural constructs is to
mediate, to domesticate—i.e., to transform terror and nothingness into
modes of value and meaning by which we may then stay human and
sane?

To confront the experience of the Holocaust directly would seem
to be possible in one way only, namely, through the straightforward
testimony of the survivors themselves. But as Wiesel observes in *One
Generation After*:

> Reading certain books by [survivors] who do not know each other,
> one wonders: they describe the same scenes, the same partings. It all
> begins and it all ends the same way. It has all been said, yet all remains
> to be said.[2]

Yes, anyone who has looked at the vast documentation left by survivors
knows that each story is the same story, one story to be told six million
times. And having told it in *Night,* Wiesel must surely have wondered
how, without merely repeating himself, he might more keenly come
to grips with his urgent feeling that having said everything sayable, "all
remains to be said."

His solution has been to mobilize silence; to use silence as a category of relation to primary aspects of the Holocaust experience; to render silence in ways that make it—and therefore what it embodies—present and meaningful to us. His job, as writer and witness, has been to make silence speak.

Referring to the documents written by survivors—the "precisely kept ledgers of horrors," the "accounts told with childlike artlessness"— Wiesel says that "they waver between scream and silent anger." The scream, which transmutes itself into the voice of the witness, is born of shock and pain, of rage and the overriding need to "let the world know," as survivors always say. Silence, on the other hand, is born of terror and sustained by the knowledge that the truth of Auschwitz can never be communicated, or that in any case a guilt-ridden world prefers to ignore this kind of truth. There is, as Wiesel notes, a "conspiracy of silence" against the testimony of survivors, in which the survivors themselves, through a socially induced guilt and through their own sense of having failed to make the world listen, are forced to join.

And thus on numerous occasions Wiesel has himself called for silence, as in his essay "A Plea for the Dead," in which he defends the dead against the kind of revilement and condemnation now current— e.g., "they went to their deaths like sheep"; they "regressed to infantile levels"; they behaved like "incompetent children"—and in which he concludes: "The world kept silent while the Jews were being massacred, while they were being reduced to the state of objects good for the fire; let the world at least have the decency to keep silent now as well." And in the same essay he says of himself: "I prefer to take my place on the side of Job, who chose questions and not answers, silence and not speeches."[3]

Yet the voice of Elie Wiesel is ever with us. The books, essays, and articles continue to appear. Wiesel's commitment to silence is countered by his commitment as a witness, the latter drawing its strength from at least three sources. First, survivors feel compelled to scream, to warn, to remember, and record. Second, Wiesel believes that unless the world's guilt is openly acknowledged and the implications of Auschwitz made an active part of general consciousness, the

Holocaust will have indeed signaled the death of man; for if this un-
acknowledged guilt is not faced, the trauma it generates will grow until
nothing less than nuclear war will suffice as atonement. A third reason
Wiesel finds it necessary to violate the silence is to avoid betraying
himself. In *One Generation After* he has one of his *personae* say: "In
the beginning, I thought I could change man. Today I know I cannot.
If I still shout today, if I still scream, it is to prevent man from ultimately changing me."[4]

## II

One of the special characteristics of Wiesel's writing is his wisdom,
and wisdom, as T. S. Eliot pointed out in his essay on Goethe, is something very few of us possess, something not to be confused with intelligence or mere worldly knowing. In Wiesel's case, moreover, it is a
wisdom born of silence and despair. He who speaks does not know,
he who knows does not speak. Certainly Wiesel knows this, and by
trying to transform silence into a mode of utterance he has revealed
to us one of the most striking consequences of the Holocaust. Here
was an experience so terrible that despair itself is inadequate; or rather,
it was an experience of such permanent disturbance that even in despair
the spirit, simply *as* spirit, continues to struggle, to respond, to confront. And in consequence, another important aspect of Wiesel's work
is his *tone*. We actually hear the silence from which he speaks, and
we cannot avoid the sense of words uttered in despair even while, by
the very act of speaking, this despair is made to join with, if not hope,
then something beyond hope, which survives and persists and is all
the more convincing because there is no false comfort. I am really
speaking of Wiesel's peculiar style; and if problems in stylistic analysis
sound grossly out of place in the presence of the Holocaust, let me at
least say that style, in literary art, is the verbal manifestation of character, of a particular configuration of spiritual being—in Wiesel's case
a strange mix of despair and something beyond despair, a mode of
utterance that includes, or is surrounded by, silence.

Some of my literary friends have remarked to me that Wiesel is not an especially fine writer. By comparison, they argue, other writers handle language better. They mean differently, of course; but comparison of this sort is suspect in general, and in this special case that kind of judgment can be made only if Wiesel's unique position—the "place" from which he speaks—is ignored. To read a book by Elie Wiesel is one thing; to read it with knowledge of the man as a survivor and a witness, and further to read it with at least some knowledge of the ghettos, the cattle cars, and the killing centers, is another, very different experience, even from the perspective of a purely aesthetic response. This is at once the weakness (from a critical point of view) and the strength (from a human and artistic point of view) of Wiesel's art. Much of the time the full impact of his prose depends on knowing *who* is speaking and *what* he is speaking of, while neither is actually clarified. Here, too, we might raise the whole pressing question of "art after Auschwitz," which is to say that any vision of the human condition will now be haunted by the Holocaust and its implications. Wiesel evokes it constantly, but often by suggestion, or seemingly innocent statements, or even by deliberately *not* identifying the source of his anguish and concern.

This, then, is what I mean when I suggest that silence is central to his art. Not silence as a vacuum or emptiness, but as *presence*—of memory, of the dead, of an evil so overwhelming and unspeakable that only silence, in its infinitude, can begin to represent it. In novels like *The Accident* and *The Gates of the Forest*, there is very little direct description of experience connected with the Holocaust, and then mostly in small bits and pieces. We have to imagine the implications, we have to recover *the story behind the story*, and it is Wiesel's use of silence that stimulates the imagination to do so. Likewise with *Messengers of God*; one reason Wiesel has been increasingly drawn to the Midrashic tradition of parable and commentary is that he can retell these tales largely by asking questions, and yet in a way that allows this bewilderment of detail to suggest—without open reference—aspects of the Holocaust or of man's relation to God and himself after Auschwitz. As if, in fact, it were all there from time's beginning.

## III

No doubt some people will object that I am "reducing" Wiesel's work to its aesthetic dimension, that I am treating matters of ultimate concern as if they were merely artistic products. I have suggested that silence is an artistic strategy in Wiesel's work, an effective solution to an aesthetic problem, which is to say the problem of meaning and communication. Let me qualify this by stating that art is one of our few approaches to truth, one of the ways consciousness is allowed to focus on otherwise unreachable kinds of experience; therefore craft and calculation in art are matters of first importance. Wiesel himself must know this: it is evident in his decision to write, to be an artist—only, in his case, an artist always in service of the witness.

Let us agree, then, that he *uses* silence. But he could hardly do this if silence did not already have profound meaning for him. Here we move from the work to the man, in particular to the man who has demanded and pledged silence over and over again, as if it were the central mode of relation to the Holocaust. I do not mean silence on the thematic level; not, that is, the dramatization of silence as a mode of behavior, as in *The Oath* and *The Gates of the Forest*, although here too Wiesel's fascination with silence is evident. No, the kind of silence from which his writing springs is more than idea or theme; it is an experience and a condition, a cause for existential response and metaphysical implication.

In *Legends of Our Time*, immediately after the passage concerning our lack of vocabulary, Wiesel goes on to say: "The survivors, more realistic if not more honest, are aware of the fact that God's presence at Treblinka or Maidanek—or, for that matter, his absence—poses a problem which will remain forever insoluble."[5] There are three phrases here that, if put in conjunction, figure in one of the primary meanings of silence for Wiesel. *God's presence*, *his absence*, and out of these two, the *insoluble problem*. This is very much like the contradictory but nonetheless authentic response that Wiesel expressed through *Night*: there is no God, and I hate him. After Auschwitz, in other words, God's presence is most strongly felt through his absence, which may indeed be an insoluble problem for the intellect but which, as experienced, is known and expressed as that eternal silence of the universe in the face of human agony. Quarreling with God is part of Jewish tradition, usually a one-sided quarrel in which God, when put to the question, answers only in the whirlwind. For Wiesel in any case—and let us not forget that he is a deeply religious man—for Wiesel this silence has become a permanent source of pain and the surest proof of God's existence.

On the human level, as I suggested earlier, silence is a symptom of our failure to comprehend and make sense of the Holocaust. But it is also, for Wiesel, the palpable presence of the dead, the purest voice of those millions murdered, who are most insistently present in their absence. One of the ways Wiesel deals with this aspect of silence is through those dialogues with the dead that continue to appear in his work. To acknowledge the dead thus, to address them as present, with respect and humility and also—as in *Beggar in Jerusalem*—with a yearning to join them, can be done, after all, only in silence.

By way of conclusion, let me repeat that silence is Wiesel's solution to questions about the Holocaust. There are no answers, no meanings to be discerned, only the intolerable weight of the event itself, to be faced in the quiet of an endless sorrow. And yet, knowing this, to stand in such a relation to the Holocaust is to take up an important, perhaps supremely important, position. For then silence and the Holocaust become one, each invested in the other—a situation in which each failure of mind and tongue, in which the stillness of despair no less than the soul's struggle to transcend its impotence, all serve to keep us in vigilant contact with the terrible truths of our century. In *Messengers of God* Wiesel makes the following remark: "One recognizes the value of a text by the weight of its silence." That is the measure of his own work as well, his burden and his aim: to evoke the unspeakable, to allow the dead their voice, to acknowledge God in His absence, and finally to make this kind of silence heard.

John K. Roth

# Telling a Tale That Cannot Be Told: Reflections on the Authorship of Elie Wiesel

Elie Wiesel has said, "I write in order to understand as much as to be understood."[1] A full understanding of Wiesel's authorship would entail a full understanding of the Holocaust. The latter, however, is not to be found. Indeed it *must not* be found. To do so would be to confer meaning on events so as to falsify them, so as to make them even more horrible and thus even less understandable. That point is one of the messages that Wiesel wants to drive home, and so a single explanation of his works will not do. Neither will a thousand. Every explanation is too little and too much, and yet we should try to tell a tale that cannot be told.

Many stories live in Wiesel's thought as it stands recorded in the books that move from *Night* (1960) to *Messengers of God* (1976).[2] Each story has its own integrity. At the same time all of them are aspects of a single tale that Wiesel wants to share. That single tale could be described by focusing on the repetition of characters met in the pages of his books: the Zalmens, the Moshes, the young men trying to find out who they are and what they can become, and the strange teachers they encounter as if by fated appointment. The tale could be summarized by analyzing events where human bodies and souls are stretched to the breaking point even as their unity is affirmed: fathers and sons embracing, one person saving another's life by sharing words, silences, songs, tears, laughter, and bread; executions and madness, acts of rebellion and violence; the drama of faith made persistent and passionate, even as its very possibility is threatened by God. Smoke, fire, day, night, the town, the forest, gates, walls, journeys, promises—tracing ideas and images such as these would be yet another path to take in exploring the many messages that are repetitions of one message, the unending variety to be found in the one account that resists every ending.

After Moses, writes Wiesel, "nothing was the same again."[3] Without Moses? Maybe no Torah, maybe nothing to set Jews apart from other human groups, maybe no Christianity and maybe no anti-Semitism and maybe no Holocaust and maybe no Elie Wiesel and maybe none of us—not even God himself. But there is Moses standing before those homeless wanderers, proffering life and death and urging them to choose well. That Moses, that mad Moshe, set history's course. The one tale that Wiesel tells has its perpetual beginnings and its non-ending conclusions in Moses' commandment to choose life.

With the Holocaust as back- and foreground, Wiesel's one story is that of how men and women under the blessing and curse of Moses (and God?) have chosen—some failing and some succeeding—to live. It is a tale that seeks to instruct not by argument, not by rules, not by offering a system, but rather by setting before us life and death. In all its variations and dimensions, it remains one tale. It also remains too big for the telling, and thus it must be told again and again so that nothing essential is slighted or left out. Its conclusion is always the same: choose life. However, as Wiesel has learned from Moses, that message is not an ending but a beginning, because the tale decides nothing for the individual reader, or even perhaps for Wiesel himself. Instead we are left with troubling questions about ourselves. More than once, Elie Wiesel has said that a Jew "defines himself more by what troubles him than by what reassures him. . . . To me, the Jew and his questioning are one."[4] To be moved by Wiesel's writings is to be moved toward that strange identity.

My point of view on Wiesel's writings, then, does not entail the thesis that they undergo some systematic evolution from one perspective to another. I find no clearly delineated stages—early, middle, and late—in his work to date. I detect no master plan that the author might explain in detail if he chose to do so. Instead there is one story told a hundred different ways. On the other hand, it is important to note that there are many books now written by Wiesel and that they are different. There is change of emphasis, perspective, and content as one piece follows another. The journey that has taken Wiesel from the despair of *Night*, where God dies at Auschwitz, to the theodicy of *Messengers of God* has been long: all the way from Sighet to New York City, all the way from smoke and ashes to best-selling editions and rave reviews. Still, it is also a journey within the same Holocaust Universe, and the development in terms of dialectical elaboration and paradoxical continuity is more striking than are the sharp breaks or turnings in his thought. Dividing Wiesel's writings into four categories, which in some cases mix and overlap the works chronologically, I shall offer one possible interpretation of his work as a whole. My analysis will focus on selected themes that emerge from his visions of a humanity that both accepts and rejects, is related to and severed from, a Holocaust God.

## Dark Nights of the Soul: The First Works

For centuries the image of "the dark night of the soul" has been used to designate the experience of passing into—and sometimes through—an abyss, an emptiness in which things taken for granted, assumptions treasured, and persons loved are stripped away, leaving body and spirit naked and sick. In *Night* (1960), *Dawn* (1961), and *The Accident* (1962), Elie Wiesel has recorded his version of that journey. It is, of course, a journey that never ends for him. The question of how to choose life in a world of wrenching losses is posed in all of the writings. The struggle with despair and hopelessness is always at hand. Wiesel's authorship is never far from the shadows that cut him off from his childhood, his family, his teachers, God, and himself—and thereby left him to battle backward and forward to find and build upon anything that was left over. This trilogy offers glimmers of success and hope, which become more definite and more determined as the literature unfolds from its origins. Those rays, however, are forever filtered through the chaos, terror, and debris of Auschwitz: "From the depths of the mirror, a corpse gazed back at me. The look in his eyes, as they stared into mine, has never left me."[5]

*Death.* In a few lines, describing the execution of three prisoners, Elie Wiesel has left an image of amazing power because it provokes so many tough questions:

> Behind me, I heard the same man asking: "Where is God now?" And I heard a voice within me answer him: "Where is He? Here He is—He is hanging here on this gallows. . . ." That night the soup tasted of corpses.[6]

Those words form a microcosm of the darkness created by the Holocaust, and I have rarely encountered a reader of *Night* who did not seize on that scene as the book's key. Nevertheless, this key is an enigma. Like any powerful image, its meaning is neither singular nor straightforward. Readers are left to wrestle, feeling that they have located a vital insight but not knowing exactly how it can be stated apart from a description of the situation itself. Perhaps it cannot be. Maybe that is why Wiesel wisely chooses the life of a storyteller and not that of a philosopher or theologian.

Who, what, is dying on that gallows? One child, all children, and Elie Wiesel among them. A world of faith and possibly all worlds of faith, whether they are oriented toward optimism about human progress or toward trust in the justice and love of God. Meanings such as these can be seen, but there seems to be much more in the scene as well. What about the God who is dying in the body of a tortured child? This death of God does not appear to be an acceptance of atheism on Wiesel's part. From start to finish, Elie Wiesel cannot get a living

God out of the picture, and that is one of the most troubling aspects—
for himself and for us—of the entire experience that he records. In
any case, the child is a picture of beauty, gentleness, and weakness,
although he may have been a violent revolutionary and certainly
showed himself to be tough and courageous in maintaining silence
during interrogational torture. Still, he does not quite fit the idea of
"The Eternal, Lord of the Universe, the All-Powerful and Terrible"
that Wiesel had learned as a boy to associate with God.[7] At most, the
child could represent a fragment, a facet of God. What part might that
be?

It is the part that transforms the universe. Wiesel writes that the
executed boy was "loved by all."[8] So the part of God that is dying
might be designated as that which can be loved—at least, the part that
can be loved easily. More than in the Christian view, Jewish visions
of God never seem to operate under the illusion that God is completely
lovable, thus making the commandment to love God more painful
and perhaps more passionate and emotional than most Christian evan-
gelism makes clear. Nevertheless, if the obviously lovable part of God
is dying for Wiesel in that Auschwitz murder, that reality does not
eliminate a creator-God, or even a God of history. A Holocaust Universe can be the result of a God who creates, and it can also be the
result of a God who watches over and even intervenes in history. But
it is extremely difficult to see such a universe as related to a providential
God who organizes and moves within history so as to reveal a care
"that means life to you and length of days, that you may dwell in the
land which the Lord swore to your fathers, to Abraham, to Isaac, and
to Jacob, to give them."[9] In witnessing the death of a child, Wiesel
suggests that to be with God is to be with a presence that leaves us
alone. That relationship makes the world unsafe: "Today anything
is allowed. Anything is possible, even these crematories. . . ."[10] How,
for what reasons, can one choose life in dark nights like that?

*Despair*. "Well, I said to myself, if in order to change the course
of our history we have to become God, we shall become Him. How
easy that is we shall see. No, it was not easy."[11] *Night* turns into *Dawn*.
But this light is hazy; as Nietzsche would advise, lanterns must still be

lit. If the world is unsafe for life, and God has chosen life in such a way that it is continually under threat, then men and women must become their own providence, their own security, their own hope. A harder task than first expected. *Dawn* shows that this attempted course beyond dark nights actually leads deeper into them.

Elisha, a young Holocaust survivor, has chosen to engage in the battle to free occupied Palestine from British rule, and thus to bring new life to a people and a nation. Apparently God will not act, but men and women can and therefore must. The twist is that choosing life in this particular situation requires choosing death as well. Elisha, once the possible victim of an executioner, is now cast in the role of having to kill. And neither from a distance nor in a direct fight for personal survival. His assignment is to execute John Dawson, a British captain, in retribution for the British slaying of an Israeli freedom fighter. Of course, there are circumstances that warrant Dawson's death. The cause of freedom for Israel is just and good, and the means necessary to achieve that end are not blameworthy. Moreover, Israel is worlds away from Auschwitz. To equate Elisha's role with that of the SS would be blasphemy. But the truth of such comparisons is not enough, not the whole truth: "The shot had left me deaf and dumb. That's it, I said to myself. It's done. I've killed. I've killed Elisha."[12]

Maybe it is good that when death took John Dawson it also took Elisha. After all, scruples against violence and murder and execution—these are folly in a world where people must be their own providence. To choose life in a Holocaust Universe one must be ready to kill, and then must not refuse when that requirement arises. Again, however, it is not that simple for Elisha. His dilemma is that Elisha lives on; he will not stay dead, not stay silent. The conclusion is that to take history into one's own hands—unavoidable and essential though that may be— is really no solution at all. It can drive one to despair, even in succeeding, unless one has chosen life in such a way that sensitivity and decency have been lost in the darkness. The latter outcome would be more a curse than a blessing, although *Dawn* does not really develop that theme. Such movement will become more pronounced in Wiesel's later works, but for now we are left in a dawn of darkness. The lines between choosing life and choosing death are fine and often dim. Established that way by God, they turn Moses' challenge into questions that defy answering, into tales that cannot be told.

*Nothingness.* Suicide might be the best answer. Respond to Moses by choosing life in a way that ends it. Thus, *The Accident* is no accident. Another in the endless line of young people—all of them the same, all of them different—doubts that he can endure his Holocaust survival. The world will not be changed; the dead cannot be brought back to life, even though they haunt the living too much, creating feelings of guilt, frustration, anger, and rebellion, which make joy and happiness all but impossible. And so in spite of the fact that he has friends, and even a woman who loves him, this young man steps in front of a moving car. "On the fifth day I at last regained consciousness. . . . I felt alone, abandoned. . . . That I was still alive had left me indifferent, or nearly so."[13]

Hope dawns in the "nearly so." Undeniably, the discovery that he can still speak sparks a choice for life, however faint, that cannot be hidden. Then, nurtured by friends, continuing under the care of a doctor who takes death as his personal enemy, life returns to be chosen again, although never without the memory of ashes. As Wiesel proposes, "the problem is not: to be or not to be. But rather: to be and not to be."[14] Life conspires to make us choose it; suicides are the exceptions that prove the rule. The issue for most of us, most of the time, is not whether to be but what to be, and we face the latter always in the midst of nothingness produced by injustice, pain, guilt, tragedy, and death. Such nothingness threatens to consume us. Not so much in the sense of leading us to end life, but in the sense of making us living-dead because we fail to care enough about how we can and should go forward from despair.

From time to time, Elie Wiesel implies that dimensions of these dilemmas may be God's as well, and perhaps that is why God and humanity need each other. Just as our power to choose life well depends on what other people—and God—have chosen, so our choices may move God. Indeed our choices may be aspects of God's own life and death, and thus the dying child-God in Wiesel's Auschwitz—as well as

the wise strangers, mad wanderers, and laughing seers of his stories—
is the result and reflection of shared tensions that both unify God and
humanity and push life forward to shatter apart again. But there are
no assurances to match the hope that either God or humanity—together or independently—is moving with a saving providence in our
world. Hope can save itself from illusion only by facing that fact head
on. Accepting Moses' challenge to choose life remains the hardest
thing in the world. It is enough to break our hearts. If such breaking
does not teach us—and God—how to be and not to be, can anything?

### Messages, Messengers, and Madness: The Novels

Elie Wiesel's first works travel through the destruction of a sup-
portive universe into the despair and nothingness that accompany a
realization that men and women must be their own providence. Life
almost succeeds in fulfilling a choice to cancel itself, but its failure to
do so becomes a turning point. The nature of that change remains
blurred, however, because reasons for living remain obscure. The effort
to discover and to create such reasons is one central thread that ties
together the four major novels that Wiesel has published thus far:
*The Gates of the Forest* (1966), *The Town Beyond the Wall* (1964),
*A Beggar in Jerusalem* (1970), and *The Oath* (1973). That battle produces a thousand conflicts—between persons, inside of persons, and
thus always with God.
  *Suffering.* " 'All I can do is to tell the story, and this must be sufficient.' And it was sufficient. God made man because he loves stories."[15]
With the concluding words of an ancient tale, we are introduced to
Gregor, another young Jew spared in the destruction of a universe.
Gregor finds refuge with a Christian, Maria, who was once a servant
to his now annihilated family. The price for his safety is silence, and
Gregor becomes a mask. He walks safely the streets of a town in which
no Jew is safe, because he is now a deaf-mute nephew come to live with
his Aunt Maria. But the disguise does not, cannot, last. Cast in the role
of Judas for the town's version of a Passion Play, Gregor finds appear-

ance becoming reality as the citizen-actors turn mad and begin to beat him to death.

Gregor saves his own life by breaking his silence, by telling his own tale. With time bought by the power of words, he manages escape to the forest, where he is able to join a group of resistance fighters. Hiding in the woods, raiding out of them, Gregor fights not merely for survival but also to locate the *why*—and thus the *how*—of friendship. Later, married to Clara (whom he meets in the forest resistance), Gregor finds their life together focused on the missing, the absent, the dead— Gavriel, Leib, Yehuda—all of whom taught worthy visions of life only to have them ended violently.

Love cannot grow in those surroundings—at least, not love for the living. Gregor decides to leave Clara. Maybe then the past, present, and future can separate themselves more clearly and more easily. But the book ends with Gregor saying a prayer for Leib, his friend and Clara's love, and with Gregor feeling renewed determination to breathe life into his relationship with Clara.

How this change comes over Gregor is left masked. Still, there are hints to be found; *The Gates of the Forest* lets in some light. More than once, Gregor heard Gavriel cry out against injustice: "If this is God's will, then deny it! The time has come for you to impose your will upon His, to pin Him to the wall. You'll have to pay, you say? What of it? You'll be damned? So what?"[16] Gregor has lived for a long time with the conviction of God's guilt, or with the recognition that the Messiah is not coming, which is the same thing. But where does one go from there? That is a torturous question. One of its results is a suffering that dwells on the past. That outcome is not wrong in itself; to forget would be a worse fate. But the need is to appropriate repeatedly the message of Yehuda: "It's inhuman to wall yourself up in pain and memories as if in a prison. Suffering must open us to others. It must not cause us to reject them."[17]

That message points us to God and to other persons alike, and one way that its tasks can be tackled is by telling "the story." Words are essential for that job. So are deeds, and once more Yehuda has seen at least part of the truth: "An act of love may tip the balance."[18] Through such acts the Messiah comes—or not at all. Thus, in the defiance of God's will—in the refusal to let events take their course— lies the possibility of revived understanding and caring between Gregor and Clara and even the chance for a reconciliation-in-tension-with-God. In the witnessing and dreaming aftermath of a Hasidic celebration that he has chosen to attend without fully understanding why, Gregor hears the past speaking with new urgency as he faces his own choice of life or death in relation to Clara. Its message, heard often before and yet never before his decision to leave Clara, informs Gregor's life and intensifies a madness, a passion, by which to live.

*Indifference.* "Pedro broke into applause, laughing: 'I like you, my friend! You're trying to drive God mad. That's why I like you.' I thought: And God too is trying to drive me mad."[19] Step back and visit *The Town Beyond the Wall.* Once Michael's home, this place is a ruin now in the vise of communist victors over Hitler's final solution. Secretly returning to see whether anyone can be found in an abyss, Michael's journey leads him to a house where a face watched silently while Jews were rounded up and deported ages ago. The face, seeking a hatred from Michael to match its own hidden guilt, informs the police. Michael finds himself imprisoned in walls within his past, tortured to tell a story that cannot be told: there is no political plot to reveal; his captors would never accept the simple truth of his desire to see his home town once more; his friend Pedro, who returned with him, must be protected. Michael holds out, but the drama inside the prison is one of madness.

"This, this was the thing I wanted to understand ever since the war. Nothing else. How a human being can remain indifferent."[20] Madness wears many expressions. One of them is indifference, and Michael seeks to understand it by returning to the past. The search also leads him to encounter God—apparently the most indifferent spectator of all. Unfortunately, there is no understanding in retrospect, at least none that rescues from abysmal absurdity the events permitted by indifference. That is a message, a tale that is also sufficient: sufficient to drive one mad. But on what terms and in what ways? How and to what ends is God driving us mad? One demonic aspect of life is that the answers are not fully in our control.

Thrust into a web of complicity not of our own choosing, our choice of life—like God's—is a choice of madness itself, whichever way we decide to go. Beyond that point, however, the message of *The Town Beyond the Wall* is that madness is reason enough to live, provided that it rebels against the forces that choose death. That lucid insight came to Michael as he returned to his past, but only in the sense that within the prison beyond the wall he was able to do his part to save Pedro from injustice, and perhaps more importantly to bring an urgency to his own life by trying to rescue his cellmate, Eliezer, from the darkness.

And what of God—never far away from any dimension of Wiesel's world, yet never clearly present either? He seems to live in all aspects of the madness, in the clash of opposites, immovable and yet moving. Neither fully deserving of trust nor fully able to have us put him aside, he prompts two prayers of madness, leaving us the task to wed them so that the many can also be one: "Oh God, give me the strength to sin against you, to oppose your will! Give me the strength to deny you, reject you, imprison you, ridicule you! ... O God, be with me when I have need of you, but above all do not leave me when I deny you."[21]

*Love.* "All of a sudden he seems a changed man. It is hard to tell whether he is blaspheming or preaching faith in the covenant. Impossible to tell whether the anger which moves him is a denial of love or the very opposite: an invocation of love."[22] Another journey to locate a home. This time Jerusalem, and our companions are a bizarre collection of tortured souls who gather to tell their tales near another famous Wall. They are also there to wait—some for understanding, some for lost friends, and all in their own ways for God. One of them seems to be the lone survivor of a Nazi mass-murder. He has heard and seen too much madness, including a teacher's counsel to accept death with quiet pride and dignity as an offering-protest to God.

If faith can no longer be faith, blasphemy is no longer simple either. When God's name is dishonored and rejected, it is reinvoked and reinstated so that there is no escape. More than that, blasphemy now becomes one of the few adequate expressions for the remnants of faith—at least that is true if its form is one of refusal to accept all that God's will tolerates or decrees. Blasphemy invokes humanity—and therefore our Creator—against God himself.

The covenant mediated by Moses has been broken—or kept—and the guilt belongs everywhere, including on God's doorstep. In spite of, because of, that fact, some refuse to let go of the promise. The reason? In it they have seen what life could be at its best. "You don't think he'll come?" asks Shlomo the Seer. "I do. He promised. That's my power over him; without me his fate would be incomplete. Whether he likes it or not, I am the keeper of his promise."[23]

Waiting continues. Even if one clings to the promise, it is difficult—to the point of immobility—to see how one can choose a future without forgetting or dishonoring the lives of one's past, and if one gives the homage due to the dead the future is poisoned by memories. Love, thought by some to heal all ills, is really the problem: "Do you understand now that love, no matter how personal or universal, is not a solution? And that outside of love there is no solution?"[24] Inside the pages of *A Beggar in Jerusalem* the waiting never ends. But it does become a prelude to action rather than a fixation on the past, and the reason is located in a message of madness: There is no solution, and love must provide it. Love must provide it by embodying the best possible in the past and by bringing it to life by caring for the living. How to do that without betrayal—that is what the issue of choosing life now becomes. Struggling with that issue becomes a reason to live. The dead and the living alike hold us to it. We choose life well only to the extent that we feel the pull in both directions.

*Protest.* "Could I have been spared in Kolvillàg so I could help a stranger?"[25] Azriel, another lone survivor of a holocaust, is bound to the past by *The Oath*. His home has been destroyed in a pre-Auschwitz pogrom incited by the mad rumor that the Jews of Kolvillàg had killed a Christian boy in an act of ritual murder. Mad Moshe, attempting to forestall the bloodshed he anticipates, offers himself as the guilty perpetrator of the nonexistent crime. Madness, however, will not be satisfied so easily. History will repeat, and the Jews prepare. A few arm themselves, and some celebrate life in the darkness; most rally strength quietly to wait and endure.

The captive Moshe is allowed to speak to his people. Neither by word nor by deed has the power of Jewish example through the centuries been sufficient to alter inhumanity. Moshe persuades his people to try a different strategy. They are captivated, and they accept his oath of silence. No survivor will reveal anything of what is about to befall Kolvillàg. Only the young Azriel survives. He becomes a wanderer, torn between speech and silence, true to his promise.

Years later, Azriel meets a young man who wishes he were dead. This young person is driven to despair because he is the child of Holocaust survivors. He has no past to match that of his parents, and that of his parents is beyond him. They cannot see him for what he is because they see others—now lost—in him. He cannot locate himself within his family or within the tradition of his people. Azriel decides to intervene, but how to make the young man choose life is the question. Azriel resolves it by breaking his oath. He tells his tale-that-cannot-be-told, hoping to instill rebellion against despair, passionate responsibility in the place of emptiness, life to counter death. Apparently Azriel succeeds: "By allowing me to enter his life, he gave meaning to mine."[26]

We can perhaps understand the young man and even Azriel. The breaking of the oath makes sense, too, but what are we to make of Moshe the Madman? Was he making any sense in calling his people to silence as death stalked them? Moshe holds that Jews "consider death the primary defect and injustice inherent in creation. To die for God is to die against God. For us, man's ultimate confrontation is only with God."[27] Clearly Moshe intended the oath as a protest to God and perhaps also as an offering that might break the hardness of God's heart. But it seems that he also intended survivors to use the oath. Life is the prize, not the oath itself, and the oath was taken for the sake of life.

**Struggles for Hope: Reports, Memories, and Dramas**

Good reasons for choosing life can be found, even in a world turned upside down by the Holocaust. Wiesel's major novels resound with that basic message. But it is not the only theme. A counterpoint is carried forward from the earlier works; memories, losses, the lack of moral progress continue to gnaw away. Nothing spared the Jews of Kolvillàg. Violence, dances of faith, quiet waiting, reason, madness— none of them was enough to guarantee that life chosen would be life left to live. Not without cause, then, Elie Wiesel has called *The Oath* his most despairing piece of fiction.[28] So in spite of, because of, good reasons to pick up the challenge of Moses and carry it forward, hope is threatened by illusion and futility at every turn. This theme—the need to regain hope because it is constantly being lost—can be found repeatedly in Wiesel's writings, but it seems to be specially accented in *The Jews of Silence* (1966), *Legends of Our Time* (1968), *One Generation After* (1970), and *Zalmen, or the Madness of God* (1974).

*Silence.* "The pages that follow are the report of a witness. Nothing more and nothing else. Their purpose is to draw attention to a problem about which no one should remain unaware."[29] *The Jews of Silence* appears straightforward. It is a report on the persecution of Russian Jews, and the author's aim is to focus on the plight of those people, whose story is not easily transmitted without special messengers. The simplicity of the account, however, turns out not to be so simple after all. For one thing, it is not so clear who the Jews of silence really are. For another, that ambiguity links all of us together in a struggle for hope in which it is no simple matter to discern who is helping whom, who is choosing life rather than death, who is acting for God or against God.

Wiesel's Soviet Jews of silence do not live in a world of flames, and "an abyss of blood separates Moscow from Berlin."[30] Theirs is a Holocaust Universe nonetheless. It is a cold-war world of spiritual destruction, subtle but firm in its reprisals for choices to keep tradition alive, to educate the young, to obey God's law. It is a world of incomparable fear because enemies are everywhere and nowhere; betrayers and informers wear no uniforms, and they even pose as friends. Moreover, one need not give up life. The only requirement is to give up Jewish spirit, although this action will not save a Jew from special passport identification and consequent discrimination. The hopelessness of Auschwitz is not so much the problem here, although the situations share the factor of isolation. Rather, there is the hopelessness of seeing a way of life crushed out, not by some killing final solution, but by the terror of being able to live—indeed of being required to do so—under terms set by enemies. And not even God himself seems to care. That knowledge intensifies the burden almost beyond belief.

To his amazement and even to his shame, however, Elie Wiesel found many Russian Jews choosing life on their own terms. Services were held, rituals observed, faith expressed in the face of threats and fears. The Jews of silence were not really silent after all. Considering the circumstances, Wiesel could honor their performance by suggesting that "today the only real Jews live in Russia."[31] By contrast, though, there are Jews of silence elsewhere in the world. And if we look beyond the Jewish community to all sorts and conditions of human life, the silence is deafening.

*Promises.* "And yet, as we listened in silence, with lumps in our throats, it was always of the future that he spoke. The truth was that we needed a future."[32] Recollections: a father's death, Yom Kippur in Auschwitz, a meeting with a Spanish Jew, a confrontation with hate. These *Legends of Our Time* deal with the past, but they are about the future. One of these tales is called "The Promise." It tells of a Holocaust victim called "the Prophet." "We loved him," says Wiesel, "because he responded to every appeal for help, he set his face against evil, he clung to his humanity in a world where humanity was denied—and he took very little credit for it."[33] He was a man with his soul set on fire by God's promises, spoken early to Moses and then later in a Messianic spirit to the prophets of Israel. Promises deal with the future, and although the hope that God would keep them was being killed night by night in Eastern Europe, the Prophet was determined that the future would not die. In Auschwitz that task could be all but hopeless.

Then a strange thing happened, which shows the thin line between hope and hopelessness, between seizing a future and letting one slip away. The Prophet was pronounced unfit for work; his future was sealed. In that hopelessness, however, energies rallied to save him because he had touched others by living for them. The future was urgent, but also hopeless. There was no reprieve for the Prophet, and his friends were left alone. Not entirely, however. They had been visited, if not by the Messiah himself at least by a human spirit that could substitute until something better revealed itself.

The example of a man giving his life for others was enough to give hopeless men a momentary future and perhaps even hope for a future beyond the camps. One difficulty remained: the Prophet was exceptional. He was not Everyone but only One. It may be that "it was its own heart the world incinerated at Auschwitz. . . . Not only man died, but also the idea of man."[34] The fate of promises seems to hinge on that dilemma. So does the future of hope.

*Irrationality.* "As a Jew, you will sooner or later be confronted with the enigma of God's action in history."[35] More recollections: dialogues rehearsed, some snapshots, a watch, a violin, the death of a teacher, excerpts from a diary. These things form a legacy *One Generation After*. Each is a tale that cannot be told, because even a past remembered is too far away from the demands, drives, and desires of the present and the future. Still, the stories burn with too much life; they must cry out against silence, even at the risk of killing hope.

One story from this collection of Holocaust tales underscores a hard lesson: There is no explanation. The Holocaust—maybe even life without it—cannot be understood without God, but it cannot be understood with him either. God can answer by pointing to his will or by pointing beyond it—to nothing. Can life bear hope in a setting like that?

The answer one generation after is yes—tentatively, defiantly, imperatively, uncertainly, all at once. But toward what does the "yes" point? What can be the nature and content of such hope? Here is where the humanism in Wiesel's theological meditation shines through most clearly. The hope cannot be located in God, at least not simply, for the double reason that God is question more than answer. On the one hand, he refuses to render an accounting to us—either because he cannot or because he will not. On the other hand, to be Jewish—to be human—is to hear that silence shoot back to us the question put to God: What are you doing? Are you choosing life or death?

Hope for a resolution beyond death, a re-creation by God in which all things are made new—such a prospect does not lure Wiesel very strongly. It is perhaps too speculative, or it is too divine an obliteration of the past, falsifying more than is tolerable. So Elie Wiesel prefers to stick with this world, battered and bruised though it is. For Wiesel, Jews carry forward best by appropriating all the good that can be found in their tradition. That base is their best chance to influence life for the better. The same lesson applies to men and women of other faiths. The odds do not favor moral progress, but without hope and urgent effort on its behalf, decay and decline wait all the more confidently to consume their spoils.

*Defeats.* "God requires of man not that he live, but that he choose to live. What matters is to choose—at the risk of being defeated."[36] We are back inside the U.S.S.R., back with madness. An old rabbi, his assistant Zalmen, a doctor, a daughter, a grandson, and a son-in-law, the chairman of a synagogue, and the rest of a fearful congregation—along with a troupe of observer-actors—are confronted by choices imposed upon them by an oppressive government intent on forcing them into silent submission. Traveling visitors from the West—some Jewish, some not—wish to witness Russian Jews at prayer. Concerned about appearances, government officials decide to permit the visit, but warnings are issued to the local Jews. There must be no disturbances, no protests, nothing to suggest discontent. Almost everyone is willing to go along. However, the old rabbi, provoked by Zalmen, or the madness of God, chooses differently. He breaks the silence and testifies to the suffering of his people.

It is a dramatic scene, but nothing much changes—at least on the surface—except that futility gains a little ground. The government investigates; the Jews' anxiety increases for a time. No plot is discovered, and fear subsides to a more normal level. The doctor dares to seek out the visiting actors to drive home the protest made by the rabbi. Unfortunately, they have already gone on their way silently. Although the possibility remains that the rabbi can have a significant relationship with his grandson, his family may be more lost to him than ever, and there is no assurance that the madness of his moving protest has not pushed him into a permanent disorientation that will be useless. Zalmen begins to doubt that his provocation was worth the pain and disintegration and emptiness it has caused. Madness compounds itself.

Such is the strand of hopelessness that runs through this drama. Yet threads of hope are intertwined with that strand. Slim though they may be, those threads direct us to the power of an example, to the courage that can be contained in a choice, to the challenge that says: We must not leave the rabbi alone; we must not allow his sacrifice to be in vain. Such threads are delicate and fragile. They are more easily ignored or forgotten than carried forward in action. Nevertheless, maybe *Zalmen, or the Madness of God* will provoke others to choose well—even at the risk of being defeated. That hope is the premise on which Wiesel's unwritten third act awaits its direction by all of us— Jew, Christian, American, or what-have-you.

### Tradition and the Faces of a Holocaust God:
### Portraits and Legends

Travel into nights of despair has offered reasons to live, but the realism of Wiesel's reports, memories, and dramas tells us that to live well is never to be far from hopelessness, and that if we do not act with vigilant compassion and protest there will be no future worth having. All of these themes find repetition in a final group of Wiesel's writings: *Souls on Fire* (1972), *Ani Maamin* (1973), and *Messengers of God* (1976). It is also in these books that the faces of Wiesel's Holocaust God come into sharpest focus. Those faces have been present throughout, although glimpses of them have been momentary and unsystematic. Such qualities are not removed in the portraits of these last three books, but the blurring is lessened. This focusing is important, because an understanding of God, while it may not control our fate, can and does influence our responses to it.

*Celebration.* "In the shadow of the executioner, they celebrated life."[37] In *Souls on Fire* Elie Wiesel relates stories about the Hasidic strand in Judaism. Born out of Jewish suffering combined with a passionate love for life and tradition that could not find adequate expression in eighteenth-century Europe, the Hasidim renewed the old and found ways to celebrate. Nourished by their example and by their stories, succeeding generations kept the flames alive, even in Auschwitz. It is not clear that their faith has survived intact, but the Hasidic tradition remains alive, stronger than anyone might have guessed. One reason is that stories can have a decisive effect on people, even though the stories are from a tradition that has not been—and will not be in any overt sense—one's own.

The Hasidism that Wiesel describes is fiercely humanistic. The aim is always to affirm the world of life here-and-now, to make it better. At the same time, the premise of that humanism is located in ties to God. Without God, man is and can be nothing. The catch—and the challenge—is that even with God man may become nothing, too. Thus, life must be lived so that it can be celebrated; it must be celebrated so that it can be lived. But what more can we see in the eternal face, and how does it relate to our Holocaust Universe?

Often the Hasidic tales recounted by Wiesel speak of the need to force God's hand. God is no weak idealist who helplessly watches the world run out of control and who cannot respond except by handwringing. He is Creator and Master of the Universe. And yet, choosing stubbornly and persistently to be the Creator and Master of *this* universe, the paradox emerges: God will not and, practically if not logically speaking, cannot move except through the characters he has brought to life to develop and tell his own uncompleted story. This God is different from all of us, and yet he is present in each of us. He has a plan, but it is the plan of freedom working out its own course as it lives in individuals. Therefore, the plan is almost no plan at all, and it can unleash the worst as well as the best that is in us. God listens and answers—usually in the mode of silence. He loves—but by needing our love because he is unlovable in his harshness, which is what we tend to experience most unforgettably. He is ally by being judge; judge, not by intervention that metes out justice in total fairness, but by letting events fall as they may to reveal the corrupt absurdity, as well as the grandeur, of what we do together. The presence of this God is like the absence of all Gods, and one response called for is that of protest against God. Depending on how that protest unfolds, we can discover in retrospect that the aim—divine and human—is indeed to celebrate life in spite of and because of the executioner.

*Faith.* "They leave heaven and do not, cannot, see that they are no longer alone: God accompanies them, weeping, smiling, whispering: *Nitzhuni banai,* my children have defeated me, they deserve my gratitude."[38] *Ani Maamin,* a song lost and found again, sings of faith in the Messiah. As Wiesel renders it, this cantata-poem tells of Abraham, Isaac, and Jacob, wandering Jews who return from earth to challenge God with their Holocaust reports. The tale is told with all the emotion and pain that the patriarchs can muster, and yet apparently it cannot be told—at least not well enough to move God toward intervention, toward sending or permitting the Messiah to work. The patriarchs are beaten. They prepare to return to their forgotten people, remembering, experiencing, and perhaps recounting once more in amazement tales of Jewish belief, inspired not by what God has done apart from them but by what Abraham, Isaac, and Jacob have done in the name of God and humanity together. Unseen, unnoticed by them, God begins to move.

The movement is in God's face. It is weeping, smiling, whispering. But to what effect? The collage of feeling expressed here is a tale too complex to tell, but perhaps it involves something such as the following. God's tears are tears of grief, guilt, remorse, compassion, and joy all at once. His smile is one of admiration, of vindication, of determining that good is balanced enough against evil to let men and women continue on their heartbreaking way alone. The whisper says: "What have I been doing? What are you going to do?" The effect overall is that the many emotions become one, and it is only God's face that moves. Once more the Messiah is delayed. The unfinished tale of his expected coming will have to move forward, so that it can be understood in retrospect that he has been on the way all along.

*Gifts.* ". . . It is given to man to transform divine injustice into human justice and compassion."[39] Abraham, Isaac, and Jacob—along with Adam and Eve, Cain and Abel, Joseph, Moses, and Job—are *Messengers of God*. The message that all their tales repeat forms the portrait of God-man painted so clearly and starkly, so ambiguously and subtly, in those few words at the end of this recent book.

Seeds of error, deception, and guilt were born with Adam. Bias, favoritism, hurt feelings, vengeance, and murder formed the tale of Cain and Abel. Promises, tests, obedience, trust, survival, hope—these did not add up to a world of rationality and justice for Abraham and Isaac, but they exist.

Jacob fought to secure a blessing, and the world has shaken to the core trying to understand its nature and what it might portend. Wily Joseph escaped the jealousy of his brothers, worked his way to the top, handled Potiphar's wife beautifully, made himself a *Tzaddik*. His success was too much; unfairly, his people paid the price. Leadership and the law—these things we associate with Moses, but even this man—closest to God of all—had to glimpse the future from so far away that he had to wonder about the One in charge. And Job, our contemporary, maybe life had been unfairly good to him and so his testing should be (unfairly?) commensurate? The face of God is the face of unfairness and injustice. It is also a mask that reveals through the rebellion of *Messengers* that God intends for us to have hard, even impossible, moral work until and through death.

So what about the face of this God who incites, permits, suffers, and perhaps endures and survives a Holocaust Universe? When everything is added up, is it a face of a friend or a foe? The answer offered by Wiesel's *Messengers* seems to be this: God is both friend and foe, but the degree to which he is one or the other depends largely on how we choose to live. As always, however, there is at least one further complication. It is that the way we choose to live cannot really be separated from the question of what we see now as we live seeking or denying God's face. What we can bear witness to in the future depends on what we have witnessed in the past and how we bear witness now. That set of circumstances is the one that forms the possibilities and burdens, the despair and hope, that we share with God.

God instructed Moses: "Say to Aaron and his sons, Thus you shall bless the people of Israel: you shall say to them, The Lord bless you and keep you: The Lord make his face to shine upon you, and be gracious to you: The Lord lift up his countenance upon you, and give you peace. So shall they put my name upon the people of Israel, and I will bless them."[40] Challenged to choose life, all descendants and followers of Moses, Elie Wiesel, and thus of their God, have been left with one challenge more. It is to discover how to receive and to give those words to each other so that they do indeed convey an affirmation of life by God and humanity together. As the Hasidim suggest, the discovery is in the creation of the fact, and so Elie Wiesel's authorship winds up where it began: with tales that cannot—and yet can and must—be told because they are in the making.

Rosette C. Lamont

# Elie Wiesel:
# In Search of a Tongue

"How did you learn to speak French?" the writer of this essay asked Elie Wiesel. "Through silence," he answered, so spontaneously that it was almost without thinking. Then he continued: "When I left the camp and was taken with other surviving children and adolescents to a special home for us, in France, I simply listened to this language. A young French philosopher, five years older than myself, would visit the home. I taught him Judaism, and he taught me French."

"What method did he use?"

Wiesel explained that they started right away to read the finest literary texts, the most difficult and demanding. They started with Racine's *Phèdre*, and went on to read all of Racine's tragedies, doing careful *explications de texte*. Recently, when the French newspaper *Le Monde* called Wiesel's style Racinian, it did so without knowledge of this early training. "Racine was my first language teacher," Wiesel said with a smile, "through the good auspices of my friend François Wahl."

"By taking the best of literary texts, your teacher used the same method Stendhal applied to his study of Italian. I suppose this would not work for every language student, but it is particularly suited to the fine literary mind and sensibility. Also you were brought up in the tradition of textual analysis, at least when it came to sacred texts, to the Bible."

"That's true," Wiesel agreed, "but Wahl also brought me Kant and Marx to read. Kant became my bedside reader. I never read novels or newspapers. Also I kept on listening. Two years later, when I opened my mouth to speak, I heard myself speaking in French. It was as though I had been brought up in the language."

## I

In his essay "My First Royalties," published in *Entre Deux Soleils* (*One Generation After*), the established author of 1970 states that if someone had told him when he was an adolescent that he would some-day become a novelist, and, what is more, a French novelist, or at least a novelist in the French language, he would have turned his back on his interlocutor, certain of being taken for another. At that time, as he explains, it seemed to him that his future was simple, clear, mapped out; he would spend his life in the study of sacred texts. To read novels, or to write them, appeared a childish, unworthy activity. What reason could there be for inventing lives and feelings, for indulging in the creation of fiction when a lifetime could not suffice to peruse the enigma of God's creation? Silence, even then, seemed superior to words. As for France, the word evoked a mythic land whose name was associated in the mind with commentaries on the Bible and the Talmud.

Elie Wiesel has not stopped wondering at the strangeness of his destiny. For those of us who, having read him in French, admire the classical purity of a style put to the service of a burning message, the thought that the writer Elie Wiesel might never have existed seems equally strange. Nor does our amazement have to do with the vagaries of human fate or the tides of history. We know that Wiesel is haunted by a very special unease, if not a feeling of guilt. The latter is strongly suggested by the following portion of Dialogue II in the work mentioned above:

> —Do you remember me?
> —No.
> —We were neighbors.
> —That could be.
> —We were friends.
> —When?
> —Before.
> —Ah, yes, it's coming back to me.
> —We went to the same school, dreamt the same dreams, admired the same teachers.
> —Ah, yes, I remember. We thought we'd be rabbis some day.
> —What do you do now? I'm a sculptor. And you?
> —I write.
> —You say it in such a way . . .
> —What can I say? Millions of people had to die for you to become a sculptor, for me to be a storyteller.[1]

Yet, if Elie Wiesel was not meant to remain in the little Yeshiva of his childhood, poring over the same page of the Talmud day after day, finding fulfillment in the strict observance of the 613 commandments of the Torah, it is because his existence was unalterably transformed by a set of events, coinciding with the Second World War, "the first massive and disastrous catastrophe since the earliest days of (Jewish) history,"[2] the Holocaust.

These events created "a temporal dissonance,"[3] as Lawrence Langer states in *The Holocaust and the Literary Imagination*, a rupture in historical tradition so final that nothing could ever be the same again. Man, as survivor, found himself in the midst of the absurd; recollection widened the gulf between him and his dead, while chronological time was obliterated together with space, both grown meaningless. Having become infected, the world of dream could no longer serve its inspirational function vis-à-vis the elaboration of literary forms. In a certain sense, one could say it became impossible to be a writer.

The problem, however, is not one of aesthetics, for if it were, neither Wiesel nor any writer who issued from the Holocaust could have reconciled the paradoxes of individual destiny with the need to testify, and to clothe this testimony with an enduring form that would imprint the event upon the consciousness of future generations. As Wiesel says: "We developed a style as terse, round, and complete as a fist, not a fist closed to strike the enemy, but one enclosed about an irreducible truth." Thus, to be a writer of the Holocaust is to transcend the ethical, taking the Kierkegaardian leap into the absurd. When Lawrence Langer states that the art of atrocity forces one to record the transformation of the familiar into the rational-irrational, he suggests that the Holocaust writer must perform the heroic act of reentering the horror he has lived through before. Yet the Jewish tradition by its very essence prepares one to coincide spiritually with the past suffering of the nation, making the tragedy of the past one's own present pain. Wiesel implies, both in his work and in his life, that for the Jew the ever-renewed need for transmission is a natural function, even when it addresses itself to the unnatural, the barbaric. In "The Story of a Promise" one of the numerous inspired madmen and prophetic seers who haunt the recent oeuvre of Wiesel exclaims:

> "Jews, my brothers, heed my words. I ask nothing else of you: do not reject my words. We do not have the right to survive. Who would testify for us, if not ourselves? One day all will have to be told, and no one will speak in our place. We will have to raise a howl against the madmen of death for no one will howl for us."[4]

This is both an invocation and a program. Since one cannot explain the mystery of evil—indeed ought not do so, for to explain the monstrous is to dismiss it, to explain it away—one must communicate that mystery in images that transcend the ordinary vocabulary of the novelist or the analytic approach of the historian. Fiction is no longer possible when the survivor becomes a celebrant. The Holocaust writer is a poet/memorialist who has reclaimed for his domain the function of medieval Kabbalists, that of mystical exegesis. He transforms his individual experience, so real in its horror that it defies human imagination, into a *corpus symbolicum*, yet he is committed to keeping his own face for, if the word of the Torah has six hundred "faces" according to the Lurianic Kabbalah, "one for each of the children of Israel who stood at the foot of Mount Sinai,"[5] the text of the Holocaust writer must be composed of six million "faces," all of them assuming the aspect of the individual witness. The one is the all, and the all live through and in the one. To return once again to Wiesel's prophet, who was doomed to die in a concentration camp, this is what he teaches:

> When misfortune strikes one of our communities, it is the Jewish people as a whole which is afflicted. . . . Oscillating between the absolutes, that of life, and that of death, the individual Jew determines the choice of his entire people. For him, everything is a sign, and every sign is destiny. While he is alive, while one of us is living, all is still possible.[6]

In an open letter to "A Young Jew of Today," one of the young "liberals" in France and in Western Europe who feels guilty in regard to the fate of the camp-confined Arabs, Wiesel equates the Jew with the act of questioning. The Jew must not only continue to posit questions but to posit the ultimate question by being. His presence is a single question: "Why and how does one survive in a universe which negates you?"[7] Although an answer to this interrogation does not exist, it could perhaps be sought in the very vitality of questing and questioning. Thus, if God had chosen to question man through the Holocaust, as some theologians seek to affirm, it is the privilege of man not to stop questioning God. "To be a Jew is to work for the survival of a people who has entrusted you with its collective memory,"[8] says Wiesel. Thus, a Jew who has survived the Holocaust is bound to become a writer in order to establish his solidarity with those who inhabit his very being. The recent dead are joined to the ancient dead, and strangers become ancestors. To the old rabbi who wonders what story-telling means, Wiesel, the mature writer, answers: "All this is not as clear cut as you would care to think. You see, certain events happened but aren't real, others are but they never happened."[9] A traditionalist might object to this reappearance of a mythic stratum within Judaism, but Wiesel knows that "the grandson of Dodye Feig"[10] must assume his rightful place again at the core of the "French" writer's life.

## II

A young man comes out of a concentration camp. He has lost his whole family, witnessed his father's debilitating illness and brutal end. There is no way back for him, no place to go, no one to go to. He will travel to that mythical land he heard of as a Yeshiva *bocher*: France. The latter, in the aftermath of the Occupation, is weak and deeply divided. It is scarred by the strife between the heroes of the Resistance and the greater majority of the people, who either collaborated with the Nazis or chose not to see what was happening around them while they went on carrying out their daily tasks. There are scores to be settled, and this is being done in the spirit of vengeance that characterizes every epoch of transition. After the silence, accusations and public confessions raise their din. Paris is slowly emerging from a long siege: students and intellectuals meet during the day at the cafés of the Left Bank, *Les Deux Magots, Le Flore*, artists have rediscovered *La Coupole* and *Le Dôme*, journalists and politicians lunch in good conscience on Alsatian *choucroute* at the *Brasserie Lipp*. Food is still scarce, clothing poor, but enthusiasm is strong, and there is a need to trust, admire, exchange ideas, and simply to have fun.

At night the Parisians rediscover jazz and American folk music, which they have always loved and of which they have been deprived all through the years of the German presence. There is a new vogue for underground cellar clubs, *les caveaux*, as though entertainment were still something forbidden, secret. One of France's most daring postsurrealist poets, dramatists, and novelists, Boris Vian, plays trumpet in the tiny *caveau Saint-Germain*, at the core of a neighborhood that is a capital within a capital. Here old rules are broken, new ones made. In 1946, capitalizing on the vogue for things American, Vian's friend the editor Jean d'Halluin asks the writer to create a "super-American" novel, so grotesque and exaggerated that it will obviously be a *canular* (practical joke). They will pretend that *J'irai cracher sur vos tombes*, which Vian writes in a couple of days, is the work of an American black, a very angry one, Vernon Sullivan. No one at first smells a rat, and since the work is a huge success, it will be followed by *Les morts ont tous la même peau*. These erotic fantasies, an Ossian-like forgery, stir public opinion, and soon Vian's "black-face" disguise is uncovered. Justice does not take kindly to this surrealist prank, and Vian and his editor are condemned to pay a fine of 100,000 francs for "outrage aux moeurs par la voie du livre."

Despite this rapping of literary knuckles, with newly won liberty comes a resurgence of interest in surrealism, a movement based on André Breton's defiant affirmation: "L'homme propose et dispose" ("Man suggests and puts into effect"). Yet, despite some brave efforts toward a renaissance of optimism, it becomes clear that such innocence is a thing of the past. The postwar generation is looking for a new definition of freedom, not the free-floating availability of the old *enfants terribles*, but a freedom that comes from moral choice, commitment. It is the epoch of existentialism.

The new *maîtres à penser* are led by the heroic Resistance fighter André Malraux and the ugly, yet charismatic philosopher Jean-Paul Sartre. The former has become De Gaulle's *ministre d'Information*, an official post that presupposes that the eternal rebel of the thirties is changing his focus and adhering to a certain image of France redefined by the liberator of his country, a dauntless fighter who had the courage to proclaim when his country was overrun: "France is where I am!" The latter is a Socrates of the *Deux Magots*, holding his dialogues with hordes of students and long-haired muses, one of whom is the singer Juliette Greco. Both men suggest that their encounter with history makes them consonant with their epoch, that the curve of their personal destiny has coincided with that of twentieth-century events. For both, experience has been transmuted into consciousness. Both have redefined the meaning of tragic awareness.

"*La Condition Humaine* of Malraux was one of the important books for me," says Elie Wiesel, "when I began to read modern novels." In *La Condition Humaine* Malraux preached a message of defiant solitude and self-definition through action. For Kyo, his protagonist, "everything is simple [since] the sense of the heroic was given him as a discipline, not a justification of existence."[11] For Malraux, as later for his admirer Albert Camus, the saint is not he who escapes from humanity but rather he who is willing to assume it.

Although an atheist, Malraux had a deep feeling for what he called the sacred. His love of art, expressed in *Les Voix du Silence*, taught him that man, through his works, transcends history. Art is not determined by the socioeconomic moment; neither does it disappear with it. It is the closest thing to eternity, the sign of a passion that, though grounded in the human flesh, is directed toward a transcendence. It is therefore the artist who becomes the true hero of Malraux's universe, for he can impart to human beings a consciousness of the greatness that is theirs but of which they themselves are often ignorant. The great lesson of the Holocaust was not lost on Malraux, who once said that the only modern setting for the Mass ought to be the barbed wire enclosure of a concentration camp. Compassion, like a rich, alluvial river, ran through the center of his being, and its deposit fertilized the parched earth of his devastated country.

For the deeply wounded young man who had been learning French from the greatest writer of neoclassical tragedies, Malraux must have appeared as the modern heir of the seventeenth-century poet, and thus a possible intellectual guide suited to his needs. As Pierre-Henri Simon points out in his magnificent book *L'Homme en procès*, it was Malraux who, in that blessedly frivolous time of respite between two wars, an epoch when the novel would not tackle anything more ambitious than salon adultery, first "raised a deep chant of human anguish."[12] Into the silence of Elie Wiesel a voice filtered through, speaking of the lucidly assumed condition of tragic existence, of reinventing life's meaning "in the full and clear consciousness of the non-sense of life itself."[13] This tragic philosophy of life, embodied in novels that now appear to us less as works of fiction than as confessional fragments from a lifelong poem, must have found in the young Wiesel a chord so vibrant that it could wrest from his dormant depths an equally tragic, yet somberly hopeful song.

If Malraux was the existentialist hero *par excellence*, the philosophic movement known as existentialism came to the fore in France only during the Occupation, and more prominently after the Liberation. Rooted in Saint Augustin, Pascal, and Kierkegaard, it is Christian in origin. Even at the start it was based on a concept of human freedom, or on the need to exercise free will in the face of determinism. In the twentieth century this urge asserted itself vis-à-vis the apprehension of the absurd.

The Second World War, prison interrogations and tortures, and the death camps taught the new existentialists that the experience of death can itself prove inauthentic. Looking at a dead flyer, Magnin, one of the protagonists of Malraux's *L'Espoir*, recalls a Spanish expression: "It is only an hour after his death that a man's real face begins to emerge from behind his mask."[14] Authenticity is then something we define for ourselves while still in this life; it comes from the anguish we experience vis-à-vis our *Dasein*. If man is present in the way that a rock, a chair, are here, then, according to Sartre, he is *de trop*. It is up to him therefore to forge his freedom, by choosing himself at every moment of his life. Nor ought he to forget that his choices involve the others, be they friends or strangers; moral decisions are drawn in with every breath he takes.

The mystique of moral involvement that was adopted by atheistic existentialism was a natural outgrowth of the years of repression. Between 1947 and 1950, when Wiesel was a student at the Sorbonne and a foreign correspondent for a Tel Aviv newspaper, Sartre and Camus were the moving forces of the new generation. At the *Café des Deux Magots*, where the first had his regular table, hours were spent discussing *L'Etre et le Néant*, *L'Existentialisme est un Humanisme*, *Réflexions sur la question juive*, the seminal novel, *La Nausée*, and later, the novels *L'Age de raison* and *Le Sursis*. There were vivid memories of the secret parable plays given under the Nazis, which had eluded censorship, *Huis Clos* (*No Exit*) and *Les Mouches* (*The Flies*). It is in the latter that the existentialist hero makes his appearance: Orestes gives up the false freedom of Enlightenment for a murderous act that transcends the ethical plane and cures the city of the plague of remorse. The French had been living in what Sartre calls *la mauvaise foi* (bad faith), and it was important to restore them to a sense of self-determined purpose.

For those who felt uneasy with the abstractions of the high priest of existentialism, Albert Camus's heroic humanism offered another avenue of exploration. As Morvan Lebesque writes in *Camus par lui-meme*: "... Camus had explored the absurd the better to bet on our reasons for existence. The battle would be won by this lucid, fearless man, against war, against the absurd, against the gods."[15] The year 1942 was crucial in French intellectual life; it was the year Gallimard published two works by an unknown Algerian journalist: a novel, *L'Etranger*, and a philosophical treatise, *Le Mythe de Sisyphe*. Both sounded the classical note of Stoicism, but in a manner so new and so personal that it was clear a major talent was surfacing.

"Although I admired Sartre's collection of short stories, *Le Mur*, I feel much closer to Camus," says Wiesel. "When I was a journalist in Paris," he likes to tell, "I would often see Camus in the *Quartier Latin*, at some of the cafés where we all liked to meet. I met him there, but I don't believe he would have remembered me. For me he was the author of *L'Etranger* and *La Peste*, two important works for my own thinking."

*La Peste* (*The Plague*) was published in June 1947 to universal acclaim. This allegory, originally inspired by *Moby Dick*, was the first complete rendering in an artistic form of the years of the Occupation, and of that condition of internal exile that divided not merely one zone of France from the other, but France from the free world, and, within France itself, a group of citizens, members of the Resistance, from the rest. The initial title of the book was supposed to be *Les Prisonniers* (*The Prisoners*). The seed of the novel is still to be found in Chapter I of Part II, a detailed account of the state of imprisonment, both physical and spiritual. It is this novel, more than any other book written by his contemporaries, that can be said to have found an echo in the mind of the young man who issued from what the French call *l'univers concentrationnaire.* Today still, when Wiesel mentions *La Peste*, there is a certain detectable emotion in his voice. In many ways he must have discovered a brother in Camus.

Like Wiesel, Camus believed that one must never forget, that one must remain a witness. In his editorial of December 22, 1944, written for *Combat* on the occasion of *La Semaine de l'Absent* (a week of charitable contributions for prisoners of war and deportees), Camus sounded the call of active remembrance:

> Only one requirement was set upon our generation, that of maintaining itself constantly on the level of highest despair.... There is one thing, however, over which we cannot triumph, and that is eternal separation since it alone ends all.... We are unable to do anything about pain; let us at least alleviate human misery.[16]

In the same piece, which is seminal in relation to the central theme of *La Peste*, the Resistance journalist defined his epoch as one characterized by separation. Both in this article and in that chapter of *La Peste* wherein Camus probes "the void" each and every one of us perpetually carries within, the concept of separation does not refer merely to physical absence but to an irretrievable metaphysical loss, that of time, of years of youth and joy, of closeness to loved ones. It is this deprivation that constitutes a major crime against the living, against life itself, one not to be effaced by survival.

The pain of "eternal separation" haunts the apprehension of Elie Wiesel, who, in 1947, must have felt that Camus's text could have been a letter written to those who had spent their childhood in death camps. In those years of emergence from hell, to have survived was no source of consolation. It was in fact a responsibility, the burden of Sisyphus. It was next to impossible to find a manner of being under the vigilant, questioning look of the others. Wiesel delineates this condition in *Le Mendiant de Jerusalem* (*A Beggar in Jerusalem*):

> Although we had survived, we knew that any victory would be forbidden. Fear followed us everywhere, preceded us as well. Fear of speaking, of being silent. Fear of opening our eyes, of closing them. Fear of loving. Marked, possessed, we were neither wholly alive, nor wholly

dead. We had no use for charity. Pity filled us with loathing. We were all beggars. Uprooted, stateless, undesirable: as time passed, people, perhaps to redeem themselves, or to protect themselves also, shunned us, holding their uneasy conscience against us.[17]

Did these people perceive the vision that confronted the refugee when he peered into the mirror: "A corpse looking at me"?[18] Within the eyes of the living dead, they could also see the dead living, the ancestors rising from the ashes of the crematoria.

Quoting a letter from a Dachau political prisoner in his *Combat* editorial of May 17, 1945, Camus records that indifference in regard to victory which characterized the survivors of the Holocaust: "In this letter, whose every line should fill the reader with both fury and rebellion, our friend writes the following about the day of victory as it came to Dachau: 'Not a shout, nor any celebration, on this day which brings us nothing.' "[19] Wiesel goes beyond this statement "one generation after," when he echoes:

And yet, for the Holocaust generation, there ought to be time to love and a time to hate. Both sentiments are human. He who does not know how to hate when he should hate will be unable to love when he meets with someone worthy of love. Perhaps, had we learned to hate during the years of tribulation, destiny itself would have been afraid. But we were incapable of it. Nothing done: hate will never be for us a cult or a commandment. If we were to hate all those who hated us, we would have lost long ago all desire to survive.[20]

Wiesel sometimes quotes Camus's letters "To a German Friend." There are four of them: July 1943, December 1943, April 1944, and July 1944. The leitmotiv of all four is the demeaning effect of hate; to give in to this sentiment is to become like the enemy, to be corrupted in some fundamental way. Camus tells his imaginary German "friend": "Despite yourself, I will preserve for you the name of man."[21] In his letter to Konrad Bieber, the French novelist insists in fact that the essential truth of the Resistance movement in France lies in the fact that it was able to operate "free of hatred."[22] If one finds echoes here of Camus's Christian upbringing, it is important to point out that what is known as a fundamental Christian virtue is rooted in fact in the ancient Jewish respect for human life. Although Camus did not write at length about *la question juive*, the latter became an intimate part of his consciousness during the war years, and played a key role in the elaboration of his symbol of the plague.

During the war Camus worked in a minor editorial position on the staff of the newspaper *Paris-Soir*, whose editor-in-chief was Pierre Lazareff. With the German army advancing toward Paris, the staff was ordered to reform itself in Clermont-Ferrand. In August 1940 the paper moved to Lyon. Shortly thereafter Lazareff, who was Jewish, escaped to the United States, and *Paris-Soir*, having moved back to Paris, became the organ of the collaborationists. Camus never followed *Paris-Soir* into the German zone, choosing to return to Algeria. At the time he was the unpublished author of the completed manuscripts of *L'Etranger* and a good part of *Le Mythe de Sisyphe*. In Oran, the newspaperman turned schoolteacher. It is a neglected, yet fascinating aspect of Camus's career, and perhaps awareness, that he found employment in a private *lycée* founded by the Jewish community of Oran for the sake of instructing not only their children but those of French Jewish refugees. His involvement with young Jews and their plight has gone unmentioned, yet it is clear that he began to give a good deal of thought to the question of Jewish persecution, both at this time and in the past. A mysterious notation can be found in his *Carnets*, one in which he seems to link the decimation of the Jewish people with the unleashing of the plague, as though the latter were a form of retribution for the first: "1342—Black plague all over Europe. Jews are being assassinated. 1481—The plague is ravaging the south of Spain. The Inquisitor says: The Jews. But the plague kills the Inquisitor."[23] These are the years when Camus is reading avidly, taking notes for *La Peste*, a novel in which the image of the concentration camp is raised to the level of myth.

In the mysterious circularity of the time/space of creation, Camus's meeting with Jewish students at a time when Jewish history and French destiny became intertwined in the death grip of common imprisonment, and the subsequent encounter of a young Jewish survivor, is one of the puzzling, richly evocative convergences of human and literary history. If Elie Wiesel recognized in *La Peste* a private message, one that helped him formulate his public plea for eternal remembrance, it is because a young Algerian writer chose to be, at the end of the war, the conscience of his time.

It is in Wiesel's *Le Jour* (*The Accident*) that one can detect most clearly Camus's influence upon the budding novelist. We must recall that Wiesel's first work, *La Nuit* (*Night*), is an autobiographical *récit*, an adaptation of the original manuscript written in Yiddish. Thus, *The Accident* is Wiesel's second work of fiction, the first being *L'Aube* (*Dawn*), a novel about the underground movements in Palestine, which prepared the emergence of the state of Israel. If its study of terrorist violence, so foreign to the ethics of the protagonist, owes a debt to Malraux's *La Condition Humaine, Le Jour* is permeated by the underlying presence of *L'Etranger, Le Mythe de Sisyphe, La Peste,* as well as by a dose of Camus's own patron saint of literature, Dostoyevsky. One feels that the young Wiesel is learning his trade and that he has picked the right European teachers.

The narrator of *The Accident* (he is named only once) is an older version of the speaker of *Night*. A foreign correspondent for an Israeli paper, he moves between Paris and New York. Although he appears to be leading an active life, he is a divided creature, existing on two levels: the everyday world of action, symbolized by his girlfriend, Kathleen, the proud, independent jet setter, and the subterranean level of past nightmares, which belongs to the ghosts that claim him. In some ways he is as detached from the concerns of the quotidian as Camus's Meursault, and as willing to go along with the lie of "normal" behavior, yet his passivity is less transparent than that of the protagonist of *L'Etranger*. The reason for this can perhaps be found in the alluring call of the dead, and in the young man's inability to feel that the life he is leading is his own. He sees himself as a child, standing on the platform of a small railway station; a train is leaving carrying his whole family; then the train rises into a smoke-gray sky. "Everything is reversed. Cemeteries are up there, suspended in the sky, and not dug in the moist earth. . . . Now everything is up there. That's the real exodus. The exodus from one world to another."[24] How can such a man continue to exist? He still recalls vividly what he felt as a survivor: "I thought I was dead. I could not eat, read, cry: I saw myself dead. I took myself for a corpse who, in dreams, imagines he's alive."[25]

It has been written that *The Accident* is a novel that begins with a would-be suicide, and that this reveals the influence upon Wiesel of the opening pages of *Le Mythe de Sisyphe*. Nothing could be further from the truth. If there is some resonance with Camus, it has nothing to do with this courting of death. Nothing is clearly spelled out in Wiesel's French text. There is of course a moment of hesitation on the part of the narrator when his attorney, Mark Brown, questions him as to whether he might not have seen the cab that hit him as it was swerving from the left. Another subtle hint as to the narrator's death wish comes at the end of the novel, when we are informed that the accident occurred on the day following the protagonist's conversation with Kathleen about his archetypal dream of abandonment in the railway station. This is also reinforced by his friend Gyula's story of his own near drowning, and his admission that, upon finding himself stretched out upon the sand, alive, he felt "terribly sad and disappointed."[26] Yet, although Wiesel clearly wants to show that for the survivor of the Holocaust the equilibrium between life and death remains precarious, he has no desire to clarify his protagonist's intentions, whether or not they are subconscious. The prose may be French, but the complexity of feeling is totally un-Cartesian.

If Meursault killed the Arab "because of the sun," then it could be suggested that Wiesel's narrator walked in front of the cab as a result of yielding to his girl's wish to see *The Brothers Karamazov* at a theatre on the other side of Broadway and 45th Street. He himself had opted in favor of *Murder in Rio*, on their side of the street, because he wished to find out "in what manner murders were committed in Brazil."[27] Kathleen's preference for the intricacies of Dostoyevsky spells disaster, but the protagonist experiences from the first what the French call *une certaine difficulté d'être.*

The latter is detected in his patient by Dr. Paul Russel, who performs the emergency operation. The surgeon of Wiesel's novel is kin to

Camus's Dr. Rieux—both names start with R—the modest, objective narrator of *La Peste*. Both Wiesel's and Camus's healers affirm the values of life with such passionate devotion that they must be seen as champions in the combat against *thanatos*.

Echoing the defiant scorn of the romantic poet Alfred de Vigny, as expressed by his solitary Christ in "Le Mont des Oliviers," Camus's Rieux explains to his friend Tarrou: "Since the world's order is regulated by death, it might be better for God if we were not to believe in him, applying all our energy to our struggle against mortality, without raising our eyes toward the heavens where he keeps silent."[28] Less metaphysically inclined, perhaps, than his French counterpart, the American surgeon is nevertheless aware that his patient failed to assist him with his will to survive, that in fact, throughout the operation, and afterwards, he placed himself "on the other side, with the enemy."[29] Since Russel does not have any knowledge of the realm of "night" whence the young intellectual he is treating has issued, he is deeply disturbed by what he has detected in the young man. He cannot understand how someone could be resigned to dying: he is unaware that his patient has sojourned in his mind among the dead, closer to them than to his friends.

There is another detail in *Le Jour* that points to a Camusian influence: for both Rieux and Dr. Russel the suffering, maiming, or death of an innocent child brings definitive proof of the absurd. Rieux experiences this confrontation when he watches the long agony of Philippe, the son of the examining magistrate, M. Othon; feeling powerless, he turns accusingly on Paneloux, the priest, shouting: "This one at least was innocent, as you well know!"[30] Dr. Russel knows a partial victory in saving a boy's life, at the price of amputating his leg. Despite the horror of the mutilation the physician feels that he held the enemy at bay: "I have triumphed, triumphed over Death!"[31]

Victories over death are but temporary triumphs. As Camus lets us know at the end of *La Peste*, the bacillus of the plague may lie dormant for centuries, and then, mysteriously, awaken again. As to the survivor of the Holocaust, guilty as he feels by the very fact of having survived, he must add to this sense of remorse the most cruel acts, the second killing of his dead, this time in his mind. When Gyula paints the narrator's portrait and captures in the young man's haunted eyes his father and grandmother, he makes the artist's supreme sacrifice: he burns the work of art in order to offer his friend the gift of freedom.

In some ways one could say that Camus had pointed in the same direction. When one reads his 1933 essay "How to Suffer," prompted by his bout with tuberculosis, one cannot help but feel that the writer of *Le Jour* could have written these lines:

> The pain that the feeling of absence gives rise to is the only thing that does not change. It is this pain which reveals its depth to experienced eyes, and about which we say we know nothing in reply to anxious questions.... To know how to suffer, to know how to love, and, when everything collapses, to take everything up once more, simply, the richer from suffering, happy almost from the awareness of our misery.

Does this not explain the expression of happiness one catches on the face of Camus's Sisyphus as he begins once more his painful ascension? Stoic joy, compounded of acceptance and lucidity, is the only form of happiness.

Wiesel acquired from his French masters a consciousness they themselves received from witnessing the Holocaust. But he would have to transcend this knowledge and their teaching to find his own voice. He is right in being impatient with Jean-Paul Sartre's discussion of Jewish identity. Although Sartre is nothing if not a noble soul, his approach to this question, as indeed to that of *negritude*, is a negative one. It is influenced by the Hegelian view that we live under one another's gaze in constantly shifting Master/Slave relationships. Thus, the Jew and the black assume their identity as a form of defiance. In his essay "A *un jeune Juif d'aujourd'hui*" ("To a Young Jew of Today"), Wiesel rejects Sartre's thesis as one that negates the intrinsic identity of the Jew and annihilates his creative powers. He writes: "Just as Man, the Jew can only be defined in his relationship to himself. Subject and not object, he is an end in himself, and not a function of what rejects him or of what he is not."[32] It is clear from this statement that Wiesel has parted from his masters, traveling back to the invisible community of Sighet, which continues to inhabit his remembrance of things past.

Had Wiesel remained a young contemporary of Sartre and Camus, one of the many French writers by adoption, he would not have become an important novelist, nor would he have brought anything new to French letters. Paradoxically—but all greatness and courage are balanced on paradoxes—it was when he was able at last to take a leap back into his ancestral past, when he became once again the boy in awe of the wisdom of the Talmud and the sacredness of the Holy Book, that he found himself as an artist and as a person.

It is not within the scope of this essay to treat the subject of Elie Wiesel as poet. As we read the mature work of Wiesel, however, we begin to realize that his ancestors in French literature are not so much the existentialists—not even a sensitive, independent thinker like Camus—but the poets: Victor Hugo, when he is not trite but allows the spirits summoned by the *tables tournantes* to speak through him; Baudelaire, with his acute sense of metaphysical rage, his "simultaneous" aspirations towards heaven and hell; Lautréamont, the dreamer tempted by madness; and before all of them, the supreme poet of passion and despair, Wiesel's first master, Racine. The author of the magnificent cantata *Ani Maamin* is kin to Claudel, Patrice de la Tour du Pin, Saint-Jean Perse, Michaux, Yves Bonnefoy. As to his unpessimistic sense of the tragic, it is not far removed from that of Samuel Beckett and Eugene Ionesco, two writers he admires and likes as people.

Wiesel's style in his novels has also begun to change, becoming looser, richer, closer to incantation. He has brought back the holy chant to literature.

What does language mean when you are evoking silence? What is the significance of place when a writer living in New York sees Sighet rising from its ashes? Those who no longer remember how to pray can at least sing and dance with Wiesel's words, like the Jews of Moscow he describes with such loving understanding:

Exuberant, they danced the *hora*, and the earth shook under their feet. Their clamor tore the night, making a wedge in the distant darkness. They sang in Hebrew, in Yiddish, in Russian, and without their knowing it, it was the survival of Israel and its continuity which they hurled as a defiance in the face of their surroundings, imposing a forgotten meaning on this ancient feast whose function it is to evoke the eternity of Israel.[33]

The eternity of Israel is connected not only with the Jewish people, but, as Wiesel suggests in every one of his books, with the living conscience of the world. It is to this conscience that Wiesel the artist addresses his message. The Jew, who for so many centuries was the Other in European literature, has been turned by the Holocaust into the symbolic figure of our tragic epoch, a quintessential Everyman. As Andrei Sinyavsky, who assumed for his writing the Jewish pseudonym Abram Tertz, writes in his *pensées* from the slave labor camp, *A Voice from the Chorus*: "Every man is a Jew."[34]

# Emil L. Fackenheim

# Midrashic Existence after the Holocaust: Reflections Occasioned by the Work of Elie Wiesel

## Absurdities

Next in magnitude only to the crimes of the criminals and the suffering of the victims, the Holocaust presents us with unheard-of absurdities. Of these we here list the following:

1. The Jewish faith teaches that catastrophe is transient and salvation final. Yet the catastrophe suffered by this generation—the Holocaust itself—is unredeemable. And the daily news testifies that salvation—in our times, not, alas, in theirs, for the creation of Israel was then still impossible—cannot even now be taken for granted.

2. At Treblinka, Jews were singled out for death as inexorably as at Sinai they had once been singled out for life.[1] Can the mind grasp the juxtaposition of Sinai and Treblinka? It grasps at most only one of the other two shocks, the groundless hatred and the singling-out of

Reprinted by permission of Shocken Books Inc. from *The Jewish Return into History: Reflections in the Age of Auschwitz and a New Jerusalem,* copyright © 1978 by Emil L. Fackenheim.

a people. Hence only the nasty people of this world tend to recognize the Jewishness of the victims, prepared as they are to imply that the hatred was, after all, not groundless, that "the Jews" deserved some of what they got. On their part—a much harder blow—the good people, horrified as they must be by the great hatred, tend to flee into the view that the victims were essentially men-in-general, and only accidentally Jews. (In 1944 J.-P. Sartre observed that anti-Semites reproach Jews for being Jews, while "democratic friends" reproach them for willfully considering themselves as Jews. This observation is still largely correct.)

3. A catastrophe surpassing all others, the Holocaust demands a moral and religious response far more insistently than did, say, the expulsion from Spain. Yet its very radicalism diminishes the likelihood of a response. The Jews expelled from Spain gave at length a new dimension to the Kabbala, for they lived; but the Jews of the Holocaust, except for a small remnant, are dead.

### The Task

To see these absurdities clearly is to understand at once that the battle still rages, that the defeat of the great hatred requires the hearts and minds and strength of us all. Is Jewish catastrophe in our time unredeemable and deliverance still precarious? Precisely this unholy combination renders sacred the existence of the state of Israel. Do the nasty and good people of this world, otherwise poles apart, act as if united in this one specific area—that of blotting out the Jewishness of the victims, whether by transforming it into a guilty secret or into an irrelevance? All the more must the Jewishness of the victims as well as that of all post-Holocaust Jews be affirmed and testified to, not only against enemies but also, and indeed above all, against friends. Finally, if the survivors are few, what of us who are not survivors but are doomed to respond to the event without the voice of those it robbed us of forever—the songs of the Hasidim, the oratory of the Yiddishists, the prayers of the scholars, the battle cries of Bundists and Zionists? Surely we must cherish their memory, study as we would Holy

Writ the diaries, books, records written in blood for our sake, relive their lives in songs of sorrow and joy. Surely we must do all this so that we may become heirs of their witness in this world and beyond.

## The "Crime" of Jewish Existence

To confront the Holocaust is to be overwhelmed by the possibility of inevitable failure. And to persist in the effort is to face a dilemma: if one seeks to grasp the whole, its horror dissipates itself into such meaningless abstractions as "the six million" or "the symbol Auschwitz"; if one seeks the truth of the horror in some particular, one encourages reactions such as the paradigm of a German woman who, having seen the Anne Frank movie, exclaimed: "At least this one should have been spared!"[2] We can avoid this dilemma only by taking hold of individual examples that, at the same time, cannot be rejected by the mind as exceptions, aberrations, mistakes, or excesses because they manifest altogether unmistakably the horror of the whole.

So totally integrated was the whole in question—rightly called by names such as "Holocaust Kingdom" or "Planet Auschwitz"—that to find the required examples is not, after all, very difficult. Raul Hilberg[3] cites two secret German army lists reporting capital punishment meted out in occupied Russia:

*Punishable Offences by Members of the Population*

### Report I

| | |
|---|---|
| Espionage | 1 |
| Theft of Ammunition | 1 |
| Suspected Jews (*Judenverdacht*) | 3 |

### Report II

| | |
|---|---|
| Moving about with Arms (*Freischärlerei*) | 11 |
| Theft | 2 |
| Jews | 2 |

The meaning of these lists is shocking but simple. All others had to *do* something in order to be subject to punishment; in contrast, to *be* a Jew—indeed, to be under *Judenverdacht*—was *in itself* and without further ado a punishable offense (*strafbare Handlung*).

One may object that the German war on Europe was one thing, the Nazi persecution of the Jews another; that while both reached a climax in Russia, they were only accidentally intermingled; and that to the end, enemies of the *Reich* were punished for their deeds, whereas Jews, even when they were murdered, were not "punished." In short, the Holocaust, while quite possibly a whole-in-itself, was an accident—for historians a footnote—in a larger whole: the Nazi-German Empire and its goals. Auschwitz, as it were, was a "mistake": not only Anne Frank, but all should have been spared.

Let those taking this view consider the following *Häftlings Personal Karte* (prisoner's identity card), which at this time of writing is on display at the Yad Vashem Museum in Jerusalem:

> *Name*: Kreisler, Andor
> *Place*: some town in Hungary
> *Religion*: Mosaic
> *Date of imprisonment*: 25.4.1944
> *Authority*: Gestapo Vienna
> *Concentration Camp*: Mauthausen
> *Reason*: Hungarian Jew
> *Previous criminal record*: none

Note, first, the archaic term "Mosaic" under the rubric "religion," a clear proof that (except in cases of Gentile converts to Judaism) religion, *as something one could freely accept or reject*, was of no interest to the authors of the form. Note, second, the utterly illogical but supremely revelatory sequence of these categories: " 'reason' for imprisonment" and "previous criminal record." The illogic is obvious. "Previous criminal record" is senseless unless preceded by the category "crime"; and any "reason" for imprisonment other than "crime"— analogous, say, to wartime internment of Germans in Britain or Japanese in the United States and Canada—is senselessly (and insultingly) followed by the category "previous criminal record." Yet precisely this illogic is revealing: the category "reason" *had* to be wide enough to include for "punishment" those who had *done* something as well as those for whom it was sufficient to *be* something. With the possible exception of the Gypsies, this latter group was composed only of Jews.

Yet a third point must be noted about the *Häftlings Personal Karte*—that it *was* a *Karte*, a form, carefully conceived, printed in countless copies and used in who knows how many cases. This decisive fact demolishes any remnant of the idea that in the Nazi system the identification of Jewish existence with criminality was an accident.

However, we may still try to understand this identification as essential only to the murder-camp system, and not to the larger Nazi system of which it was a part. What gives us pause in this attempt is the fact that, though concealing the camps themselves, the Nazis made no attempt to hide the *beliefs* enacted in the camps. Indeed, years of propaganda concerning the "hereditary criminality" of the Jews had preceded a progression of actions that escalated until finally, so far as this crucial point is concerned. S.S. murder-camp forms and army lists of executed "criminals" can no longer be distinguished.

Disdaining to hide their beliefs from the populace outside the camps, the Nazis disdained even less concealment from the victims inside. At least as far back as 1938, concentration camp prisoners had their respective categories emblazoned on their uniforms in the form of triangles—red for "political," green for "professional criminal," brown for "unemployable," pink for "homosexual," and yellow for "Jew." Once again with the possible exception of the Gypsies (who were sometimes considered as inherently unemployable), everybody had to have *done* something in order to land in a concentration camp. Only Jews had simply to *be*. And, as if to underscore this distinction, when finally all Jews had conspired to do something—for such was the official theory about the assassination of Freiherr vom Rath by Herschel Grynszpan in November 1938—those Jewish members of the conspiracy who were incarcerated in concentration camps had *two* triangles on their uniform, neatly arranged into a star of David: a red one for the political crime in which they had conspired, and a yellow one for "Jew." Significantly, Jews in the camps at the time seem to have had no adequate understanding of the explosive distinction of which they themselves were victims. The present writer, at any rate, did not have it. Indeed, on a visit to Yad Vashem just half a year ago he understood Andor Kreisler's *Häftlings Karte* sufficiently to copy it, but still not sufficiently to copy it in its entirety. This is why he cannot report the name of the town in Hungary that had once been Andor's home.

The distinction, then, between criminals-by-dint-of-actions and criminals-by-dint-of-birth not only was uniquely explosive but also was applied with an insidiousness that even in hindsight staggers the mind. We must now face this insidiousness in its full scope. The late Leo Strauss has rightly observed that the Nazi regime was "the only German regime—the only regime ever anywhere—which had no other clear principle than murderous hatred of Jews, for 'Aryan' had no clear meaning other than 'non-Jewish.' "[4] If the "non-Aryan" was a criminal-by-dint-of-birth, then "man" no longer was, as once he had been, innocent-by-dint-of-birth. Each and every person was presumed to be guilty-by-dint-of-birth until he had proved his innocence, and this he could do only by proving his "Aryan" ancestry. So openly yet insidiously did the Nazi Reich implicate in its crime against the Jewish people not only its direct agents and their accomplices but each and every person proving, or even prepared to prove, his "Aryan" innocence. Indeed, even those surviving on the presumption of innocence of *Judenverdacht* are implicated. Only those rejecting outright the whole system of "non-Aryan" guilt and "Aryan" innocence are wholly pure, and they were sure to become honorary Jews, i.e., victims themselves.

We are thus forced to give up the comfortable conventional wisdom that the Nazi tyranny was much like all other tyrannies, except of course for the shocking murder camps; and that the Nazi murder camps were much like other murder camps, except of course for treating a whole people as a "race" of hereditary criminals. The uncomfortable truth is rather the reverse. The murder camp was no accident of the Nazi system but its inmost essence. And what made the

murder camp into a kingdom not of this world—the Holocaust Kingdom—was an unheard-of principle: that a whole people—Jews, half-
Jews, quarter-Jews, honorary Jews—were guilty by dint not of actions
but of existence itself. The process governed by this principle climaxed
in an apocalypse. It began before the first Jew was ever "punished" for
his "crime." Hilberg writes: "When in the early days of 1933 the first
civil servant wrote the first definition of "non-Aryan" into a civil
service ordinance, the fate of European Jewry was sealed."[5] So, one
must add, was the moral fate of the twelve-year Reich—the twelve
years equal to a thousand—which has no analogue in history but at
most only in the imagination when it pictures hell.

*Apocalyptic Manicheanism ...*

## Hell Surpassed

History provides many examples of the strong vanquishing the
weak without scruple, and of ideologies, recently taking the form of
"social Darwinism," that endorse such unscrupulousness. But neither
in such struggles nor in the ideologies endorsing them is weakness
ever considered a *crime*, or the conquest or even "extermination" of
the weak a *punishment*.

Again history shows no dearth of societies governed by unjust laws.
Yet the "criminals" of such societies are always punished for something they have *done*, namely, the breaking of the unjust laws. Hence
even the most unjust society cannot but recognize the free will, responsibility, rationality, and thus humanity of its purported criminals. It is
this circumstance that caused Hegel to remark—controversially but
intelligibly and even defensibly—that a bad state is better than no
state at all.

The Nazi state was no mere quasi-Darwinian, quasi-natural state,
recognizing no right other than might.[6] It was not a merely unjust
state, forced to recognize, if nothing else, the responsibility and hence
humanity of its victims.[7] The identification of existence itself with
criminality, involving as it did *all* human existence, "Aryan" and "non-
Aryan" alike, caused *this* state to be neither a subhuman quasi-state

nor an imperfect human state but rather an antistate, that is, a system absolutely perverting all things human. Indeed, since the perversion is surpassable not in quality but only in quantity, the Nazi state was *the* antistate *par excellence*. Hegel would condemn it as worse than chaos. As we have said, it has an analogue, if anywhere, only in hell.

Yet as one ponders this possibility one wonders whether even hell is adequate. The devil is insidious in the ways he tempts us but does not place us into a kingdom, onto a planet, of which insidiousness is a built-in feature. He punishes sinners beyond desert but cannot so much as touch the innocent. He may have an infinity of time. But he has only finite power. Perhaps this is why Roy Eckardt has said that sooner or later the devil becomes a bore.[8]

We ask: what will limit the power of the devil if existence itself is a crime? If he can and does touch the innocent—indeed, them above all? What of a hell in which the question of punishment according to, or beyond, desert no longer arises? What will then limit the innocent suffering of the purported criminals, or the criminal actions of the purported judges and law enforcers?

There can be no limit, or would have been none, if, by good fortune, Planet Auschwitz had not been destroyed. Hence, a whole generation after, we still accept its possibility only because of its brute facticity. We do not accept it because we understand it. Though the misbegotten creature of our civilization, Planet Auschwitz transcends the resources of our imagination, those pagan on the one hand, those Jewish and Christian on the other.

Wisest of the pagans, the Greek philosophers confronted the brute facticity of filth but could not conceive of an enthusiasm fired not by good but by evil.[9] In contrast, biblically inspired poets and theologians did indeed imagine such an evil, a fallen angel saying to evil, "be thou my Good!" But on their part, believing as they did in a divinely created world, they could not confront the facticity of filth.[10] One must therefore summon the resources of both our Western traditions to begin to grasp a kingdom that was *anus mundi* and hell in one; ruled in an eerie compact by "disgusting" pornographic Streichers and "fanatical National Socialist" idealists whose "cause" was "serious anti-Semitism";[11] and run by a wholly new species of human beings: men and women who performed by day their quite new "jobs," and yet by night continued to relax as men and women have always relaxed—playing with their dogs, listening to fine music, and celebrating Christmas.

Commemorating the twenty-fifth anniversary of the liberation of Bergen Belsen in nearby Hannover, Norbert Wollheim, a leading spokesman of the survivors, referred in his memorial address to Hitler as Goethe had referred to the devil—"misbegotten creature of filth and fire." Perhaps only the wisest of Germans—close to Christianity and classical antiquity and yet identified with neither—was able, if not to predict, prophesy, or imagine, at least to find words adequate to describe him who, of all the Germans, was the most depraved. It is not certain how long the world will be inspired and instructed by the wisest German. But we must live with the grim certainty that the shadow of the most depraved German will never cease to haunt it.[12]

## Midrashic Existence

How does a religious Jew respond to Planet Auschwitz, a place of limitless crimes and limitless suffering, surpassing hell?

> Never shall I forget that night, the first night in camp, which has turned my life into one long night, seven times cursed and seven times sealed. Never shall I forget that smoke. Never shall I forget the little faces of the children, whose bodies I saw turned into wreaths of smoke beneath the silent blue sky.

Pious Jews always dreamed of a time when "wickedness" would "vanish like smoke."[13] Now a wickedness never dreamed of snatched their symbol, turned it into a weapon of terrifying literalness, and used it to murder their little ones and their prayers. Hence Elie Wiesel continues the above passage—there is none greater or more relentless in his writings—with these words: "Never shall I forget those flames which consumed my faith forever."[14] *How can a Jew say anything religious thereafter?*[15]

The religious Word may be in flight from the world, into the soul within or heaven above, or even from this world altogether into a world-to-come; a Jew, however, even when he is sorely tempted, cannot flee from the world, for he belongs to a flesh-and-blood people—a people with children. Again, the Word may despair of the world and yet stay with it; but then surely the despair is of God as well, and the Word is no longer religious. The religious Word, then, seems no longer possible within Jewish existence. Yet, prior to Buchenwald, some Jews have always found it possible to hold fast to God, hold fast to the world, and affirm a bond between them with their lips and, indeed, with their very lives. The most authentic Word expressing this bond is Midrash, and a life witnessing to it may be called Midrashic existence.

To affirm a bond between God and the world is always problematical. Midrash, however, is aware of this fact. Radically considered, a bond between a God who is truly God and a world that is truly world may well be considered as not merely problematical but nothing short of paradoxical. For its part, however, Midrash does not shrink from paradox, but confronts it, and in the very act of confrontation reaffirms the bond.

This stance requires closer inspection. Philosophical reflection may find it necessary to choose between a God who is divine only if he is omnibenevolent and omnipotent, and a world that is truly world only because it contains elements contradicting these divine attributes, namely, evil and human freedom. Midrash recognizes the tension yet refuses to choose. Thus when the Israelites do God's will they, as it were, strengthen his power, and when they fail to do his will they, as it were, weaken it. Thus, too, redemption will come when men have become good enough to make the Messiah's coming possible, or wicked enough to make it necessary. It would be wayward to regard such Midrashim as insufficiently demythologized fragments of philosophizing, the first groping for a "finite God-concept," which would at one blow "solve" the "problems" of evil and freedom, the second struggling with two conflicting views of history, the one "progressive," the other "catastrophic." Midrash cannot embrace a progressive view of history, for such a view would dispense with the need for God's acting in history, nor a catastrophic view, which would destroy the significance of man's actions. Nor can Midrash accept a "finite God-concept" but must rather sweep aside all God-concepts so as to confront God himself—a God absolute yet "as it were" (*k'b'yachol*) finite in the mutual confrontation. The term *k'b'yachol* alone—a full-blown technical term in Midrashic thought—suffices to show that Midrash does not grope for concepts in order to solve problems and dissolve paradox. The Midrashic Word is story. It *remains* story because it both points to and articulates a life *lived with* problems and paradox—the problems and paradox of a divine-human relation. This life is Midrashic existence.

Midrashic existence acts as though all depended on man and prays as though all depended on God. It considers itself worth nothing so that it can only wait for redemption; and worth everything so that a single pure deed or prayer may have redemptive power. It holds all these aspects together because it knows itself to stand in a mutual, covenantal relation—mutual even though the partners are radically unequal. Climactically, Midrashic existence endures the strain between these extremes without palliatives or relief. It cannot seek refuge from the real in a "spiritual" world, for it is the existence not of souls, monks, or sectarian individuals but rather of a flesh-and-blood people— a people with children. Thus it is not surprising that during the trimillennial history of the Jewish people individuals and whole groups should always have failed to endure this tension. The truly astounding fact is much rather that endurance of the tension has been continuous; that prior to the Holocaust it had never been broken.[16]

Does this endurance extend as well over Planet Auschwitz? One cannot answer this question lightly. For one dare not ignore or belittle the fact that countless and nameless Jews persisted even then in acting as though all depended on them, and in praying as though all depended on God—all this as if nothing had changed. Nor dare we ignore the fact that everything *had* changed. The Midrash sees Israel, as it were, augment or diminish God's power. Elie Wiesel's most famous Midrash tells of God hanging on the gallows with a dying child,[17] despite prayers of saints meant to augment His power and because of acts of criminals meant to destroy it. The Midrash sees the Messiah come when men are either wholly righteous or wholly wicked. On Planet Auschwitz the Messiah failed to come even though both conditions were fulfilled. The "judges," "law-enforcers," and "ordinary employees" were wholly wicked, for the antiworld that they ruled, administered, and ran was wholly wicked. The "punished criminals" were wholly righteous for, as a statement wrongly attributed to Maimonides rightly says, a Jew murdered for no reason other than his Jewishness must be viewed as if he were a saint.[18] Hence the protagonist of *The Gates of the Forest* asserts that it is too late for the coming of the Messiah— that a Messiah who can come, but at Auschwitz did not come, has lost his meaning.[19]

Midrash is meant for every kind of imperfect world. It was not meant for Planet Auschwitz, the antiworld.

### Mad Midrash

What then makes Elie Wiesel's work possible? No matter what its content—Israel, Russian Jews, Hasidism, the Bible—the Holocaust is always part of its hidden agenda. And no matter what its form— eyewitness reports, essays, a cantata, a play, to say nothing of the novels—it always has recognizable Midrashic elements. The first dimension is not accidental, for Wiesel cannot relate himself to *any* Jewish reality before and indeed after the Holocaust as though the dread event had not happened. The second is not accidental, for Wiesel cannot respond to the event by rejecting or fleeing from Jewish past and future—both informed by the hallowed tradition—but only by affirming both, and the most authentic and unmistakable verbal expression of this affirmation is Midrash. Indeed, precisely this fusion of a relentless self-exposure to the Holocaust and a Jewishness steeped in tradition has given Wiesel the stature of a teacher.

This seemingly impossible fusion produces the unprecedented phenomenon of mad Midrash. Moshe the mad *Shammash* appears on the very first page of *Night*, and no matter what guises he assumes in subsequent works he never disappears. At times he is only behind the scene. At other times his presence is manifest even though he is not the speaker. Thus the God who hangs on the gallows of the dying boy may seem close and assimilable to the Christ, but there is no suggestion of the death of God, let alone of his resurrection: this God is part not of the Christian message but of a mad Jewish Midrash. Again, the outburst "it is too late for the coming of the Messiah!" may seem close and assimilable to a tragic humanism, but becomes a mad Midrash through the sequel "precisely for this reason we are commanded to hope."[20] The madness of mad Moshe is most unmistakable when he speaks with his own voice. This he does when he enters a small synagogue in Nazi-occupied Europe, listens for a while to the worshippers, and warns them not to pray so loud lest God hear them; lest He notice that some Jews are still alive in Nazi Europe.[21]

What is this madness? Not insanity, if insanity is flight from reality. It is just because it dare not flee from *its* reality that this Midrash is mad. This madness is obliged—condemned?—to be sane. Not irrationality, if by this term we designate ignorance or lack of discernment. There is, to be sure, a rationality of a lesser sort, which is displayed by discerning the ways of one's world, by going about in it, going along with it. But such a rationality shows its own ultimate irrationality when it goes along on a road descending into hell and beyond. After all is over, this rationality can only plead that it "did not know." Midrashic madness, in contrast, *knows*, in some cases has known all along. Its discernment is informed by a Truth transcending the world of which it is a victim. Irrational by the standards of lesser rationalities, its rationality is ultimate.

Third, Midrashic madness is not mysticism, if mysticism is a rise to a divine ecstasy in which innocence and guilt, joy and anguish, good and evil are all indiscriminately transcended. Midrash must hold fast to the world; mad Midrash cannot but hold fast to *its* world, the anti-world.

How then can it retain this stance and *remain* Midrash, that is, hold fast to God as well as to its world? Only by dint of an absolute protest against the antiworld and its God—as it were, an anti-God over and against mad Moshe, a God mad with him, or a God torn between these extremes. This protest is serious only if it turns into a determination to *restore* the world. To be sure, the world-to-be-restored will be, as it always has been, an imperfect world. But although tarnished by a thousand blemishes, it is neither part of nor heir to the antiworld. On the contrary, the attempt to restore it strikes at the very core of the antiworld, aiming at the absolute overthrow of the latter. Thus the mad Midrashic Word turns into a Kaddish for all the victims of the antiworld, "that solemn affirmation full of grandeur and serenity, by which man returns to God His crown and sceptre."[22]

## Mad Midrash and Post-Holocaust Jewish Praxis

Midrashic madness is not insanity, not irrationality, not a flight from the world into mysticism. These negations must forever be emphasized if Midrashic madness is to preserve its integrity. But still a fourth negation—this one in a class by itself—is necessary. The negations made hitherto oppose threats and temptations from without. The negation to be made now opposes a threat arising from within the sphere of Midrashic madness itself. This threat is its last temptation.

The Midrashic Word was seen to point to, and be the linguistic expression of, Midrashic existence. For this relation between Word and existence, however, Midrashic madness can have no counterpart. Midrashic existence is lived in and with an imperfect (albeit ever perfectible) world. The existence to which mad Midrash points, the antiworld, cannot be lived in and with, but only opposed. To be sure, as we have seen, this opposition is already built into Midrashic madness itself. Yet, no longer having an existential counterpart, the Word is tempted to withdraw into inwardness, to expand this inwardness into a self-contained quasi-existence, and thus descend from literature into aestheticism.[23] Already theopolitical in its own right, mad Midrash must overcome this last temptation by pointing beyond the theological Word to a praxis whose politics forever questions all theology even as it remains itself theologically questioned. Thus a clear road leads from

*Night* to the *Jews of Silence*—a road understood only if its ultimate goal is not characters divorced from all else in a book, but also people outside and beyond the book. A people that (in no small measure thanks to *this* book) he ceased to be silent. A road too—though this one not so clear—leads from the final Kaddish for Leib the Lion in *The Gates of the Forest* to the final argument with Gad, the Israeli officer in *A Beggar in Jerusalem*. Leib has fought against, but has been killed by, the Holocaust when it murdered his people. Gad is killed only after having helped save the state which is the heir of the murdered people. The Kaddish for Leib can do no more than restore to God a crown and sceptre that have little power and majesty so long as the world remains unrestored. Gad helps restore the world—or at any rate, what after the antiworld has become its indispensable center—when he helps save the Jewish state, the heir of the exterminated Jews, from being itself exterminated.

This act on Gad's part is preceded by an argument with the protagonist. The latter knows (to paraphrase his words) that the world has not changed, that they would let it happen again, that Jews are still expendable, and that, what with superiority of arms and men on the side of an implacable enemy, to expect victory—or, what is the same thing, survival—is irrational. (As we have said at the very outset, although the existence of the Jewish state, after what has happened, is sacred, it is not, to put it mildly, secure.) Gad in no way challenges these facts. Yet he affirms that "the national funeral" of the Jewish state "will not take place. Not now, not ever." He admits the protagonist's murmured protest that a faith such as this borders on madness yet insists that not madness but only death is to be feared and, indeed, that death can be driven away, some wars be won, by invoking madness.[24]

Gad wins this argument even though, as an individual, he is killed in the war "shortly thereafter." For Midrashic madness points to *an existence in which the madness is transfigured*. Midrashic madness is the Word spoken in the antiworld that ought not to be, but is. The existence it points to acts to restore a world that ought to be but is not, committed to the faith that what ought to be must and will be, and this is its madness. After Planet Auschwitz, there can be no health without *this* madness, no joy, no life. Without this madness a Jew cannot do—with God or without him—what a Voice from Sinai bids him to do: choose life.

## Epilogue

Almost a century ago Friedrich Nietzsche—not the wisest of Germans, but the one best equipped to understand madness—let a madman appear on the scene, crying that God is dead, that God stays dead, that men are his murderers, but that despite this fact the deed has not yet come to their ears.[25] Somewhat later he let Zarathustra—a sage beyond madness—prognosticate two possibilities. The one hoped for—his "last will"—was: "Dead are all gods ... now let the superman live."[26] The one dreaded was the "last man":

> Alas, the time is coming when man will no longer give birth to a star. Alas, the time is coming of the most despicable man who can no longer despise himself.... A little poison now and then: it makes for pleasant dreams. And much poison in the end, for it makes for a pleasant death.... One still works, for work entertains. But one takes care lest the pastime cause fatigue....
>
> No shepherd and one flock. Each wants the same, is the same. He who feels differently enters the madhouse of his own accord.[27]

But Nietzsche's wisdom was not wise enough. A century after, the Nietzschean madness—mad because God is dead—is joined by a madness that is mad because He is alive.[28] And both are joined—surpassed?—by a new maturity, which, amusedly or wearily but in either case condescendingly, dismisses the whole question.

This new maturity fancies itself as representing Nietzsche's prophesied superman. Yet in fact the notion of a superman fit to take the place vacated by God has become a sad joke. For Planet Auschwitz murdered, along with men, women, and children, the idea of Man itself. And from Gulag and all the other heirs of Auschwitz resounds the daily cry: "Man is dead. Man stays dead!"

Thus of Nietzsche's three prognostications only the third has been borne out, and even this fails us in the end. It is not hard to recognize Nietzsche's "last man" in features of contemporary life, among them grey uniformity, computerized pleasure, an inability to create, and an unwillingness to sacrifice. But behind such characteristics of decadence lurk far more ominous dangers. There is callous indifference to murder abroad and on the streets at home. There is an infatuation with death and perversity. And pleasure seeks escape from boredom, not just (as Nietzsche naïvely imagined) in a poison making sweet dreams, but in quite a different poison, which produces an ever accelerating search for ever new depravities. The spectre of the Holocaust is quite unmistakably behind these phenomena. And it was only to be expected that sooner or later someone would make Auschwitz into a joke.[29]

In the beginning was the universe, and with it came man, the animal capable of laughter. He laughed at small incongruities—a man slipping on a banana skin—but stopped laughing when the incongruity became large—when the man broke his neck. Then came the Holocaust universe, and with it the S.S. man. He laughed only at large incongruities—the smashing of a non-Aryan baby's skull. Now the post-Holocaust universe has arrived, and it has produced a species of post-Holocaust man, Aryan and non-Aryan alike, who laughs at all the incongruities once considered large—the crimes of the murderers, the anguish of the victims, and above all his own previous "unliberated" inability to laugh at either.[30] Man becomes human through his capacity to laugh. With *this* laughter, his self-destruction is complete.

Or so it would be if the new maturity had really heard what it laughs at. However, though it wearily fancies itself as having heard everything, it has as yet understood nothing. The deed is done, but it has not yet come to men's ears. If a few feel differently, it is because their ears have heard, if indeed they are not survivors who have seen with their own eyes. These few will *not* enter the madhouse of their own accord. Never! They *must* not enter the madhouse. The post-Holocaust universe is in need of them. It needs them if man is to become, not a superman replacing God, or a "last man" replacing man, but rather, after what has happened, once again human.

Yes, it *is* necessary for us who are not survivors to become heirs of their witness in this world and beyond.

Byron L. Sherwin

# Wiesel's Midrash: The Writings of Elie Wiesel and Their Relationship to Jewish Tradition

### Wiesel's Midrash

Midrash is a search, an inquiry, a description, an exegesis. It attempts to fill in and to fill out the terse nature of the biblical text. Both Halakhic (i.e., legal) and Aggadic (i.e., nonlegal) Midrash frequently endeavor to find biblical precedent for unprecedented problems and events. In so doing, Midrash provides a link between a biblical text and a contemporary situation. It binds the experiences of the patriarchs and the prophets to our experiences, to our lives, to our times. Midrash provides a means by which our story may become incorporated into the continuing story of Jewish experience. Midrash insures a relationship between an ancient text and a modern problem, between ancient events and contemporary experiences.

By means of Midrash our perplexities become assuaged. Seeking a "sign" in the turbulence of our confusion, Midrash reminds us that "The events of our ancestors are a sign to their descendants." In early Midrash we witness the personalities of our ancestors unfold. In modern Midrash we establish our links with them. When we read about Abraham being thrown into a fiery furnace, about the crematoria of his six million descendants, we ask—Why was he spared? Why were they not spared? By raising our questions we provide beginnings for a new Midrash, for *our* Midrash.

In Midrash we find a framework for testing the genuineness of our response to events. Through Midrash we either find that our forefathers' problems were our problems or we *make* our problems their problems. Midrash comments upon a text. The text often precedes the commentary, but sometimes the commentary must seek the text.

God provides the text that Midrash attempts to explain—history. In history, God casts us in a role and we play it. In Midrash, we write the script. We provide God with his role.

Halakhic Midrash aims at telling us what to do. Aggadic Midrash tries to tell us *why* and *how* events have happened. Halakhic Midrash answers our questions. Aggadic Midrash poses our questions.

Midrash embarrasses the philosophers. It evokes the associational mind but provokes the logical mind. Midrash defies cogency; it repudiates systematic thought. Its bold imagery inspires the mystic but shocks the philosopher.

The medieval philosopher sought to encapsulate wisdom in a comprehensive but closed system. Midrash forces the tradition to remain open. Philosophy seeks finality. Midrash seeks new beginnings, new ways of understanding. Philosophy often seeks to explain away new problems and harsh events by redefining them. Midrash confronts them.

For the philosopher, evil may be explained away as the privation of the good. Hence experience must be made to conform with theory; theory interprets experience. Contradictions between idea and event must be removed; consistency must prevail. Midrash, on the other hand, seeks only to express and not to resolve discrepancies between concept and event.[1] Midrash represents theological expression while philosophical theology offers theological reflection. Midrash tells our theological story while philosophical theology formalizes the doctrinal beliefs of that story.

One may, therefore, suggest that Jewish theology operates on three levels, corresponding to the three levels of phenomenological analysis. On the pre-reflective level are the events of faith and the events that challenge faith. On this level—before we describe, before we reflect—we *experience*. Abraham J. Heschel refers to this primal theological experience as "depth-theology."[2] On the descriptive level we attempt to tell—both for our own self-understanding and as a legacy for those who will come after us—our story of the events that engender, expand, or challenge our faith. This is the level of Midrash. On the third level, the reflective level, we try to analyze, to concretize, to formalize, to systematize that which has been experienced by us and by others. We ponder and examine the story we have been told. Thus, Midrash may not organize our ideas, but it expresses our feelings. Through Midrash we seek self-understanding within the framework of tradition. We try to link our story, our experiences, and our problems to those of the past, without the formal discipline of logic or the clinical precision of philosophical theology. Through liturgy and ritual we enact our story, our Midrash, and make past stories our stories.[3]

Elie Wiesel's writings provide a Midrash for our times. In composing his Midrash, Wiesel ties the experiences of our days to those of the past and binds his story to the Jewish story. Though he persistently claims that the Holocaust is a unique, unprecedented event, Wiesel's writings belie this claim. By writing a modern Midrash, he connects the Holocaust and the State of Israel to past events, past experiences, past personalities. For, as he says, "Midrash mirrors both the imagined and lived reality of Israel, and it continues to influence our lives."[4] For Wiesel, no event in Jewish history completely stands apart. "No thing in Jewish history is unconnected. In Jewish history, everything is linked."[5]

Though Wiesel denies he is a theologian and claims he is only a teller of tales, it is precisely those tales, his Midrash, that bestow upon him a central place in contemporary Jewish theology. Though Wiesel's work is characterized by a constant tension between the devout Yeshiva student he once was and the skeptical Holocaust survivor he has become, it is this very tension that qualifies his work as a modern Midrash. Like earlier Midrashim, Wiesel's work manifests an attempt to relate new experiences to former faith. The complexities of the Holocaust survivor confront the simple faith of the Wishnitzer hasid.

The Auschwitz story is juxtaposed to the Hasidic story. The biblical story confronts the Holocaust story. Wiesel's spiritual pilgrimage brings these stories together.

Each person perceives his reflection in Adam.[6] Concerning the patriarchs, Wiesel writes, "Fathers of a people, Ancestors of Israel, your faith is our faith. To be a Jew is to believe in that which links us one to the other."[7] Abraham, the first Jew, becomes a contemporary of the modern Jew; he is cast into a crematorium; he dwells in the Land of Israel; he challenges Divine injustice.

Isaac is the survivor of a holocaust, as are Wiesel and so many others.[8] The story of Isaac "contains Jewish destiny in its totality." Isaac teaches the survivor of the Holocaust to suffer and despair, but not to surrender the art of laughter. The contemporary Jew, like Job, confronts God out of a whirlwind, out of a *Shoah*. Job teaches the survivors of catastrophe to live in spite of themselves. Like Jacob, the contemporary Jew represents the first post-Holocaust generation, the first witness of the Holocaust. He sees the ladder at Auschwitz as a Jacob's ladder on which "an entire people was climbing, climbing toward the clouds of fire." Like Joseph, the Jew today confronts the question of how to live as a Jew in the Diaspora. Moses seeks the redemption of his people from Egyptian bondage, the contemporary Jew seeks the redemption of Soviet Jewry from Russian bondage. Thus Wiesel's Midrash makes the Jewish past the Jewish present. It is a seance, allowing the dead to speak to the living and the living to try to understand the dead. In Wiesel's Midrash, the legends of past times become *Legends of Our Time*. "The legends he brings back are the very ones we are living today."[9]

Like I. L. Peretz, Wiesel searches for the *niggun*, the melody of past times, in order to find the appropriate melody for our times. In Wiesel's writings, the *niggun* of the past is transmigrated into the present.

## Wiesel's Challenge

Elie Wiesel's Midrashim are his prayers. All his stories are one story; all his prayers are one prayer: "Why was God's prayer not answered?" And what does God pray? "May My attribute of mercy suppress My anger; may it prevail over My other attributes."[10] The Holocaust is evidence that God's prayer was not answered, that the perennial prayer of the Jew was not answered.[11] Has Wiesel's prayer been answered? Like Levi Yitzchak's, Wiesel's prayer is a Kaddish—both a challenge and a praise. Wiesel's Kaddish is a mourner's Kaddish, which indicts while it affirms.

The great Hasidic master Levi Yitzchak learned his tactics from Honi, the rabbinic master: " 'I will not move from this place until Heaven answers.' If Honi had not been successful, Shimeon ben Shetach would have excommunicated him for apostasy."[12] Unlike Honi and like Levi Yitzchak, Wiesel has not been answered, and to some, perhaps even to himself, he walks the thin line between faith and heresy.

The hero of *Dawn* bears the name Elisha—simultaneously the name of the prophet[13] and of ben Abuya (Aher), the excommunicate heretic, the paradigmatic blasphemer.[14]

Some have found Wiesel's theological kinship in Elisha the heretic and his rejection of the tradition epitomized by Elisha the prophet. However, if Wiesel is a blasphemer, his "blasphemy" is a traditionally defensible, uniquely Jewish blasphemy with deep roots in classical Jewish theology, specifically in rabbinic and Kabbalistic sources. It is based upon disappointment, not rejection, inspired by sympathy and love of God, precipitated by love of man. In this regard, Wiesel writes:

> Jewish tradition allows man to say anything to God, provided it be on behalf of man. Man's inner liberation is God's justification. It all depends on where the rebel chooses to stand. From inside his community, he may say everything. Let him step outside, and he will be denied this right. The revolt of the believer is not that of the renegade; the two do not speak in the name of the same anguish.[15]

Wiesel holds membership in the fellowship of those reconstructionists of faith who have arisen among traditional Jewish blasphemers after each major tragedy in Jewish history. After the destruction of the Temple, the Talmud was committed to writing. After the expulsion from Spain, the Kabbalah flourished in an attempt to explain what had occurred. Wiesel is the *Tanna Kama* (master-teacher) of the new Talmud, trying to explain why God's prayers, as well as man's, remain unanswered. He is the *Ari*, the "Lion" of our generation: he roars at God, he purrs at God. Perhaps it would be more correct to say that he is writing a new Bible. For the Holocaust claims Wiesel: though it is the antithesis of Sinai, it is its equal in significance. This new Bible would have as its major theme not God's disappointment with man but man's disappointment with God.

The tradition of Jewish protestantism was begun by Abraham— "Shall the Judge of all the earth not do justice?" (Gen. 18:25)—and developed by the prophets: "Wherefore does the way of the wicked prosper?" (Jer. 12:1). ". . . Lord, how long shall I cry and Thou wilt not hear, even cry out unto Thee of violence and Thou will not save. . . . The wicked encompass the righteous, wrong judgment proceedeth. . . . Wherefore holdest Thou Thy tongue when the wicked devoureth the man that is more righteous than he?" (Hab. 1:1-3). When did Habakkuk say this? A Midrash suggests this answer:

> Habakkuk drew a figure of a circle and stood in the middle of it and said to the Holy One, blessed be He, "Master of the Universe, I shall not stir from this place until Thou declarest to me how long Thou wilt continue to show forebearance to the wicked in this world?" The Holy One, blessed be He, replied: "You have cried out to Me but you have not doubted Me. As thou livest, I shall answer thee and cause thee to understand. I show forebearance to the wicked in this world so that they may come back to me in repentance and their willful sins will then be reckoned as unwitting sins. . . ." When the Holy One lets the righteous envision the trials that are to come upon Israel, the righteous stand up and protest to Him.[16]

Moses, the greatest prophet, also protests. Moreover, he goes further and defends even the guilty against God's wrath. God plans to exterminate the Jewish people for the sin of building the Golden Calf, but Moses intercedes and convinces him rather than the people to repent. As a result, God changes his mind and does not punish the people with death (Exod. 32: 7-14). The rabbis comment upon such a phenomenon as follows: "God says, 'I rule mankind. Who rules Me?—The righteous. For I make a decree and they annul it.'"[17]

Job, when he had nothing else to lose, protested to God. In rabbinic times the school of Rabbi Ishmael cultivated protest:

"Who is like unto Thee among the mighty (*elim*) O Lord?" (Exodus 15:11). Said Rabbi Ishmael: Read rather "Who is like unto Thee among the silent (*elmim*), O Lord—seeing the suffering of His children and remaining silent?"[18]

As the Midrash concerning Habakkuk stated, these protests arise from the guts of faith and are not mere skeptical asides. Such protests to God come out of love for and disappointment with God. In our own time, Elie Wiesel voices this view of Jewish protestantism. He writes:

"You are blaspheming," he repeated gently, as if he were envious, as if he would have liked to blaspheme as well. "God's victory, my son, lies in man's inability to reject Him. You think you're cursing Him, but your curse is praise; you think you're fighting Him, but all you do is open yourself to Him; you think you're crying out your hatred and rebellion, but all you're doing is telling Him how much you need His support and forgiveness."[19]

Only after Jacob struggles with God is he called "Israel." Israel is a people by virtue of its eternal struggle with God to make him remain faithful to his covenant, to force him to run his world with justice and to temper his justice with mercy.

Perhaps the greatest protester of all was the aforementioned Levi Yitzchak of Berditchev, who stood in the center of the circle he had drawn and brought a suit for breach of contract against God. The Talmud says that Israel is the *tefillin* of God. And so one day in the midst of his prayers Levi Yitzchak said to God:

Master of Worlds, when a simple Jew drops his *tefillin* he picks them up and kisses them. Lord—Israel are your tefillin. They lie in the dust. Do what even the simplest Jew knows he should do—Pick them up. Pick us up and redeem us.

In another time of great persecution Levi Yitzchak said to God: "We have had enough of suffering. If to be a chosen people means to experience incessant suffering, then Master of the Universe, choose someone else!"

Wiesel joins this tradition of calling God to justice, which expresses the Jew's perennial struggle to believe in God in spite of him.

### The Covenant

The right to challenge God, as the privilege of judging God, is implicit within the covenantal relationship between God and men in general, God and Israel in particular. Wiesel's indictment of God assumes that God can be indicted and tried by man for His failure to abide by His agreement, by His covenant.

Like most theologies of the Holocaust, Wiesel's Midrash rejects the applicability of the classical interpretation of tragedy as punishment for sin, as divine retribution.[20] With R. Simeon B. Elazar, Wiesel assumes, "There *is* a death without sin and suffering without transgression."[21] To explain the Holocaust as punishment for sin is to assume that Israel alone has broken the covenant, not God. It presumes that by exacting such severe retribution, God is fulfilling rather than denying his part of the covenant.

For Wiesel, however, the Holocaust calls the covenant into question, especially where God's obligations are concerned. When man breaks the covenant, God judges his deeds. In turn, when God breaks the covenant, man may judge God. According to the Talmud, the covenant was imposed upon Israel by force; man was compelled by God to accept the covenant.[22] As God initiates the covenant, his breaking it entails greater implications than when man breaks it. Does

God's breaking the covenant mean that the covenant is discarded, at an end?

While Wiesel raises this question, his position is that the covenant, while broken by God, has not been terminated. Echoing Jacob Glatstein's poetic statement that God gave the Torah at Sinai and took it back during the Holocaust,[23] Wiesel adds that God returned the Torah to Israel at the Western Wall. For Wiesel, the Holocaust does not cancel the covenant, nor does it affirm the covenant. Nevertheless, Sinai and Auschwitz are interlinked. They represent the zenith and the nadir of Jewish experience. Wiesel parts company with past traditions in his implicit refutation of Saadya's view of the nature of the relationship of the Torah to the people of Israel. For Saadya, Israel is a people because of the Torah. For Wiesel, the Torah exists because of Israel. Jewish existence guarantees the Torah. Without Israel, the Torah cannot survive.[24]

The Holocaust, therefore, represents God's assault on his Torah through his people. "It is the Bible that is being killed, the prophets that are being massacred."[25] Nevertheless, God's breaking his covenant does not free him from the covenant. He is punished by watching his people suffer. To assert that the covenant is no longer in force is not to grant a posthumous victory to Hitler, but to grant a total victory to Christian theology and an undeserved victory to God.

In Jewish law, God can be tried for his crimes because he is a party to an agreement, i.e., the covenant. In this respect he is a "person" in Jewish law.[26] The trials of God narrated by Hasidic literature, Holocaust literature, and by Wiesel are not only aggadically (theologically) defensible, but halakhically viable. As man is required to bear witness before God, he may also bear witness against God.[27]

The assumption that God sins and requires expiation has Hasidic and even rabbinic roots. Levi Yitzchak of Berditchev, for example, claims that the Day of Atonement is known as *Yom Ha-Kippurim* (in the plural), because it is a day of atonement both for man *and* for God. According to rabbinic literature, God unjustly diminished the size of the moon; He sinned. Therefore, one is required to bring a "sin offering *for* God" (Numbers 28:15)—to atone for God's sin.[28] The notion that God requires man to atone for His misdeeds is related to the equally bold idea that God, not being omnipotent (at least in our world), requires man to redeem Him.[29]

Wiesel is a partisan of the long-standing tradition that calls God's justice into question. He rejects the tradition that understands such questioning as being tantamount to heresy. (For example, the claim of R. Yudan that "He who says that the Merciful One is loose in the administration of the world gets loose bowels [i.e., he who questions how God runs the world gets the runs].")[30] Wiesel rejects Rashi's stance, which allows one to say to God, "Even if you annihilate us we shall praise you forever."[31]

If God's trials of the pious are in some way an expression of his love,[32] then the faithfuls' trials of God are also an expression of their love. The moral challenge to God does not manifest arrogance but profound disappointment in a loving parent. It is an encounter that assumes a deep intimacy with the Divine. As in the lawsuit of Levi Yitzchak against God, for example, Wiesel, too, prays to God to aid him in his unbelief. The trial is harsh, but its purpose is not to chastise the defendant but to express the advocate's desire that He at least offer a plea on His own behalf.[33]

Only once in Wiesel is such a plea heard—God's answer is an answer that speaks with silence. The answers come but are not understood.[34] In a way Wiesel is apprehensive of the answer. He yearns to "know God" and is afraid to do so. Here, too, Wiesel is like Elisha. He is entering the Garden (*pardés*) of forbidden knowledge, aware that this may bring insanity or apostasy. "You can love God but you cannot look at him. . . ."[35] "If man could contemplate the face of God, he would stop loving Him." But Wiesel continues to love him despite disappointment.[36] Despite all his yearning for God and for an answer, he must condemn God for the most unforgivable crime—useless murder. Man can live with a cruel God, who creates men to murder them, who chooses a people to have them slain on a sacrificial altar, but he cannot live in a world without God. Better to be insane, better to blaspheme, than to be without God.[37] Better to search for the hidden God, the eclipsed God, than to be without him.[38]

In *Ani Maamin* God is silent throughout. Job received an answer, which was no answer. Perhaps silence is the only answer. Wiesel echoes the Talmudic episode in which Moses is shown the flesh of Rabbi Akiva being weighed in the marketplace. He protests and God answers: Such is my decree—BE SILENT![39] Rabbi Akiva departs both from the *pardés* and from torture by the Romans in peace, but Moses' question still remains.

Possibly influenced by André Neher's reflections on the silence of God, Wiesel rejects the possibility that divine silence entails the termination of the covenant. Neher writes, "With the same force used to announce a rupture of His covenant, God cries out that such a rupture is inconceivable."[40]

*Ani Maamin* concludes not with God's silence but with his compassion, with his empathy for human suffering. It concludes, not with God's word, but with his tear. This is not the omnipotent God of the philosophers but the empathetic God of the prophets and of the Midrash. This is the God whom the Midrash describes as crying at the destruction of the Temple. This is the God to whom is addressed the question: Why did you allow the Temple to be destroyed? The God who answers: "Is not my Temple destroyed and my children thrown into chains. I am in anguish, as it is written—I am with him in anguish." This is the God about whom the Midrash reports: "It must be concluded that the Holy One, blessed be He, was saying to the prophets: 'You weep,' and was saying through them, 'I weep with you.' "[41] This is the God who must weep rather than be silent.

"When Israel was banished and the Temple destroyed, and the Sanhedrin was removed from its seat, the Holy One wept bitterly. He lifted his voice in lamentation for Israel, and like one who is stunned, He said about Israel—Surely, My tent is spoiled—foes have entered it and despoiled my sanctuary. How can I sit and be silent?"[42] God is not unaffected by Israel's sufferings: " 'When Israel is in exile,' says God, 'I am as one who is ill.' "[43] This is the God of Wiesel's Midrash, *Ani*

*Maamin.* "He (God) weeps over his creation—and perhaps over much more than his creation."[44]

Thus, for Wiesel God is both an apparently apathetic witness to and a passionate participant in human suffering. God in his essence, the omnipotent God of the philosophers, the Infinite God (*En Sof*) of the mystics, must be challenged for not exercising his omnipotence to assuage the radical evil of the Holocaust. However, God as he is manifest in our world, the empathetic God of the prophets, the *Shekinah* of the Midrash and later of the mystics, participates in suffering and affliction. The omnipotent God redeems us; the empathetic God, conditioned by the human plight, requires us to redeem him as well as ourselves. Wiesel, knowing that the Infinite Unmoved Mover will not respond, turns toward the *Shekinah*, the manifestation of the Godhead, which, in a way, shares our finiteness.

### Redemption: Human and Divine

Perhaps the central idea of Kabbalah is the ability, indeed the destiny of man to play a central role in the life of God. Hegel suggests that world history is God's autobiography.[45] The Kabbalah disagrees: world history is God's biography as written by God and man; God supplies the letters—man writes the sentences. The interdependence of man and God, i.e., man and *Shekinah*, is best articulated in the chapter of the Jewish story on Messianic redemption. According to Jewish mystical thought, man need not be a passive spectator to the cosmic drama of redemption; he can be a participant, a liberator, a protagonist.[46] Until the final redemption, insists the Jewish mystical tradition, everything in the natural and the supernatural spheres remains alienated from its true essence. God himself is no exception. The *Shekinah*, his presence in the world, is in exile—like his people—alienated from its true essence.

The rabbinic notion of the exile and redemption of God and man was further developed in the sixteenth century by R. Isaac Luria. According to Lurianic mysticism, the harmony that characterized existence on all levels—human, cosmic, divine—was disrupted by the "breaking of the vessels" that contained the Divine Light. As a result of this event, the *Shekinah* was cast into exile and part of the Divine Light flowed downward into the cosmos. Thus sparks from the Divine Light are to be found throughout creation. But these sparks, which belong reunited with their Source, are now mixed with the evil elements that surround and imprison them with "shells." The purpose of human existence is to restore the primordial harmony and unity. Redemption is acquired through man's attempts to liberate the sparks through the performance of good deeds and to rejoin them with their Source.[47]

Luria formulates a similar theory concerning the soul of Adam, the first man. According to this view, after Adam's fall, which intervened when he should have completed the restoration of harmony by lifting up all the divine sparks from the broken vessels, the great and all-embracing soul that was his was shattered too. The souls of all men, symbolized as sparks, originally constituting the soul of the first man, were scattered throughout the world. The human sparks, like the *Shekinah* and its sparks, are in exile, dispersed. The reunification of the sparks of the First Man brings about the advent of the Last Man, the Messiah.[48] In this view, the Messiah is not one who brings redemption but one who comes as a sign that redemption has arrived.[49] The Lurianic notion that each of our souls contains a spark of the soul of the primordial Adam, which is identical to the soul of the Messiah, means that each individual shares in the drama of bringing the Messiah because he shares in being the Messiah. Luria's system often fails to distinguish between these two kinds of sparks: human and divine.[50]

Luria's perspective, with this characteristic absence of a clear differentiation between the human and divine sparks, appears in Wiesel. Wiesel writes:

> An aspect of God was concealed even in evil, and the theory of the *Nitzotzot* said so poetically: every man possesses a divine spark. The *Shekinah* is the sum of the sparks. Let the *Shekinah*—the divine emanation—be reunited with God and the world will have achieved its final liberation.[51]

In rabbinic and Kabbalistic thought, therefore, the idea persists that man may redeem God. Thus the roles of God and man are reversed. God is imprisoned, the sparks are trapped in the shells, and man must liberate them to secure his own redemption as well as the redemption of God's presence in the world. "That is the best-guarded secret since the creation. . . . The criminals of the world, the forces of evil, know this secret. It is for that reason that they seek imprisonment. For once in prison they can kill God."[52]

God awaits redemption from his confinement. He awaited it in Auschwitz, and he awaits it today as he dwells among the Jews in Russia. The truest Jews share in the plight of God. They await the redemption of God and of man. The genuine Jew not only awaits the Messiah but is the Messiah.[53]

Wiesel restates the Kabbalistic notion that the internal unity of the Godhead is to be equated with redemption. Unity, the "collection of the sparks," restoring the primordial unity of the divine forces in the cosmos, stressed in Lurianic thinking, is reiterated by Wiesel:[54]

> Once I asked my teacher, Kalman the cabalist, the following question: For what purpose did God create man? I understand that man needs God. But what need of man has God? . . . The holy books teach us, he said, that if man were conscious of his power, he would lose his faith or his reason. For man carries within him a role which transcends him. God needs to be ONE. . . . man who is nothing but a handful of earth is capable of reuniting time and its source and of giving back to God his own image.[55]

## Conclusion

While one waits and works for future redemption, the past remains a mystery. The Holocaust defies solutions. The story may be recounted but not understood. Questions may be posed, but only responses and not answers should be expected.[56]

The most extensive theological analysis of the problem of evil after Auschwitz has been that of John Hick. In his erudite and thorough study of the literature on the subject in Western Christian tradition, Hick concludes:

> Our "solution" then to this baffling problem of excessive and undeserved suffering is a frank appeal to the positive power of mystery. Such suffering remains unjust and inexplicable, haphazard and cruelly excessive. The mystery of dysteleological suffering is a real mystery, impenetrable to the rationalizing human mind.[57]

It is significant that Hick's conclusion, apparently reached primarily through methodological conceptualization, is identical to that of Elie Wiesel, whose response is primarily based upon experience.

> Perhaps some day someone will explain how, on the level of man, Auschwitz was possible; but on the level of God, it will forever remain the most disturbing of mysteries.[58]

And so, like Pinhas of Koretz, Wiesel's questions remain questions; his doubts are still heavy with anguish, but he is compelled to continue, to tell the story, to provide the link between our past and our future, between man and God.[59]

According to the Talmud, when the Romans executed R. Hananya ben Teradion, they burned him to death in a Torah scroll. The rabbi is reported to have said, "I am burning together with the Torah scroll. He who will have regard for the Torah will also have regard for my plight." His disciples called out: "Our Master, what seest thou?" He answered them: "The parchments are being burnt, but the letters are soaring aloft."[60] Wiesel's Midrash attempts to retrieve the words burnt in the Holocaust, the letters that have soared aloft. The Talmud also relates:

> When the First Temple was about to be destroyed bands upon bands of young priests with the keys of the Temple in their hands mounted the roof of the Temple and exclaimed: Master of the Universe, as we did not have the merit to be faithful treasures, these keys are handed back into Thy keeping. Then they threw the keys upward

toward heaven. And there emerged the figure of a hand which received the keys from them. Whereupon they jumped into the fire.[61]

Wiesel's Midrash attempts to recapture the keys surrendered by those who perished in the Holocaust. With these keys he has begun to open a door that links past to present. In so doing, to use Wiesel's own words, "he only tries to wrest from death certain prayers, certain faces, by appealing to the imagination and the nostalgia that made man listen when his story is told."[62]

Sidra Ezrahi

# The Holocaust Writer and the Lamentation Tradition: Responses to Catastrophe in Jewish Literature

Most of the European literature of the Holocaust focuses on the individual in his struggle for survival, or on the degrees of his acquiescence to the concentrationary system. The self in its anomy is, then, the primary reference, personal survival is the ultimate goal, and death, disintegration of the self, or submission to the system is the ultimate defeat.[1]

In this context certain writers appear unique in that they rely not on biography but on Jewish history to infuse their work with the structural continuity between past, present, and a possible future. The historical vision that anchors the meaning of the self in the fate and the cultural resources of the group, and that places theodicy rather than the struggle for survival at the center of its exploration of the concentrationary universe, generates symbolic responses that are profoundly different from the existentialist perspective. The writers I am about to consider reflect and draw upon a literary and philosophical tradition in which centuries of persecution and a codified system of beliefs have generated specific cultural responses to collective catastrophe and the absorption of "facts" and historical "events" into an inherited valuational framework. The Hebraic lamentation tradition derives from biblical sources and can be traced through two millennia of Hebrew texts.

Not unlike the writers for whom the self is the primary arbiter of experience, the Holocaust survivors writing within the Hebraic tradition are motivated at least in part by the need to convey and legitimate their own sufferings and to commemorate the lives and deaths of their companions. Additionally, they are responding to the imperative to link their own fate to the destiny of Israel, wherein the self, even in death, is submerged and retained in the collective consciousness—to locate the Holocaust along the spectrum of Jewish suffering. In some cases, they also commemorate the way of life and the cultural values that were extinguished along with those who held them.

Those European writers who share this perspective, such as Elie Wiesel, Manès Sperber, André Schwarz-Bart, Nelly Sachs, and Paul Celan, should be read with reference to Hebrew and Yiddish writers, all of whom draw upon a vocabulary that has been incorporated into the lexicon of Jewish martyrology. Adolf Rudnicki, a non-Jewish Polish writer, wrote in one of his stories that "no other nation has so many synonyms for suffering as have the Jews.... Everybody knows that what the Germans did during the Second World War has no equivalent in history, yet it was all contained within the Jews' ancient vocabulary."[2] The works of writers who can be located within this tradition seek resonance, then, within an identifiable constituency of readers, and invite judgment not only as reflections of the creative ability of the artist or even as authentic versions of reality but also, or especially, in terms of the ways in which, as Maurice Samuel put it, "the event is establishing itself in the Jewish people."[3]

The term "constituency of readers" should be used advisedly: the decimated, displaced survivors of the Holocaust in the Diaspora can no longer be regarded as constituting a cultural unit capable of absorbing, judging, and preserving the works of its artists. As the Yiddish writer Rabi has observed, what has replaced the "Jewish public" as a heterogeneous but still organic community is the "mass media," which arbitrates Jewish literature for Jews.[4] Outside of Israel, anyway, acclaim and censure are no longer an internal process but a derivative one, by which Jewish readers are guided largely by standards of the non-Jewish community. André Schwarz-Bart and Nelly Sachs reached Jewish readers in large numbers only after they had received the Prix Goncourt and the Nobel Prize, respectively. Nevertheless, these writers draw upon a common heritage and may be regarded as performing specific cultural tasks as witnesses to the slaughter not of six million individuals but of one third of the Jewish people.

Whether or not the individual survivor succeeds in isolating and containing his experience in the camps and in rebuilding a post-Holocaust life for himself—and most of Holocaust fiction testifies to the failure of such efforts—the Hebraic writer cannot regard the Nazi epoch as unrelated to, or isolated from, the issue of both social and metaphysical continuity. What is at stake here is not only the belief in divine justice, which had been the ultimate reference for generations of persecuted Jews, but the entire fabric of society and culture that upheld that faith. Here it may be necessary to recall, perhaps, that we are studying constructs of literary response that are derivative from but not necessarily mimetic of the reactions of the actual victims to the actual persecutions—that is, they are meant to be in some way instructive in a post-Holocaust future. Ultimately there came a moment in the life of nearly every inmate of the ghettos and camps when all supports collapsed and life came to mean nothing but the struggle for a crust of bread. In an autobiographical fragment, Elie Wiesel writes that this "miserable crust of moldy bread came to contain more truth, more eternity, than all the pages of all the books put together."[5] There are writers—powerful, compelling writers like Tadeusz Borowski—who have concentrated on that struggle. But the writers I would like to discuss are those who *have*, after all, attempted to put the pages of the book back together—to absorb the agony into the collective consciousness of the surviving remnant. And that is achieved, especially in the case of Wiesel, Sperber, and Schwarz-Bart, not primarily through realism but through a kaleidoscope of history, a contemporaneity or simultaneity of events that places Auschwitz within the context of centuries of martyrdom. As Sperber writes in his novel . . .

*Than a Tear in the Sea,* Hitler was "none other than Haman whom they knew so well from the Book of Esther."[6]

These writers, then, still conceive of themselves and are received as public scribes, as the heirs of the prophets and elegists of what Sachs calls "Das Leiden Israels" (the suffering of Israel).[7] Although direct lines of influence cannot always be drawn between their poetry and fiction and lamentational literature, they should be studied with reference to that tradition.

The massacres, forced conversions, Crusades, expulsions, and pogroms that punctuate Jewish history from the time of the destruction of the First Temple till modern times have been commemorated in a chain of liturgical elegies—"selihoth" and "kinoth"[8]—and in folktales or "midrashim."[9] When we consider the paucity of historical records of the time,[10] the mnemonic function of such poems and stories becomes even more apparent. Of course historiography as we know it—secular history—had no place in a society in which study of and commentary on the Torah, rather than on the vicissitudes of human fortunes, were meant to reveal eternal and recurrent truths.[11]

Lamentation literature helped to preserve sacred communal memory in a number of ways. In a community in which a mythic view of history prevailed, the kinoth provided the footnotes to update the biblical revelation of divine purpose. The poems take not only their historical analogues but also their form and idiom from biblical elegy, especially from the books of Jeremiah and Lamentations. Many of the kinoth are written in variations of the alphabetical acrostic of the book of Lamentations, a form common to much of the poetry of the Middle Ages.[12] The purpose of the poems is generally twofold: to commemorate the martyrs and to praise and petition God. The names of important persons and of whole communities are woven into the verses, as well as other details, such as the date ("on the Sabbath day, the eighth of Iyar";[13] "in the year 1391"[14]) and even the means of torture ("their feet and hands they severed / and cut the corpse in half"[15]) and the various forms of desecration of the Scriptures.[16] On the whole the paytanim (liturgical poets) demonstrated more passion than poetic talent; many of these poems have simple, almost ludicrous rhyme schemes governed by a greater commitment to selected facts than to form.[17] A. M. Haberman admits that the community did not always inquire as to the poetic quality of the kinoth; many of these poems exercised their power over the people not because of their aesthetic merit but "by dint of the truth in them."[18] An occasional elegist did, however, produce verses of lasting power, which were incorporated into the liturgy.[19] It is of course an ancient bardic method of preserving communal memory to recite names and historical events in verse, but in the medieval and postmedieval Jewish communities the kinoth and selihoth served the additional and more immediate purpose of providing the information that could enable survivors to recite the Kaddish for their dead on the proper day.[20] And specific poems were often integrated into the prayer service of local communities—for instance, one selihah that commemorated the local victims of the Chmielnicki massacre was incorporated into the Lithuanian selihoth liturgy and contributed over the years to a unique sense of continuity of place.[21]

Occasionally a single act of bravery took on mythic proportions in midrashim or poetry, and in its variation one can trace the growth and uses of legend. Such, for example, is the story of the woman—variously called Miriam or Hannah—whose seven sons refused to eat swine, or, in another version, to bow down to idols, and were tortured and killed. The story is related, with different details and emphasis, in the apocryphal Second Book of Maccabees, in Lamentations Rabba, and in other contexts.[22] Through the literature such stories were transformed into paradigms of the agony and heroic faith of the entire community and were meant to provide instructional models for the victims of future persecutions. Writing within such a well-defined normative framework, the paytan was careful to avoid mention of acts of betrayal or cowardice on the part of the martyrs.[23]

Although the paytan often wrote in the first person and described particular events, his poems, as specific or autobiographical as they might be, usually illuminated one of two fundamental axioms: that Israel was suffering because it had erred[24] or because certain innocent persons or communities had been singled out to sanctify God's name through martyrdom.[25] There were also frequent and impassioned pe-

titions to God for vengeance and numerous instances of desperate and
even defiant indictments of divine silence or indifference.[26] Nevertheless, the poet spoke with a prophetic or collective voice and concluded
his lament with an affirmation of faith. The kinah, then, was both a
poetic reflection of and a constitutive response to history. As a sustained
literary genre it is, according to Haberman, unique among comparative
literatures: "the community of Israel, which had forgotten what celeb-
ratory poetry was, raised up its voice in one terrible kinah—a long and
bitter shout which incorporated the sorrow and the tears of the generations."[27]

Even the diffusion of the Enlightenment ideology and the erosion
of monolithic religious beliefs did not significantly alter the image of
the poet in the eyes of the people. Struggle as he might against the
summons to a public, prophetic voice, a poet like Haim Nahman Bialik
could not escape into an exploration of his private soul so long as his
people needed him as comforter, chastiser, and national poet.[28] But
already Bialik represents the lamentation tradition in transition. He
was no longer strictly bound by the religious authority of the tradition
or by the formulas with which it had confronted historic crises. His
God is elusive and many-faceted: in some poems God has turned a
deaf ear to man;[29] in others it is man who has lost the way to Him.[30]
Bialik's elegies are far more complex than the traditional kinoth, not
only in their theodicy but also in their exploration of the responses of
the victims. In the long poem "In the City of the Slaughter," written
in 1905 as a response to the Kishinev pogrom, the speaker displays
neither pure piety nor unmitigated compassion; he is as repelled by
the cowardice of the victims as by the brutality of the victimizers. In
this poem it is human behavior, as well as divine providence, that is
being tested.[31] Yet Bialik registered his protest not by a retreat from
but by subtle inversions of the traditional responses to catastrophe;
by retaining familiar symbols and constructs yet altering their context
and significance, he succeeded in conveying the ambiguities and complexities of a new spiritual reality while satisfying the community's
need for an elegist.[32]

When the Jews in the Nazi ghettos and camps looked for a writer who would bear witness to their catastrophe they again looked for an elegist. Even as meticulous an historian as Haim Kaplan felt that historical record alone could not provide the kind of commemoration that a dying people wanted to leave behind. If we consider the social dimensions of elegiac literature, even in an increasingly secular community, the poem that is invested with mythical or ritualistic functions can also provide a contemporaneity that historiography, in its remoteness, cannot:

> Our forefathers [Kaplan wrote in his Warsaw Diary], who were experienced in adversity, immortalized their sufferings in lamentations. . . . The national splendor inherent in religious poetry is not expressed in newspaper reports. . . . A catastrophe that becomes part of poetry, even non-religious poetry such as Bialik's "The City of Slaughter," which commemorated the Kishinev pogrom, spreads among the people and is transmitted to future generations. A poet who clothes adversity in poetic form immortalizes it in an everlasting monument.
> Who will write of our troubles and who will immortalize them? Poet of the people, where art thou?[33]

One man who might have become—given the time and tranquility needed to perfect his craft—the "poet of the people" was the Yiddish poet Yitzhak Katzenelson. By the time he perished in Auschwitz he had already written his monumental "Song of the Murdered Jewish People." He was regarded, even by secular resistance fighters such as Mordecai Tenenbaum, as the one who could immortalize the agony and the struggle: "All that we thought, felt, or imagined, he wrote about," Tenenbaum wrote in a letter from Bialystok to his sister in Palestine. "We furnished him with the debris of our misery, and he made it eternal, sang of it, it was our common property."[34] The terror of Katzenelson's poetry is not only in the atrocities he relates, some of which are even surpassed in their gruesome details by poetic accounts of medieval pogroms, but in that it reflects a world that has lost its center, a world from which God has receded and the community of worshippers who might have found their way back to Him has been destroyed, root and branch. The echoes of phrases from lamentation literature appear all the more terrible in these poems because the ulti-

mate source of meaning and consolation that informed the interpretation of catastrophe throughout the generations has been withdrawn.
In the Midrash, as in the Bible, all of nature, all of the cosmos, participates in the suffering of Israel. One Midrash recounts that when the
Temple was burning and the Jews were being slaughtered, Moses
reprimanded the sun for shining on such devastation. The sun replied,
in sorrow and shame, that it was forced by higher powers to shine.[35]
Compare this with Katzenelson's poem of the stars whose indifference
twinkles at the poet in his everlasting night.[36] The outside world—
nature, the cosmos, Divinity—appears either as a memory or a mockery.
Although a defiance that borders on apostasy accompanied the response to catastrophe in nearly every generation, never, I believe, in
the lamentation literature does man's loneliness appear so vast and
implacable or the desolation of his world so total. In Katzenelson's
poetry, as in the Yiddish poetry of many of the survivors, tradition
flounders like a boat whose course was charted long ago but which
has lost its compass—and its crew.

And yet these themes continue to reverberate through Yiddish po-
etry—to whom, to what force can the Jewish poet appeal other than to
the God of his fathers, even in the hour of His eclipse: "In whom can
I believe, / If not in Him, my beloved God of Cataclysm," asks Aharon
Zeitlin in his poem "Ani Maamin." "I am a Jew, as He is God."[37]
And Ya'acov Glatstein seems to answer him in his poem "Ohn
Yiddn": "Without Jews, there is no Jewish God."[38]

Hebrew literature has undergone a somewhat different development. A long chain of literary precedents and the historic consciousness
of the only socially coherent and articulate community of Jews left in
the world generated the expectation that Hebrew poetry would produce the "definitive" elegy that could encompass and assign meaning
to the latest and most terrible chapter in the chronicle of Jewish suffering. The Jews of Palestine, sharing with other Jews the same heritage
and the same regard for the evocative power of poetry under critical
circumstances, removed from the continent on which the annihilating
hosts were gathering—though not from the global conflict that threatened to engulf Palestine as well—responded variously to the condition

of their European brothers. In the years preceding the war, a surprising number of Hebrew writers had warned of impending disaster in a series of poems and stories that can, perhaps, be read not only as clairvoyant but also as reflections of the ideological bias of a community disengaging itself from the ways and the fate of the Diaspora. Some of the major poets, including Zalman Shneur before World War I and Shaul Tchernikovsky in the thirties, invoked grotesque images of medieval torture and mass murder to suggest through an analogous and cyclical reading of history the imminent encroachment of the forces of destruction upon the world in general and the Jews in particular. Even Uri Zvi Greenberg, who later became European Jewry's chief Hebrew elegist, was one of the most prominent prophets of its destruction in the thirties, referring to himself as a creature not quite dog and not quite jackal, "who sniffs out disaster and barks in time."[39]

During the war itself a fairly large number of poems appeared that expressed the sense of helplessness and horror that the Jews in Palestine were experiencing. The tone of much of this poetry was strident and declamatory, uneven in quality and nourished by both unfounded hopes and the trickles of real news that filtered slowly into public consciousness. Attentive not necessarily to aesthetic standards, but to a tradition of public poetry in times of national crisis, a large segment of the community reproached its poets for not sufficiently fulfilling their role as spokesmen. Much of the unease expressed in the community issued from a pervasive sense of the disparity between the relative security enjoyed by Palestinian Jewry and the nightmare that raged in Europe.

The post-Holocaust generation of Hebrew writers continued to struggle with the elegiac mission against constraints that they shared with other Jewish writers as well as circumstances peculiar to their own historical situation. A number of writers who had survived the war immigrated to Israel, but their influence, and the impact of the events themselves, began to be felt among the younger writers only in the early sixties; the Eichmann trial proved to be a watershed in Israeli perceptions of the Holocaust. In the years between the war and the trial, the impact of secularization, the preoccupation with nation building, and the identification of the Holocaust with the remote condition of "exile," as well as what Robert Alter has called the increasing "concentration on private and quotidian experience,"[40] may account in part, at least, for the initial resistance of Israeli writers to the summons to become the vessels of collective Jewish commemoration. Nevertheless, the subject has engaged an increasing number of writers; the voice they adopt is frequently that of the spokesman, and the themes and symbols derive from the motifs and imagery that prevail in lamentation literature. Uri Zvi Greenberg, in his epic poem *Streets of the River*, participates in the lamentation tradition through the same kinds of echoes and inversions of the conventional formulas and concepts that we have come to recognize as characteristic of both the ancient and the modern kinah and Midrash. Yet the personal voice is not lost even in this literature, as the speaker or narrator usually strains to find the meeting ground—or the point of departure—between his present and the past he is seeking to recover. Even where a writer, such as Abba Kovner, may not ostensibly assume a public stance, his very language reverberates with national memories and attitudes toward destruction and redemption. As Kovner himself admits, "I inherited many things from my ancestors. One is the teaching that a man should not say his own prayer before the prayer of all the people. In the Talmud it was stated that a man should always participate with the community. This is a moral code in creating art."[41]

An Hebraic writer such as Elie Wiesel, writing in a European language (although *Night* was written originally in Yiddish,[42] Wiesel chose early in his career to become a French writer) cannot avail himself of the resonances inherent in Hebrew or Yiddish and must make other compromises with tradition in order to be accessible to a wider audience. Nevertheless, writers like Wiesel, Sachs, Schwarz-Bart, and Sperber associate themselves deliberately with the tradition and can be discussed in terms of it. It should be emphasized that the use of historical values in the search for signification does not ensure the continued reaffirmation of those principles, but it does, at the very least, inform the quest.

Wiesel works from within two literary traditions—the lamentation tradition and the genre of the modern French novel—and those readers who make a direct leap from ancient Midrash to Wiesel's fiction tend to oversimplify the complexities of religious or religious-oriented responses in a secular world and in a genre that has rarely accommodated the issues of theodicy and collective destiny. The contradictions between the literary tools and perspectives that were his pre-Holocaust heritage and the medium of the modern novel in which he has chosen to write are the source of both the unique power and the weaknesses in Wiesel's writing.

Wiesel's fiction is grounded in fact, yet its value is primarily spiritual rather than documentary. Unlike some of the lamentation literature cited above, Wiesel does not choose to dwell on the sordid facts, as if the aesthetic forms he is using and the religious categories he is probing cannot stand on a substructure of atrocity. What emerges as significant, then, is not the events per se but their function in raising questions and generating legends. The role of the witness or transmitter of collective Jewish experience is to establish at least a degree of verisimilitude and then to interpret and explore the event and to assign it a place in Jewish history. Yet the balance between reality and legend is a very tenuous one, and Wiesel's narratives are often in danger of being subverted by too much or too little realism.[43] There must be constant reminders that, as in Midrash, the theatre is the human arena but the drama is cosmic. As Wiesel writes in one essay:

> Without God, the attempted annihilation of European Jewry would be relevant only on the level of history—another episode in another inhumane war, and what war is not inhumane? and would not require a total revision of seemingly axiomatic values and concepts. Remove its Jewish aspects, and Auschwitz appears devoid of mystery.[44]

Yet the traditional rationale for martyrdom is hardly applicable: neither purpose nor meaning can be assigned to Auschwitz, Wiesel keeps insisting—neither in religious terms (for the sake of our sins . . .), nor in terms of a dialectic of Jewish history by which reconstruction follows destruction. In this conviction Wiesel differs from a poet like U. Z. Greenberg, who claims a kind of causal relationship between the

Holocaust and the establishment of the State of Israel.[45] In his own version of an ancient Midrash in *Ani Maamin,* Wiesel deliberately alters the rabbinic conclusion in which Rachel's pleas to God prevail and He agrees to return the people to Zion.[46] Avoiding the temptation to link recent historical events through a claim of redemption that would assign some sort of design or purpose to the suffering of the Holocaust victims, Wiesel concludes his Midrash with the pitiful gestures of a God who can only commiserate with His people in their suffering.[47]

Even without these traditional supports, Wiesel perseveres in his attempt to reveal the links by which the individual can continue to orient himself to the collective destiny. These are, ironically, among the few instances in Holocaust literature where the survivor does not have to "invent" the historical or moral coordinates by which the events can be scrutinized and transmitted. He proceeds by a method of transmutation and chastisement reminiscent of the powerful inversions, petitions, and rebukes of the rabbis and paytanim in Midrash and in lamentation poetry. In *Night,* when the kapos come into the barracks at Auschwitz to collect any new shoes that the inmates may have brought with them, Eliezer's own pair of new shoes are so coated with mud that they are not noticed: "I thanked God, in an improvised prayer, for having created mud in His infinite and wonderful universe," he says, in a prayer that comes out sounding like a curse.[48] In *Ani Maamin,* Isaac invokes his own willingness to be sacrificed against the sacrifice of the Jews of Eastern Europe:

> You made me climb, then descend
> Mount Moriah—
> Crushed and silent.
> I did not know, my Lord, I did not know
> It was to see my children,
> Old and young,
> Arrive in Majdanek.[49]

Such writing, which in the magnitude of the task Wiesel has set for himself leads to occasional excesses and redundance, is nevertheless a persistent effort to transmute reality into legend that can abide within the canon of lamentational literature. It attempts to convey in secular fiction the manner of thought and the literary modes practiced by believing Jews who perished—to apply, that is, to the most cataclysmic event of all the internal methods by which the Jews of Eastern Europe traditionally grappled with and assimilated collective tragedy—while revealing the strains that both the modern mind and the enormity of the evil impose upon the tradition.

Manès Sperber is another writer who, especially in . . . *Than a Tear in the Sea*, reveals the tensions generated by the Holocaust in the inner fabric of Judaism. The essence of this writer's novel is the challenge to the ultimate significance of martyrdom posed by such an unprecedented threat to the body as well as the soul of the Jew—and the struggle for the proper Jewish response to an opportunity for resistance. It is, in other words, the drama between the traditional summons to martyrdom for the sanctification of God's name—Kiddush haShem—and the call to arms, which is both an ancient and modern alternative to self-sacrifice—what one rabbi during the Holocaust called *Kiddush ha-hayyim.*[50] The lesson that the protagonist, an assimilated Jew named Edi Rubin, ultimately learns from a young rabbi with whom he fights against the Nazis is that "one must understand events as parables."[51] What emerges, then, is a story that is, in the Midrashic tradition, a clash of spiritual attitudes *in history*, under the aspect of eternity.

For a writer like Nelly Sachs, it is also a version of history that provides both the precedent for and the response to martyrdom. Biblical, Hasidic, and Kabbalistic themes and symbols are woven into Sachs's poetry and drama, but they are for the most part *sources* rather than *traditions* serving the search for an attitude towards death. Unlike what we find in the writing of Wiesel and Sperber, it is death—the enormity, the mystery, the place of death—that is at the center of Sachs's poetry. When Wiesel and Sperber do concentrate on dying, it is more for the legacy that the manner of dying leaves to the living than for the repulsive—or redemptive—power of death itself. The Bible and Jewish history appear here not as the epic of a living people en-

gaged in a dialogue with God, but as a kind of compendium of the
signs of martyrdom that will furnish the references for future sacrifice.
In that sense there is no *history* in Sachs's universe—there is rather a
recurrence of archetypal events and relationships. Jewish existence
becomes a series of reenactments of the pageant of death, which takes
place not in a civilization but in a barren landscape of screams. There
is a kind of inexorable relationship between victim and victimizer,
which is destined to be reenacted in every generation. In this pageant
the Nazis remain anonymous, often becoming no more than the dis-
membered instruments of a transcendent will. A recurrent synecdoche
in the poetry is the "fingers of the killers": in the play *Eli* each finger
represents a different form of death (one finger strangles, another
administers injections, etc.[52]), and in the poem "O the Chimneys"
the "fingers" are the agents that build the chimneys for Israel's
"Smoke."[53] Compare this with the image of "fingers" that appears in
a Midrash in which Jeremiah returns from captivity to Jerusalem and
finds the fingers of the dead exiles on a mountaintop. These are the
limbs of the body of his beloved Israel, whom he chastises even as he
mourns: "He collected them, embraced, fondled and kissed them,
placed them in his cloak, and said to them, 'My children, did I not
warn and tell you, Give glory to the Lord your God, before it grow
dark, and before your feet stumble upon the mountains of twilight.' "[54]

Death in Sachs's universe is, somehow, consecrated by divine will,
but not by the God of revelation and covenant, not by the God who
is called into dialogue with man. Wiesel's poem, quoted earlier from
*Ani Maamin*, bears a striking resemblance to one of Sachs's poems,
in which Moriah and Majdanek are also linked.[55] But whereas Wiesel
links the two events in bitterness and irony, as if in an effort to force
God to honor His covenant with His people as they have honored
theirs with Him, in Sachs's poem God is unreachable and unaccounta-
ble, and the recurrence of martyrdom is accepted as part of a transcendental synthesis. In a manner that recalls the seventeenth-century
metaphysical poet, Sachs lifts the real historical properties, the arti-
facts, of Israel's martyrdom—such as the numbers engraved on their
arms—and assimilates them as components of an organic universe:

When your forms turned to ashes
into the oceans of night
Where eternity washes
life and death into the tides—

there rose the numbers
(once branded into your arms
so none would escape the agony)

there rose meteors of numbers
beckoned into the spaces
where light-years expand like arrows
and the planets
are born
of the magic substance of pain—
numbers—root and all
plucked out of murderers' brains
and part already
of the heavenly cycle's
path of blue veins.[56]

Sachs's poems are, then, a volume of consolation that seeks refuge in a Divinity whose ways are inscrutable and in a humanity that fulfills its tragic mission in death.

Paul Celan uses many of the same images and invokes many of the same associations as Sachs, yet he constructs a world as bleak and rudderless as hers is whole and mysterious. Sachs's repeated invocation of the dust of martyred Israel—the dust of ancient sacrifices and the ashes of contemporary incinerations—is echoed in repeated poems of Celan's, but whereas for Sachs the dust of today's sacrifice mingles with the sand of Sinai and the wisdom of Solomon and finds its resolution in the eternal process by which "the fingers" (of the murderers) that "emptied the deathly shoes of sand" will tomorrow "be dust / In the shoes of those to come,"[57] Celan can offer no consolation in the cosmic design, or even in the artistic reconstruction of the event:

There was earth in them, and
they dug.
They dug and dug, and thus

> Their day wore on, and
> their night. And they did
> not praise God,
> Who, they heard, willed all this,
> who they heard, knew all this.
> They dug and heard no more;
> they did not grow wise, nor contrive any song
> or any kind of language.
> They dug. . . .[58]

The God whom they "did not praise" is the God of the covenant, the God who must be held accountable for the operations of history. In another poem the victims' silence, their refusal to pray, is transformed into a prayer of defiance that strains the lamentation tradition to the breaking point:

> No one kneads us again of earth and clay,
> No one incants our dust.
> No one.
>
> Blessed art thou, No-one.
> For thy sake we will bloom
> Towards
> thee.[59]

Celan acknowledges directly the gap between Sachs's quiet faith in an inscrutable Deity and his own angry prosecution of an accountable God, in a poem dedicated to Nelly Sachs:

> The Talk was of your God, I spoke
> against Him, I
> let the heart that I had,
> hope:
> for His highest, His deathrattled, His
> angry word—[60]

Yet whatever his brief against God, Celan casts his lot with the folk of Israel. When he speaks of the victims he usually speaks in the first person plural, and his identification with the suffering lot of his people is nowhere more apparent than in his masterpiece, "Todes-fuge": "Coal black milk of morning we drink it at evening / we drink it at noon and at daybreak we drink it at night."[61] Celan's legacy is not a consolation or a resolution but a confrontation and a defiance.

A pattern begins to emerge from a comparative study of the most visible of the Hebraic writers—a pattern that may be surprising but that derives from the immeasurable trauma that the Holocaust wrought not only in the flesh of Israel but also in its spirit, and that finds expression in the poetry and prose of its lamentation. For those writers such as Wiesel—and Celan and Sperber in their Holocaust works—who remain within the bounds of the tradition, the attempt to recreate the Holocaust in terms of its collective legacy is accompanied by the risk of exposing the ruptures, the challenges, and contradictions in the fundamental codes of Jewish faith and conduct. A different kind of resolution is reached by a writer such as Nelly Sachs—and here I would add, parenthetically, André Schwarz-Bart, whose *Last of the Just*[62] may appear to belong to the tradition of the chronicles of Midrashim of catastrophe, a kind of latter-day fictional *Emek ha Bacha*, but whose designation of Ernie Levy as a self-proclaimed expiatory martyr in the context of some sort of communal redemption is essentially Christian in origin and presents Jewish history as an adjunct to or whipping boy for Christian history. As in Sachs's poems, the roles of victim and victimizer appear in *The Last of the Just* as preordained, the Nazis become the latest in the necessary succession of executioners, and their partners in this passion are the willing victims, the Just Men. The lyrical element of reconciliation wrought by pity and of the transcendental harmony that concludes this novel is absent in writers such as Wiesel, Sperber, and Celan and is extrinsic to a tradition in which no man can relieve the sins or the suffering of another. Writers like Schwarz-Bart and Sachs, who would "conquer" the Holocaust by seeking in the abyss the sparks of redemption or consolation, have done so by going beyond the tradition, beyond the covenantal relationship between God and Israel, and beyond the internal literary and philosophical dialogue through which Israel has confronted catastrophe throughout the ages.

André Neher

# Shaddai: The God of the Broken Arch (A Theological Approach to the Holocaust)

In its primary sense, the term *Shaddai* is an attribute of the *promise*. Weightily presented by Rashi in his commentary on Exodus 6:3, this idea is a classic one, finding its most striking confirmation precisely in this verse, on which the evolution of biblical history hinges decisively. Previously, we are told, the divine revelation had been manifested only through the dimension of *Shaddai*. Abraham, Isaac, and Jacob had no relationship with God except through this dimension; a divine "secret" eluded them, which it remained specifically for the Mosaic revelation to bring forward into history. At this privileged moment when the waters of the covenant divided, one passed through from *promise* to *realization*, and a sheet of water, hitherto subterranean and hidden, welled up onto the surface and now issued forth, plain for men and all the world to see.

*Promise—realization*: a dialectical pair whose inner movement deserves to be investigated! Our biblical text, moreover, invites us to do so in that it expresses the process in terms of *memory*: "Now [suddenly] I remember the Covenant" (verse 5). It is as though, during the long first phase of the biblical revelation—the first four centuries of patriarchal history—something had been "forgotten," which now, suddenly, at this decisive moment of the Exodus, was reactivated in the memory of God. Theologians of the Aristotelian school might describe the change as a transition from power to action, from the virtual to the real, or from the unconscious to consciousness. Psychological or logical, ethical or metaphysical, all these images have but one and the same purpose: to show the disconnection between the phase of promise and that of realization, the latter possessing a sense of positive fulfillment that is absent from the former. The promise is defective by its very nature: like forgetfulness, like unconsciousness, like virtuality, it can only be located and defined by a second term— memory, consciousness, realization—which, establishing its own posi-tion, also situates the other. As against realization, the promise is only a "pro-missus" (something sent out), a forerunner, a preface; like these, it has meaning only in relation to a subsequent message, to a text that underlines and follows it. It is a thing offered up to chance, having value only if something or someone retrieves it. As against realization, whose light ray summons it into existence, the promise is only a shadow. It *is* shadow. Rashi suggests it is silence.[1]

Indeed, the defectiveness of the patriarchal revelation is evident precisely in that it was confined to the dimension of the promise alone. No doubt it offered something, but more than it offered it refused, it withheld. It concealed, notably, the Tetragram (Exod. 6:3), con-cerning which Moses learnt, by way of an answer to his questioning, that it was identified with the *Essence* (Exod. 3:15). The promise, by virtue of the very fact that it *was* only a promise, thus hid the *essential*, deprived the patriarchs of their access to the roots and placed them apart in a limited zone, in a sort of reserve, where revelation might just be described as vision ("I appeared to Abraham, to Isaac and to Jacob," [Exod. 6:3]), but not as a word. Something had been offered to the patriarchs, but that something could not boast of having been a word. It is as though the many *spoken* revelations of God to the patriarchs had been only the shadow of a word, a groping, a mum-bling, something so very pale that, relative to the word as finally realized, it could be only in the nature of a *silence*.

And, taking this analysis further, we must submit to the evidence: the promise is not only a "minor" with regard to the realization that brings it to birth as a mother her child, but it carries an additional risk, that of never seeing the light of day, of being the stillborn infant, the abortion whom nobody or nothing receives or has in remembrance. If the realization does not come to pass, then the promise has never *been*! If, in the history of biblical revelation, the Exodus had not come about through the unfolding of Moses' career, the patriarchal period would have lost its meaning as a whole. It would have been literally "forgotten," and all the many words spoken by God for the benefit of the patriarchs and intercepted by them would have come to nothing. God might just as well have remained silent! To put it boldly, the promise is the *energetic dimension of silence*, and this is what Rashi is trying to teach us in singling out one of the senses of the term *Shaddai*, which thus means at once God of the Promise and God of Silence.

But this silent promise, or if one prefers, this promising silence, may not this also be identified, in a wider theological compass, with that culminating moment of the patriarchal existence that the Bible theology calls *the test*?

Does not the test presuppose a period of time during which it *appears* as if God has forgotten who the man is on whom He has imposed the test? Is not the test an intermission, an interval of silence during which God refuses the slightest echo of a word, the smallest sign lightening the empty scene? But, at the same time, does not the test gain its character precisely from the fact that it *is* only an intermission, that it stores up a potential that seeks only to emerge, and whose emergence is, in fact, inevitable? Did not Nachmanides, one of the Jewish theologians who, in the Middle Ages, submitted the test to the most searching analysis, propose identifying the test with power, in the philosophical significance that we have given it; and is not the test a sort of demonstration of the *transition from power to action*, since the forces hidden or ground under during the test are kept so only in order that they may be restored in the end and the better revealed?

Every test, indeed, is limited in time. It has a beginning and it has an end. At the beginning, God and the man who is tested know one another, speak together, possess mutual esteem. At the end, God and the man who is tested know one another, resume their dialogue, regain their mutual esteem. But in the interval there is rupture, silence, defiance. Yet the defiance cannot be reciprocal, for if, on the side of the proven man, the rupture appears to be real, on God's side it can only relate to a fiction: God, in the test, withdraws none of his esteem from the man whom he tests. Quite the contrary, remarks Nachmanides; God chooses for testing only men of whom he is certain. God pulls only on solid cords, he tempers only that which is already steel. And Nachmanides continues: there is no instance in the Bible of a test's having failed. Not because historical or psychological circumstance arranged matters in such a way that there would be no failure, but because a failure would go contrary to the very purpose of the test, which is to bring men's potential for faith through into action. It was not through any subjective effort of heroism that Abraham endured the test of the *Akeda*. No. Abraham was chosen by God for the test because God knew in advance that Abraham would hold out. The frightful possibility that the test might fail, concludes Nachmanides, one can put out of one's mind without fear. The test always succeeds, not because the man who is tested endures, but because, in the test, *God takes no risks.*

Let us call this God of testing the God of the *suspension bridges*. The man left out on these bridges risks dizziness, certainly, in sizing up the silent and obscure depths over which he makes his way. But he risks neither life nor destiny, for Another keeps watch over the two ends of the bridge, firmly anchored in solid ground. And the man sent out will reach his destination and will hear the Other say to him, "Here I am!"

But there are in the Bible, notwithstanding, bridges laid out for suspension that give way. There are men sent out on these bridges who are seized not only with dizziness, but with madness, despair, and death. With all respect to Nachmanides, there are tests in the Bible that fail. Unless, that is, we assert that we read badly, that one has to "interpret between the lines," that people we thought dead are not really dead, that madness is not really madness and evil not evil but a variant of good. Yet that, most precisely, is what Nachmanides claims when confronted with the biblical man whose testing, if testing there was, was mathematically and structurally opposite to that of Abraham. I am referring to the man called Job.

It is not with a lowered head, like Abraham, that Job goes through his testing, if testing there was, but he confronts it in an athletic but vain hand-to-hand combat. To the silence of God, Job does not oppose, as Abraham does, his own human silence: he counters Him with his cries, harassing but useless.

We have already indicated the underlying reasons for this characteristic isolation of Job as compared to Abraham.[1] One of them is that Abraham was ready to offer up his son; Job never offered up anything, for the brutal reason that he was never asked for anything. God's attitude toward him takes on the character of robbery or even duplicity, since the aggression was not even committed by God himself, but only by one of his deputies—Satan. The other reason, which we have not yet mentioned, is that if Abraham received back his son, Job, for his part, did not get his own children back, but *other* children. The inexorability of death slices Job's existence in two, and the plenitude of the second half does not compensate the violence of the first.

In this respect, Job does not differ from Naomi, who had her husband and children torn away from her without any consultation prior to the robbery, which might have turned it into a test, and to whom were also given back *other* children, but not her own sons Mahlon and Kilyon, who were never to rise again. From a point of view one might describe as tragic and not simply formal, there is reason to differentiate between the testing of Abraham and that of Naomi and Job. Abraham's test was authentic, because everything depended, in the final reckoning, on Abraham's conscious will and also because, in the ordeal, there *was* a final reckoning, a calculable restitution whereby the beginning (Abraham holding Isaac by the hand) was exactly parallel to the end. Conversely, it would be improper to speak of a testing in the case of Naomi or of Job: a destiny was imposed on them from the outside, which neither the one nor the other was able to accept or to refuse, a destiny that left them mutilated, and one where the final reckoning was unjust, since neither of them was restored to their condition previous to the tragedy. Does not this important distinction, marking the difference between a *true* test and a *false* one, suffice to explain why the term *Shaddai* is absent from the account of testing of Abraham, which is genuine, and appears only in the chapters on the false tests of Naomi and of Job?

But, this being the case, if we are to attempt to understand the Silence of God in the test—whether true or false—we can no longer bring our analysis to bear on human attitudes alone but must turn our attention to something in the attitude of God that we may assume to be connected with the *other sense* of *Shaddai*, which it is now time to examine.

Before the philosophers took it up, the Midrash (Bereshit Rabba, 46:2) had already given shape to this other sense of *Shaddai*, declaring that it meant *He who is sufficient unto Himself*, or the *Almighty*, as the Greeks, the Christians, and the Moderns were to translate it, so confirming the Midrashic interpretation. Now, in rabbinical theology, the Almighty is not only he who can do everything, but he who, being capable of everything, is capable also of nothing, that nothing which then becomes only a vehicle for everything. The whole weight of emphasis falls on the side of this *nothing*, on this power of negativity and passivity, God being, in this boldly mystical concept, not the Being from whom one expects everything, but the One of whom nothing is to be expected. The God who is sufficient unto himself—*Shaddai*—is the God who has no need of men, no more than he needs any being other than his own. He is the God of the farther slope, of the inaccessible, of the unfathomable, the God who eludes creation, revelation, communication. This God who is sufficient unto himself is likewise self-sufficient in his Word: He is the *God beyond dialogue*. He requires no partner, neither to whom to address the Word, nor from whom to receive a reply. He is the God without an echo, without yesterday and without tomorrow, the God of absolute Silence.

The grave theological point with which we are now confronted is that this God of absolute Silence persists in speaking even across this

Silence; that this God beyond dialogue provokes man and dares him to take up the challenge of dialogue; that this God without echo, without yesterday and without tomorrow, imposes his intolerable presence on the very instant, on the *hic et nunc*.

For in both the Book of Ruth and the Book of Job, *Shaddai* is ever-present, not suspended on the wings of the promise but deep at the heart of an irremediable failure. No doubt one could try to eliminate this absolute, challenging dimension of *Shaddai* from the Book of Ruth, where the term, which makes a significant but fleeting appearance (1:20–21), seems to fit well enough into the framework of a promise that would make of the story of Naomi a plain and simple test (i.e., "the dead are not really dead, and the God who does me evil, by means of this evil prepares me good"). Moreover, Naomi complains and groans quietly, referring to God only in the third person. She does not call upon *Shaddai* directly, engaging him in a dialogue, but speaks of him as of someone who one knows is hidden temporarily, but who is waiting out there somewhere along the paths of the *toldot* (generations) of history. Thus Naomi, too, appears to be walking on a suspension bridge.

But what of Job? He calls and cries out, addressing himself directly to God. Faced with the absent *Shaddai*, he screams, "*Shaddai*, it is You who persecutes me!" And furthermore, in the Book of Job, the name of *Shaddai* lodges itself deeply, structurally, architecturally, in just that part of the book (chapters 3 to 37) where the Silence of God is as repellent as it is absolute, as unjust as it is inflexible, as long as it is intolerable. In these chapters, it is as if God wished to bring to the point of rupture the impossible yet inexorable dialogue between man and God. Here, with Job, it is as if the test had necessarily to fail.

It is not surprising if, in order to save the concept of the test in the drama of Job, Nachmanides felt himself constrained to tell us a fairy story. The children taken away from Job in the first chapter—why, they are not really dead at all! Satan, the dear fellow, had hidden them behind a bush, and it is they who come back to Job in the last chapter of the book, just as the living Isaac was brought back into the arms of Abraham.

The Sleeping Beauty! We will not accept this fable in order to save, at any price, the testing of Job. No! With Job, the test has *failed*. At a certain moment, on the suspension bridge, something gave way, and from that point onward the test only *looked* like a test. *Shaddai* now manifested himself in all the aggressiveness of his challenge. The risk that God refused to take in the testing of Abraham, he has taken here, in the temptation of Job. It was not harmoniously preordained or mathematically foreseeable that Job would hold out in his experience, as Abraham did in his. With the rope stretched so tight, something might give way. And give way, indeed, it did, if not with regard to Job himself, then at any rate with regard to his children. For let us restate the fact with all the gravity it now commands: Abraham was not alone in his silence. Isaac, his son, accompanied him, and three times the text of the *Akeda* repeats insistently that the father and the son walked *together*: in the beginning, when only the father knows (verse 6), then when the son knows together with the father (verse 8), and finally, in that redemptive instant of reunion when the suspension bridge is crossed, and father and son clasp hands within the Word and in the Light (verse 19). But, from chapter 3, from the first instant of his encounter with the silence of *Shaddai*, Job is *alone*, cut off from his children by the hurricane of death, and till the end of his experience and of his book he will remain *alone*; if he is given other children, none of his dead children will ever be given *back* to him. Thus, across the Book of Job death traces a diagonal bar of silence. The testing of Job is marred by a failure, that supreme failure which is death.

Thus our study brings us, beyond a simple consideration of the phenomena, to the critical point where two theological concepts, divided by impassable limits, confront one another.

One concept, serene in the assurance of a conciliatory ending, places opposite the Alpha of one bank an Omega on the other, as firmly anchored in solid ground as the symmetrical arches of a suspension bridge. Come who may on the bridge, and even if it sometimes shakes so as to give the impression of yielding, it still holds good! And a man may go across without fear of coming to grief.

The other concept introduces into this too fine a structure the element of insecurity: there is no protecting the bridge against any accidental knocks, no guaranteeing the man who crosses it against any risk, *even a mortal one*. No assurance is provided as to the final outcome: an Omega is as little certain of appearing as man is of attaining it. We have said that the God of testing is the God of the suspension bridges. Let us now say that the God of the false test—*Shaddai*—is the *God of the broken arch*.

As soon as we attempt to transcribe this theological predicament into terms of history, we are irreparably drawn toward the second concept, that of the broken arch. Indeed, did we not point out at the very start of this work that we need only to delve into the structure of the Bible in order to learn that the Word is not constructed in the manner of a suspension bridge? No, the Word, in the Bible, is neither at the beginning nor at the end; it lies at both extremities, but overflowed by silence, since silence is at the *beginning* of the Bible, in the chaotic prologue ("pro-logos," before speech), where no word has yet been known and whose essential points of reference are night and death, and there is silence also *at the end*, beyond the Bible, in the zone where the prophetic dialogue was abruptly broken off, and whose night envelops us still. Immersed thus in silence at both ends, is not the Bible the most disturbing theological document ever offered up to human reflection? And could Jewish thought remain impervious to this sense of anxiety? In the interval between the two end silences, do not the biblical outcroppings of silence suggest a theological idea far more troubling than those of *inertia* and *energy*, an idea depicted by Isaiah in the Bible itself as the idea of the *hidden God* (Isa. 45:15)?

Our analysis now leads us to the boldest questions raised by these ideas, and we shall make no attempt to evade the challenge of their impact, because we sense in that challenge not just the echo of an abstract revelation, piercing though it be, but the shock-effect of a brutal, experienced reality, the throbbing trace of an *event*. This event, whose very name is the most tragic invitation to an encounter with *Shaddai*, this new extremity of the history of the covenant, is the *event of Auschwitz*. *Shaddai* is God in the "test" of the Holocaust.

# A. Roy Eckardt

# The Recantation of
# the Covenant?

I offer a few comments upon just one phrase within a tale from Elie Wiesel. The words read: "in the kingdom of night, when it [the Torah] was taken back."[1]

I am unsure who utters these words. Is it the beggar of Jerusalem, in whose tale they appear? Is it Katriel? Is it the personage called "I" in the novel? Perhaps we are not to know for certain. It is painful and it is hard to comprehend the beggar. Yet he has put forth his hand, and we are obligated to reckon with him.

More than once I have made reference to the above phrase, for it has pursued me over the nine years since it was first expressed.[2] I find that I have even overstated the wording. I have written that, according to the beggar's testimony, "at Sinai God gave Israel the Torah, and then in 'the kingdom of night,' the Holocaust, he took it back again."[3] But the phrasing of our text is more circumspect than this. Thus the passive voice is utilized: "they were given the Torah," and then "it was taken back."

The present opportunity for constructive searching ought not be dissipated in semantic maneuvers. Therefore, I shall be categorical. In the precise context of our phrase, there was a kind of *kairos*, a kind of appointed time-space, if a dread one, when a recantation of the covenant ostensibly occurred. That time-space was "the kingdom of night," the *Endlösung* ("Final Solution"). According to our theological tradition, God responds to human events with total seriousness. He is, indeed, deeply involved in such events. This means that if the Torah was "taken back," certain human beings must have had a part in that event. Of course, insofar as the power to recant depends alone upon the power to bestow, any final recantation could only come from God himself. But *has* God recanted? Or did he receive back the covenant only to offer it once more, to incarnate it in some fresh or strange form? These questions try our souls.

## I

An initial interpretation is that of simple negation. The bond with Israel is severed. For that matter, there never was any bond. He who bears witness to this interpretation will insist, nonetheless, that all we have is one legend being called forth by a previous one. Our context reads: "Just like long ago, at Sinai, when they were given the Torah. Just like a generation ago, in the kingdom of night, when it was taken back." But in truth, so attests the proponent of this first view, no Torah was ever given. How ludicrous, then, to declare that it could be returned. No owner is to be found to receive it. In the end as in the beginning, the great world, out there, remains a dark and empty thing.

How can we, contemporary people *par excellence*, arbitrarily strike out this first possibility? The logic may be marked by wistfulness, yet, hauntingly, it stands its ground: There was in fact no singular kingdom of night, for there never was a singular kingdom of day. (Perhaps there might arise little kingdoms of night, relative kingdoms of night, but there is none possessed of *Einzigartigkeit*, of absolute and transcendent uniqueness.)

## II

A second possibility is that God (who is here, here in all his hiddenness) recanted because of the acts of his people. Israel betrayed the divine statutes and had to be judged.

In *A Beggar in Jerusalem* there is much laughter. For the most part it is terrible, maniacal laughter. According to Rabbi Nachman of Bratzlav, somewhere in the world there is a certain city that encompasses all other cities. In the city is a street that contains all the other streets of the city; on that street is a house dominating all the other houses; it contains a room that comprises all the other rooms of the house. "And in that room there lives a man in whom all other men recognize themselves. And that man is laughing. That's all he ever does, ever did. He roars with laughter when seen by others, but also when alone."[4] Is there something special for him to laugh about now? (By now I mean, of course, 1933 to 1945.) Yes. The man is especially laughing at this moment because of the very context of the phrase that occupies us: It was *in the kingdom of night* that the Torah was taken back. I think—and hope I am not unkind—that someone who identifies the *Endlösung* as an act of judgment by God upon his people is subject to confinement in that room, where he will have to listen, without surcease, to the laughter of that man.

## III

There is a third alternative, the inclusion of which is prompted in part by recent residence in Germany. This alternative clearly transcends any intention either of the beggar or of his creator. Yet the alternative does muster a certain theological relevance by virtue of the reputed historical opening of the covenant to the non-Jewish world. I shan't examine here the shattering possibility that the Torah was finally taken back because of the eternal assaults of Israel's enemies upon her, although some later remarks will bear upon that eventuality.[5] What I will allude to is a possibility that takes into some account the Christian viewpoint. Yet I do not intend to violate the Jewish presuppositions of A Beggar in Jerusalem.

My allusion is to the possible taking back, or replacement, of the Torah in association with the event of the cross of Jesus of Nazareth. The interjection of Pauline theology is evident. This theological complication could be elucidated in any number of ways. There is, for example, the Christian theological truism that long before the kingdom of night, the covenant with original Israel had already been taken back. That is to say, the Torah was soteriologically fulfilled or even abrogated on the basis of faith in Jesus as the Christ. Reputedly, Jesus is the divine Word, or the Torah—as the prologue to John's Gospel has it.

I shall only mention some recent argumentation from Jürgen Moltmann of the University of Tübingen. In a work entitled The Crucified God, Professor Moltmann—a dominating figure among contemporary Christian theologians—puts the cross of Golgotha in unique association with Jesus' (allegedly) total Godforsakenness. Jesus' abandonment and deliverance up to death are held to constitute the very torment of hell.[6] This is a way of declaring, in effect, that the twentieth-century kingdom of night marshals no crucial theological significance, but possesses at most only ancillary significance, simply because the very hell of Godforsakenness long preceded it and, indeed, furnishes prototypical substance for the Holocaust itself. The Endlösung is viewed under the aspect of Golgotha, rather than the possible other way around. In consequence, God need not have any special concerns with the reputed kingdom of night. Any relating of the kingdom to the taking back of the Torah becomes meaningless, or at least gratuitous, from this Christian perspective.

I shall never forget the account that follows, as it was read in a memorable paper of Irving Greenberg's at the Conference on the Church Struggle and the Holocaust, held in Hamburg in 1975. The scene is Auschwitz in the late summer of 1944. The gas chamber near the crematorium was out of order; it had been wrecked in a Jewish commando operation in August. "The other gas chambers were full of the adults and therefore the children were not gassed, but just burned alive. There were several thousand of them. When one of the SS sort of had pity upon the children, he would take a child and beat the head against a stone before putting it on the pile of fire and wood, so that the child lost consciousness. However, the regular way they did it was by just throwing the children onto the pile. They would put a sheet of wood there, then sprinkle the whole thing with petrol, then wood again, and petrol and wood, and petrol—and then they placed the children there. Then the whole thing was lighted."[7]

Jürgen Moltmann, though he writes today, lives virtually in the time before the kingdom of night. His is pre-Holocaust theology— understandably so, within its own frame of reference. For him the event of Golgotha remains the solely decisive event of salvation-history. Yet how is it possible for us to remain bound by that single event? How can we stop at that place? Are we not called to find in the subsequent unfolding of events an acting out of the divine-human encounter, and hence of the human understanding of God?

Even though my own rejection of the Christian supersessionist view of the Jewish Torah preceded my involvement with the Holocaust, that involvement has effected a crisis in my thinking on the covenant (as it has for some others). It is just not so that the event of the cross of Golgotha remains an absolute horror upon which the Christian faith will and should build, dialectically, its faith. It is no longer possible, if it ever was possible, to make the passion of Jesus of Nazareth the *locus classicus* of Christian faith. Jesus was a man with a mission, a courageous man, who set his face to go up to Jerusalem. Professor Moltmann is a theologian of Germany. But he does not comprehend that there is in this world an evil that is more horrible than every other evil. This is the evil of children witnessing the murders of other children, while knowing that they also are to be murdered in the same way, being absolutely aware that they face the identical fate. The Godforsakenness of Jesus has become non-absolute, if it ever was absolute, for there is now a Godforsakenness of Jewish children that is the final horror. It was *in the kingdom of night* that the

Torah was taken back: this fact determines eschatologically all other presumed transformations of the covenant.

## IV

A fourth eventuality is that God recanted because he found that he could no longer live with himself. The kingdom of night proved too much, even for him. In *A Beggar in Jerusalem* a young madman, one of only three survivors who had escaped the deportation, asks: "How does God justify Himself in His own eyes, let alone in ours? If the real and the imaginary both culminate in the same scream, in the same laugh, what is creation's purpose, what is its stake?"[8]

In recent thinking, Jewish and Christian, no one has put these kinds of questions more relentlessly or persuasively than Richard L. Rubenstein. I now raise the question, not of the impossibility or objective negation of all divine-human covenants, but instead of the obliteration of Israel's covenant of demand (this in contradistinction to a covenant of promise, of assurance).

From the standing ground of our fourth alternative, a moral indictment is entered against the very King of the universe. For once upon a time God mandated that his elect be "a kingdom of priests and a holy nation" (Exod. 19:6). Yet at the last, in the kingdom of night, his chosen ones were transubstantiated into vermin, and to less than vermin—and by his permission.

The end of the covenant of demand is the consequence of the juridical-moral trial of God. The charge entered against him is no less than implicit Satanism. No plea of innocence is open to him. No appeal is available to him. All that is possibly left for him is an act of penitence.

This penitential act is suggested in Elie Wiesel's *Ani Maamin: A Song Lost and Found Again*. God stays silent there, it is true, before the remorseless pleadings and terrible denunciations of him by Abraham, Isaac, and Jacob. Yet when Abraham snatches a little girl from before the machine guns and runs like the wind to save her, and she tells him, weakly, that she *believes* in him, in Abraham, then at last a tear clouds the eyes of God (though Abraham cannot see that). When Isaac beholds the mad Dayan singing "of his ancient and lost faith," of belief in God and in the coming of the Messiah, yet a second time God weeps (though Isaac cannot see that). And when Jacob finds a death camp inmate declaiming that the Haggadah lies, that God will not come, that the wish to be in Jerusalem will never be granted, but that he will continue to recite the Haggadah as though he believes in it, and still await the prophet Elijah as he did long ago, even though Elijah disappoints him, then yet a third time (though Jacob cannot see it) God weeps. "This time (he weeps) without restraint, and with—yes—love. He weeps over his creation—and perhaps over more than his creation."[9]

According to this fourth viewpoint, the original sin of God—a sin in which Christians, Muslims, and others were to become most ready and available accomplices—was the sin of applying absolute divine perfection to the lives of ordinary human creatures. But it may be that the penitence of God has come. Is he, perhaps, promising now to do his best not to sin again, not to have anything to do with allowing such torment? For the loathsome myth of the Jew as "suffering servant" will surrender its horror only as the erstwhile covenant of demand is given a fitting burial.[10] Was the Torah of demand in fact taken back in the kingdom of night? If so, release came with it.

# V

A fifth possibility is the reincarnating of a covenant of promise through a new, or a renewed, political-secular bond. In the kingdom of night, there is the recantation of the Torah; after the kingdom of night, a transformation, a *metanoia*, is needed if the Torah is to be reconstituted, if it is to be vindicated.

Our final theme may be identified as the christology of the resisters. "Christology" stands here only for messianic thinking as such; no invidious comparisons are entailed. And the "resisters" are simply those Jews who fought back. The general christological/messianic significance of the Holocaust has been obscured in a certain measure by a fixation upon death and suffering. Thus it was possible for a typological link to be more or less assumed between the Jew of Nazareth, who reputedly went as a lamb to the cross, and the Jews of the *Endlösung*, who allegedly went as lambs to the slaughter. Most Jews, obviously, had no choice but this. They were trapped. In their very death agonies the Torah was obliterated. However, the recent historiography of Yehuda Bauer, Yuri Suhl, and others has made us forcibly aware of the Jews who responded to their would-be annihilators through combat.[11] This historiography is of some aid in the formulating of a fresh christology.

We have remembered the burning of the Hungarian Jewish children at Auschwitz. Now let us recall a different kind of burning, but one that is just as constituent to the Holocaust. I refer to an event inspired by the revolt of the Warsaw Ghetto. On the second of August 1943, at the annihilation center of Treblinka, a sprinkler normally used for disinfectant had been filled with petrol. The contents were sprayed about the grounds of the camp. At a signal, hand-grenades were thrown and a great fire was soon raging. The arsenal exploded. Two hundred or more Jews managed to escape. Most of them were later captured and killed. A major objective of the revolt was to destroy the murder center. At least obliquely, this aim was achieved. In October of 1943 the Germans razed the remaining parts of the camp.

I speak here only of the men who actively fought the German Nazi antichrist—not of the children and the rest who went to their doom. Who are these other Jews? Many of them are two persons in one. Here is a man who, by betraying his brothers, had lived. For he had been one of the "winners" in the competitive "race of the dead," physical endurance contests held at Treblinka and elsewhere that made his survival literally realizable through his brother's extinction. But now, through his sacrifice, others would live, would escape, would know. Only in rising against the Enemy could he emerge from the absolute despair that was his for having bought his life with the lives of others. (Neither of these things is to be said of Jesus of Nazareth.

He did not live by having to destroy his brothers. And he did not engage, subsequently, in that act of resistance which enabled others to live.)

Messiahs retain special followers, a special apostolate. Who, in the present context, are these apostles? In the Christian tradition, the works and person of the disciple do not exactly replicate the saving function of the Christ. The disciple's cross is not the savior's cross. Yet there is always a link, an act of witnessing. Today the heirs of the Holocaust saviors are the members of the Israel Defense Forces. These men and women are not Holocaust messiahs, for they have not committed the requisite and qualifying sin of betraying their fellow Jews. Yet they remain special messianic heirs, for they carry forward the other aspect of the messianic office. They enable Israel to live.

Among its many other roles, the sovereign State of Israel remains the assenting voice, the perpetuation of the *Widerstand*, the *Résistance*. It comprises, so to say, the dowry brought to the new marriage, to the new covenant of promise. It is the rainbow set again in the clouds. Yet the rainbow that was seen after the recession of the flood waters meant the divine remembrance of the covenant with *all* living creatures (Gen. 9:16). One messianic query reads: "Are you he who is to come, or are we to look for another?" (Matt. 11:3). Has a messiah come? Traditionally, the Christian answers "yes," the Jew answers "no." But the German Nazi *Endlösung* brings a partial reversal: the Jew may answer "yes"—though not, of course, a "yes" to the one from Nazareth, lest he fall prey to the cynic's definition of Christianity: that religion which teaches that the Jewish people are to turn the other cheek. And the Christian? As the poor pagan redeemed—hopefully— into the covenant of promise (cf. Ephes. 2:12–13), the Christian has answered "yes" to the messianic query. But what is this to mean in the frame of reference of the kingdom of night? Is he or is he not a child of Israel? Is he among the company of those who act to return the Torah? Or is he a resister against that? Is his history restricted to only a part of the history of Israel, or does the Christian's history enshrine Israel's total history, which is pierced by, but then prevails over, the German Nazi *Endlösung*?[12]

## VI

All that has been sought here is to single out the "taking back" of the covenant, its possible recantation, and then to ask: Where? Where was it taken? To oblivion? If not to oblivion, then to what place?

There is a passage from Reinhold Niebuhr, written twenty-five years ago, that, I think, conjoins him and Elie Wiesel. It brings as well a little focus to these poor midrashim upon the phrase of that strange beggar who reaches out to us from the deep shadows of Jerusalem. "Nothing that is worth doing can be achieved in a lifetime; therefore we must be saved by hope. Nothing which is true or beautiful or good makes complete sense in any immediate context of history; therefore we must be saved by faith. Nothing we do, however virtuous, can be accomplished alone. Therefore we are saved by love."[13]

# Michael Berenbaum

# The Additional Covenant

Traditional Jewish self-understanding maintained that God and Israel were intertwined in a covenant of trust, fidelity, and protection, a moral covenant that demanded the best of God and Israel.[1] It was this covenant that gave Israel a sense of mission to the world and served as Israel's *raison d'être* during the millennium of its existence.[2] The question for the contemporary post-Holocaust Jew as he relates to this tradition of covenant is how to affirm Israel's sense of mission without relying upon a God who failed his people in their hour of greatest need. A detailed and thorough examination of Elie Wiesel's writings suggests a partial resolution of this dilemma. Wiesel confronts the theological void in his treatment of Israel, yet he is able to maintain Israel's centrality and mission through an additional covenant forged at Auschwitz, a covenant that renews Israel's mission despite the void. It is this doctrine of an additional covenant that unifies all of Wiesel's pronouncements on the Jewish people both in their fictional and nonfictional forms. Furthermore, this additional covenant becomes the necessary direction for all covenantal theology in the wake of what Wiesel understands to be the collapse of the covenantal framework.

Wiesel's particular struggle with the covenantal framework of traditional Judaism, which posited a crucial relationship between God and Israel, was intensified by his early exposure to two of the doctrines of the Jewish mystical tradition, the doctrine of *Tikkun* and the doctrine of chosenness, doctrines that not only formed his consciousness of the meaning of Israel but that still fascinate his imagination concerning Israel.

According to the first mystical doctrine, found in the tradition of Lurianic Kabbalism,[3] Israel was charged with the ontological responsibility for the reunification of divine sparks scattered by the cosmic catastrophe of creation. The doctrine of *Tikkun*, or restoration, implies that Jewish observance of the commandment reunites the cosmic sparks with their divine source. According to Gershom Scholem, in the mystical tradition "*Mitswah* became an event of cosmic importance, an act which had a bearing upon the dynamics of the universe. The religious Jew became a protagonist in the drama of the world; he manipulated the strings behind the scenes."[4] According to the doctrine of *Tikkun*, seemingly insignificant acts take on cosmic dimensions in the redemption of the universe. Israel comes to occupy the center stage in the human drama.

The second mystical doctrine contributing to Wiesel's dilemma is the doctrine of Israel's chosenness. Perhaps the clearest statement of this chosenness is found within the Hasidic tradition, in the writings of Rabbi Scheneor Zalman of Liadi. Scheneor Zalman maintained that Jews possess two souls, an animal soul and a divine soul. The divine soul is part of the *En Sof*, the *deus absconditus*, whose purpose is to purify the animal soul. Scheneor Zalman believed that only Jews receive divine souls.[5]

Wiesel's early exposure to the mystical doctrines of Israel's chosenness and centrality solidified his estimate of the innate superiority of the Jewish people, both ontologically and historically.[6] Wiesel is currently estranged from both the cosmic and ontic dimensions of Israel's mission, but his initial acceptance of such dimensions precludes a sociological solution. His imagination cannot be kindled by the dimension of history alone. He constantly searches for that lost dimension of ontology only to retreat from its implications, for these implications make him painfully aware of the void.

Wiesel partially resolves this dilemma with his concept of the additional covenant. This covenant can no longer be between humanity and God or Israel and God, but rather between Israel and its memories of pain and death, God and meaning. The covenant cannot be between God and Israel, for God has proved an unreliable partner in the convenantal bondedness. Therefore, if we are to continue as Jews, our self-affirmation must be based on our choice to remain Jews and to assume the past of Jewish history as our own and as in some way determinant of our future.

The elements of Wiesel's additional covenant are threefold: solidarity, witness, and the sanctification of life. (I have deliberately avoided the term "new covenant" not only because of its theological implications, but also because of the implication that a new covenant entails the negation or fulfillment of the old.) Wiesel suggests that the threefold covenant is an additional obligation for those Jews to whom the original covenant is still relevant and meaningful. To other Jews, for whom the original covenant is no longer relevant, the threefold covenant can function as the basis for their self-affirmation as Jews.

The need for an additional covenant was precipitated by the Holocaust, which represents a rupture with the Jewish past, a rupture that is theological as well as historical. The Jewish communities that were most continuous with the past, those that had avoided the inevitable secularization following the Enlightenment, died in the Holocaust. The magnitude of the Holocaust, its scope and its radical inhumanity, marked the end of both the covenant between people (in traditional language between man and man) and the covenant between Israel and God. Auschwitz was the terminus of a tradition that began at Sinai, and if in the future there is to be a new beginning that can offer some continuity with that tradition, it must begin at Auschwitz, where both man and God combined to renounce all that had previously been regarded as sacred. All affirmations, all sanctifications of life, all endeavors to begin again, must commence with a realization of the destructive powers of man and God and of their respective creations.[7]

Theologically, the rupture with the past can clearly be seen in the collapse of the Midrashic framework. Wiesel concurs with Emil Fackenheim that the distinctive feature of all Jewish theology has been the persistence of Midrash, which assumed God's presence in history as well as the allegiance of both God and Israel to the original covenant at Sinai.[8] For Wiesel, the most terrifying theological implication of the Holocaust is the collapse of the Midrashic framework. Wiesel cites a Midrash that speaks of the difference between Hanukkah and Purim —Hanukkah, when Jews chose military means to defend themselves against a spiritual threat, and Purim, when Jews chose spiritual means to defend themselves against a physical threat.

> The Midrash explains this paradox in the following way: The Jewish people entered into a covenant with God. We are to protect His Torah, and He, in turn, assumes responsibility for Israel's presence in the world. Thus, when our spirituality—the Torah—was in danger, we used force in protecting it; but when our physical existence was threatened, we simply reminded God of His duties and promises deriving from the covenant. . . .
>
> *Well, it seems that, for the very first time in our history, this very covenant was broken.* That is why the Holocaust has terrifying theological implications. . . .
>
> *In the beginning there was the Holocaust.* We must start all over again.[9]

There are two reasons why the Midrashic framework of covenant and divine presence was shattered for Wiesel. First, the traditional images of God relating to the covenant and God's presence become so difficult and torturous when applied to the reality of Auschwitz that we might prefer to abandon them entirely rather than retain them. Second, the covenant implies a posture of trust leading to an acceptance of the historical reality as God ordained.[10] If there is to be a protest, it must be a cosmic protest, for the major participants in the

drama are God and Israel and not Israel and the nations. An acceptance of this framework ultimately points toward God as the principal
actor in the Holocaust, a position that Wiesel illustrates as antithetical
both to Israel's conception of God and to the aggressive posture assumed by the Jews in creating the state of Israel.

Theologically, the demise of the covenanted past can also be seen
in the emergence of the state of Israel. Elsewhere I have argued that
in *Dawn* Wiesel maintains that the cost of the historical existence of
the Jewish people has been the functional death, if not the deliberate
murder, of Elisha, the God who is salvation.[11] Israel was founded because man chose to become God, to take his fate into his hands and
grapple with the life and death decisions of historical existence.

The radical break with the past is not limited to religious language but extends to the forms of historical existence. The emergence
of the state of Israel brought an end to the Diaspora conditions of
landlessness and powerlessness, which had been the marks of the traditional Jew. Wiesel is aware of the dramatic shift in the character of the
Jewish people as a result of their transformation from landlessness and
dependence to landedness and independence. Recalling his first meeting with Gad, Elisha recounts: " 'I am Gad,' he said in a resonant voice,
as if he were uttering some cabalistic sentence which contained an
answer to every question. He said 'I am Gad' in the same way that
Jehovah said 'I am that I am.' "[12] The Israeli, as depicted in *Dawn*,
has no need for self-justification, no need to respond in categories that
have been externally imposed upon him. He is stereotyped as self-
assertive and future-oriented. Gad promises to give Elisha his future
almost as abruptly as the Nazis had robbed him of his past. Elisha
recalls the stories of Jewish battles and triumphs, which Gad had related to him, and comments: "This was the first story I had ever heard
in which Jews were not the ones to be afraid. Until this moment I had
believed that the mission of the Jews was to represent the trembling
of history rather than the wind which made it tremble."[13] This transformation from weakness to strength was not without its cost. Nearly
all of the Israeli characters in Wiesel's novels are self-assertive and

confident; however, they are unable to approach the depths with the author or with any of his other major characters.

The rupture with the past is also reflected in Wiesel's fascination with Soviet Jewry and with the secular Israelis, as well as in his own distance from the Hasidic world of his youth. There is always a sense of estrangement in Wiesel's treatment of Hasidism. Although he is attracted to the ecstatic forms of Hasidic celebration and to the authenticity of that world, he conveys a sense of distance except during that transcendent moment when the character is transformed by song. The Hasidic world is the world of the past, a world that has maintained its quest for eternity—as Wiesel could not—despite the vicissitudes of history. In contrast to this estrangement, Wiesel is very much at home with those Jews who have unconsciously developed new forms of Jewish life that either illuminate the void or preserve a love for the Jewish past even in the face of the void. His attraction to Soviet Jewry is not only based upon their plight of suffering and persecution (though that would be sufficient), but is more profoundly rooted in his desire to participate in a cultural renaissance of Jewish identity, albeit without a faith in God. Wiesel came to the Soviet Union to witness Jewish suffering. He returned a year later to participate in Jewish joy.[14]

Wiesel is more attracted by the secular Israelis' rediscovery of their own Jewishness in the wake of their historical experience than he is by the religious affirmations of the self-consciously traditional community. In his writings Wiesel captures the sense of history and the sense of continuity that the secular Israeli felt when he experienced the return to the Western Wall as a return to his place of origin and as a fulfillment of the hopes, prayers, and legacies of past generations.[15] He is aware that both the secular Israelis and the Soviet Jews will not become observant Jews remaining within the four cubits of the Halachah. Nonetheless, these secular Jews have discovered a sense of the Jewish spirit and are creating new forms of Jewishness.

For Wiesel, as we have seen, the traditional covenant has collapsed, the forms of Jewish existence have been altered, yet the task of the Jew must still be to retain some continuity with the past. This continuity is to be found in the additional covenant, which contemporary Israel forges with the past of Israel, with its memories of pain and suffering, joy and ecstasy, God and meaning.

## I. Solidarity

Solidarity is the first element in Wiesel's additional covenant. For Wiesel, the solidarity of the Jewish people is not a necessity turned virtue, but a virtue that is also necessary. Solidarity is a persistent and honored tradition in Judaism. In the liturgy the Jew recites, "All Israel is intertwined in friendship."[16] The Talmud dictates that Israel is responsible one for another.[17] Beshtian Hasidism, as Wiesel sees it, is founded on the solidarity of the Jewish people,[18] on a recognition of the overriding importance of mutual responsibility. Wiesel follows an honored tradition of *Aggadah* by creating a moral legend out of this solidarity. He claims, for example, that the Six-Day War was won because the Jewish people were united. That is why the state of Israel survived. At times it seems that Wiesel has shifted his early sense of omnipotence from the Zaddik to the community as a whole. There is an obvious danger involved in this position, for in the historical world wars are won because of an imbalance of power. However, Wiesel is not a politician but a storyteller, and the story he tells of unity is both cogent and mysterious. He argues that if people can no longer say, "In the beginning God created" and must say, "In the beginning there was Auschwitz," then they must no longer pray, "Because of our sins we were exiled from our land"[19] but rather, "Because of our solidarity we regained the land and were restored to Jerusalem." The psychological potency of these myths should not be underestimated, although it should not be confused with military power.[20]

Wiesel's theology must be considered (like much of recent black, women's, and Jewish theology) a theology of survival. Wiesel writes: "To be a Jew, therefore, is to ask a question—a thousand questions, yet always the same. . . . Why and how to survive in a universe which negates you?"[21] (The parallels between Wiesel's questions and the questions of James Cone, William Jones, and Mary Daly are striking.

For all three theologians and the movements they represent, the questions are the same; the concern with theology is more existential and political than it is metaphysical.) History assumes a critical dimension and becomes the significant datum for theology, while the suffering community of the oppressed can never be denied and the significance of human suffering cannot be mystified or obscured. Finally, even the images of God must be altered if such images lead to powerlessness or acquiescence to oppression. Solidarity is the cornerstone for all survival theology, for it is the prerequisite for self-reliance.

Wiesel contends that in the face of hostility a minority people must unite. He advocates a plurality of paths within the Jewish community, but dissent can never exclude or endanger other Jews. His emphasis on solidarity at times even leads him to distort Jewish tradition. For example, Wiesel takes the rabbinic condemnation of the wicked son in the Passover Seder and exaggerates it to the point where it becomes the primary heresy in Judaism.

> Jewish tradition allows man to say anything to God provided it be on behalf of man. Man's inner liberation is God's justification. It all depends on where the rebel chooses to stand. From inside the community he can say everything. Let him step outside it, he will be denied the right. The revolt of the believer is not that of the renegade.[22]

Recent history has revived the sense of Jewish solidarity that previous history had created and that was weakening within the past two centuries as the processes of emancipation and assimilation developed. The Holocaust has exposed the raw nerve of Western civilization by exposing the awesome potential for violence and inhumanity and the absence of effective traditions that would constrain such inhumanity. Israel now stands united as a victim of Western civilization and knows the culture's limitations as well as its lures. Ironically, Wiesel's perception of the Holocaust as the central event of the twentieth century, if not of the entire modern period, thrusts Israel once again to center stage of the human drama. Although Wiesel does not and cannot celebrate this state of affairs, he is not unaware of the fact that the Holocaust renews Israel's centrality while radically altering the content of that centrality.

There is an additional dimension to Jewish solidarity, and that is the continued dissent of the Jewish people from Christianity, which still remains (albeit in secularized form) the dominant culture of Western civilization. For Wiesel, the Holocaust has only heightened the theological antagonism that the Jew holds for Christianity.

Wiesel's basic antipathy toward Christianity for its role in anti-Semitism is strengthened by his understanding of the crucifixion of Jesus. Wiesel's rejection of that myth is threefold. He argues that by considering the death of the innocent as an atonement for humanity and a prerequisite for salvation, Christians blunt the impact of human suffering. Like Albert Camus, Wiesel fears that suffering can become tolerable as a meaningful part of the religious structure. In *The Rebel* Camus writes: "In that Christ had suffered and had suffered voluntarily, suffering was no longer unjust."[23] Wiesel too does not want any solution to the problem of suffering other than the elimination of suffering wherever possible. Furthermore, the suffering of the innocent is, for Wiesel, the central mystery of human existence and a mystery that encourages the individual to confront both man and God. If Jesus of Nazareth is not a God or if his death was not an atonement, then his death must stand as a question before both man and God. We are far more comfortable with a God who suffers than with the innocent and unwarranted suffering of the individual.

Wiesel also rejects the notion of death as ultimate redemption. The difficult choice for Wiesel is life rather than death. It is easy to die; it is far more difficult to live. Wiesel's imaginative contrast of Jesus and the Jewish concept of the Messiah reveals his attitude toward death.

> Man is incapable of imagining his own death; he imagines that of his fellow man. The survivor resents his survival. That is why the Christians imagine their Saviour expiring on the cross. They thus situate him outside the circle of shame; he dies before the others, instead of the others. And thus the others are made to bear his shame. A Messiah, as seen by the Jews, shows greater courage; he survives all the genera-

tions, watches them disappear one after the other—and if he is late in coming, it is perhaps because he is ashamed to reveal himself.[24]

Wiesel's symbolic antagonism to the Christian myth is also intensified by the reenactment of the crucifixion that Jews have witnessed. Jews have been killed, the innocent have suffered, and the world is not yet redeemed. By cosmitizing evil, we run the risk of becoming blind to the immediate evil that surrounds us.

> Any messiah in whose name men are tortured can only be a false messiah. It is by diminishing evil, present and real evil, experienced evil, that one builds the city of the sun. It is by helping the person who looks at you with tears in his eyes, needing help, needing you or at least your presence, that you may attain perfection.[25]

In summary, Wiesel maintains that the solidarity of the Jew is based on a common kinship, a common memory, and a common historical experience. This solidarity is intensified by anti-Semitism, by a sense of alienation from Western Christian civilization, and by an affirmation of alternate myths and values. Solidarity is a virtue that possesses enormous power and leads to self-reliance. Wiesel's appeal to solidarity does run the risk of blinding one to the real divisions of class, religion, and politics, differences that divide the Jewish people. Personally, Wiesel sees no conflict between his sense of solidarity with the Jewish people and his role as a man in the world, for only by affirming a particular community can he reach out and embrace mankind.

## II. Witness

The first element of the additional covenant forged at Auschwitz was solidarity. The second is witness. For Wiesel, to be a Jew in the post-Holocaust world is to be a witness to a sacred past of some four thousand years of history and to the ability to soar to the heights of holiness and descend to the depths of inhumanity. Jewish eyes have seen and Jewish ears have heard the awesome revelation at Sinai and the equally awesome (anti-) revelation at Auschwitz. For Wiesel, Jewish voices must testify to both moments in human history. It is through this element of witness that Wiesel partially resolves his duties to the past without either returning to the world of the past or denying its legitimacy.

Wiesel himself is the witness *par excellence*. Viktor Frankl has argued that the chances of an individual's surviving the concentration camp psychically intact dramatically increased if his life had a sense of meaning and purpose.[26] Throughout the first part of his ordeal, as depicted in *Night*, Eliezer was sustained by his father, and he sustained his father as well. The relationship of father and son gave him some semblance of meaning in a world bereft of it. After his father's death, Eliezer became apathetic. It was only when he came to regard himself as a witness that he reachieved a reason to live.[27]

For Wiesel, the role of witness is immensely complicated. The struggle is between the impossibility of not bearing witness and the attraction to silence. Wiesel writes: "For the fact that he has survived commands him to bear witness. But how can he speak up without committing treason against himself and others. A dialectical trap from which there is no escape: the true witness must be silent. . . ."[28] Wiesel is frustrated by the futility of the role of witness and intrigued by the possibility of silence; however, at the same time he is convinced that a sacred opportunity to alter the world's relationship to the Jews was lost by bearing false witness, premature witness, or violating the canons of strict silence. In *One Generation After* he expresses the fear that words might betray the dead, for words threaten to destroy the mystery behind the experience as well as the immediacy and intensity of the experience itself. If the world has changed so little, little has been learned. The continued persecution of Jews and the persistence of crimes against other peoples leads Wiesel to question the efficacy of the role of witness and the ultimate faith in humanity that such a witness implies.[29] In *The Oath* Wiesel again returns to the theme of witness and the tension between silence and witness, witness and guilt. The witness must tell his tale not to save the world but rather to save a single soul.

Wiesel's personal role of witness is twofold. He is both the witness of the Holocaust for the post-Holocaust world, insisting upon a total confrontation with what transpired in the kingdom of night, and a witness to the victims of what transpires in the modern world. He presents the world of the victims to us and judges our world by the laws of the dead.

For Wiesel the role of witness involves even more than a mutual representation of one world to another. It also involves the telling of tales that would otherwise be lost to history. Eastern European Jewry was destroyed, so if their world is to make some contribution to ours, their stories must be told, their yearnings shared, and their inner resources uncovered. Their memory must be kept alive in order to enrich ours and in order to preserve some sense of continuity with the past. In *The Oath* Wiesel attempts (without real success) to reject this role for the witness.

In the broadest sense, the role of witness is not limited to the actual victims or the actual survivors. All Jews are survivors and all Jews are victims. If we follow the tradition of the Passover Haggadah— "In every generation each man must regard himself as though he personally went forth from Egypt"[30]—then every post-Holocaust Jew must regard himself as though he personally went into the camps and emerged. The quality of a person's testimony depends upon the degree to which he accepts this past as his own and thereby allows it to alter his future perceptions of reality. The quality of Israel's witness will be determined by its willingness to confront both moments of the Jewish past, Sinai and Auschwitz, and to relate both of them to the future. Part of the task of witness that stems from this confrontation is to ask the right questions.

Wiesel insists upon the pursuit of difficult questions, and thus affirmations are replaced by questions. This mode of questioning is not just a circuitous way to affirm a sense of meaning without confronting the specific conclusions reached or the course that led to the conclusions. The questions themselves are genuine, for, according to Wiesel, all that is left after Auschwitz is questions. Wiesel contends that commonalty and community are now the result of shared questions rather than answers. When there are answers they are personal. The bond that can now unite Israel is not the bond of affirmative commitment but rather the bond of shared questions produced by a common root experience. The fact that today the Jew must stand without answers and reassurance underscores the pervading sense of the void in Wiesel's writing. The Jew who once felt trust and fidelity toward the universe must now face a universe of unanswerable questions.

## III.  Sanctification

The Jew is left to confront the abyss and charged to witness a cosmic absence, but it is in the depths of this emptiness that the battle for meaning begins and the struggle for sanctification is born. This experience of the depths and the kindling of the spark of sanctification is described in *The Town Beyond the Wall*, in Wiesel's contribution to the Symposium on "Jewish Values in the Post-Holocaust Future," in *Souls on Fire*, in *Zalmen, or the Madness of God*, in *The Oath*, and in *Messengers of God*.

It is this affirmation of life and the possibility of human meaning in the face of the void that is the third element of the additional covenant, *kedushat ha haim*. The term can be used in two different ways. Literally, *kedushat ha haim* means the sanctification of life and can signify that the very act of survival is holy. Quoting a Russian Jewish student, Wiesel writes: "Our answer lies in the fact that we continue to survive and that we wish to go on surviving."[31] Survival itself can be a sanctified response to an inhuman world. Survival is a fundamental act of faith for the Jewish people, our basic commitment to the Jewish future.[32] However, there is a second, more pervasive sense in which the term "sanctification of life" can be used, and this second sense most accurately describes the third element of the additional covenant. In this sense *kedushat ha haim* entails an endeavor to sanctify not merely the very act of survival but the quality of that survival. Wiesel writes of this second sense of sanctification in the traditional context when he speaks of the covenant that all Jews share: "Are we not brothers in the same ancient tradition sharing a common belief in the eternity of Israel? Do we not observe together the commandment bidding us to sanctify our lives?"[33] Wiesel's Moses in *Messengers of God* tells us what the rabbi who goes mad in *Zalmen, or the Madness of God* also knew: "Through centuries and generations to come, that to live as a man, as a Jew, means to say yes to life, to fight—even against the Almighty—for every spark, for every breath of life."[34] In the mad rabbi's words: "God requires of man not that he live, but that he choose to live. What matters is to choose—at the risk of being defeated."[35]

The endeavor of Israel to make life holy, to sanctify the quality of human existence, began at Sinai and remained within the tradition for more than three thousand years. Wiesel maintains that although the ground rules have now changed and the ontological support for this endeavor is no longer credible, the endeavor itself should still continue. Wiesel is uncertain how it will continue or why it should continue, but if the effort to sanctify life were to end, madness would ensue. Wiesel writes: "We have not survived centuries of atrocities for nothing. This is what I think we are trying to prove to ourselves, desperately, because it is desperately needed. . . ."[36] Though the commitment to sanctify life is a positive and hopeful decision, the desperation that prompts this position must not be overlooked. For Wiesel covenant, chosenness, and *Tikkun* are no longer genuinely credible concepts that serve to legitimize the sanctification of life.

In the Symposium "On Jewish Values in the Post-Holocaust Future" Wiesel writes of the role of the Jewish people:

> In a world of absurdity, we must invent reason, we must create beauty out of nothingness. And because there is murder in the world—and we are the first ones to know it—and we know how hopeless our battle may appear, we have to fight murder and absurdity and give meaning to the battle, if not to our hope.[37]

In *Souls on Fire* Wiesel similarly states: "For whoever creates affirms that the creative act has a meaning, a meaning which transcends the act itself."[38] Perhaps, for Wiesel, to be a Jew after Auschwitz is to hope for a Messiah and to work for a Messiah while knowing full well that the hope is for naught.

The dimensions of human aspiration have been scaled down with respect to sanctification as they were with respect to the role of witness. Sanctification no longer leads to the messianic moment of redemption but is rather an individual's or a community's act of solidarity, designed to rout momentarily the void.

The desire to sanctify life expresses itself in various forms. It is a desire that permeates the experience of Soviet Jews. Wiesel also considers the establishment of the state of Israel just such an endeavor to sanctify life: "But Israel, for me, also represents a victory over absurdity and inhumanity. And if I claim it for myself, it is because I belong to a generation which has known so few."[39] For Wiesel the foundation of the state of Israel was a victory over death, though not an unqualified victory. Israel's existence is also a question, one that the Jewish people ask of their past and of their future, even as it is a testament to the durability of the Jewish people. The triumph of 1948 expressed a Jewish desire to create in the face of devastation. It also functioned as a tranquilizer for the conscience of Western civilization. The victory of June 1967 was different from that of 1948, even though, according to Wiesel, both battles were fought for survival: "One does not win battles without paying a price and it is usually one's innocence. Whatever the triumph, sooner or later it begets conditions which call it into question."[40]

Wiesel is pleased with the behavior of the Israelis and with the relative humaneness of the Israeli occupation, although he is displeased that such military measures were necessary to insure the survival of Israel. According to Wiesel, Israel's behavior underscores the continuing determination of the Jewish people to sanctify life despite life's injustices.

Wiesel's reaction to criticism of Israel's behavior in the wake of the Six-Day War illustrates his dual commitment to solidarity and sanctification. Wiesel wears his Jewishness as a badge of justice in a manner similar to the way that James Cone wears his blackness or Mary Daly her feminism. Wiesel attacks the moral purity and the shortcomings of Western society and thereby challenges the right of Western nations to act as judges. In order to insure their silence, Wiesel, like Cone, plays upon the guilt that Western man feels toward his innocent victims (Jews, blacks, Indians, and women, among others). Wiesel views criticism of Israel by Western people as arrogance. He argues that those who were silent when the Jews needed their voices should also remain silent now. Only the Jew in solidarity with his people has the right to demand higher standards from Israel. This right stems from the other commitment of the Jew to sanctify life.

The existence of the state of Israel poses an ideological question with respect to the Jewish past and future. The foundation of the state of Israel was the product of two conflicting ideologies. On the one hand, the state was born in order to insure a people's survival, while on the other hand it was the heir to three thousand years of tradition and morality that placed different demands upon its demands of sanctification. Ronald Sanders has stated the problem clearly, and his own sentiments mirror Wiesel's. He writes:

> These questions are ways of stating the dilemma of Jewish history. Anyone who recognizes clearly what happened to the Jews of Europe during the Second World War, anyone with the slightest knowledge of the long *Leidensgeschichte* that preceded it back through the centuries of pogroms, humiliation, blood accusations and burnings at the stake, knows why a Jewish state must survive. Anyone with a sense of the innate values of Jewish history knows why it should continue as such, why Jews shouldn't simply become absorbed into the existing populations wherever they can and eventually disappear as an entity. But isn't there a conflict of principles here? Are the innate values of Jewish history, the persistent Jewish contributions through millennia to the conscience of mankind, compatible with the Realpolitik of a Jewish state?[41]

Wiesel also sees this problem as the fundamental challenge confronting the Jewish people. He once hoped for a messianic solution, but with the demise of this hope he substituted the concept of a moral Jewish state and a people charged with the sanctification of life. The fact that this sanctification is difficult only highlights the distance between the contemporary world and the messianic hope. The Talmud argues, "In a place where there are no men try to be a man."[42] Wiesel would argue, "Where there are no gods, man must become God." In the process, man becomes aware of his own humanity and his own fragility.

## L. Eitinger

## On Being a Psychiatrist
## and a Survivor

The topic "being a psychiatrist and a survivor" allows me to start with a few personal remarks. Any person who has been exposed to extraordinary events in his life and at the same time has been used to working systematically will feel the need to see these experiences in a more general context and in the total frame of reference of his life. This was indeed true in my case. I studied medicine and made plans for a future in a milieu that could be considered safe, but suddenly I found myself a refugee in a foreign country where I did not know anybody and where nobody was interested in knowing me or anything about me. Without any psychological preparation, I was confronted with the problems of the prewar refugee, i.e., a person who was considered with suspicion because nobody would believe what he had to tell about the persecutions he had escaped from. After a few months, however, the Nazis were in Norway too, and I was on the run again. Eventually I was caught. In the beginning I went through several Norwegian prisons, which at the time I considered terrible, but which later on I remembered almost as convalescent homes. Afterwards there were prisons in Norway administered by German police, then several

186

concentration camps in Norway, and at the end Auschwitz. Here one lived literally in the shadow of the chimneys of the crematoria and their steady stream of smoke, which became fatter and darker and more threatening every time a new transport of prisoners arrived, which happened nearly every day. But every day one could also see hundreds of killed and thousands of maltreated prisoners in the most hopeless conditions and situations. Even here there were some who were able to keep their fighting spirit, in spite of everything. Others gave in, overwhelmed by the seemingly desperate situation. Brutality, under-nourishment, diseases, vermin, the prisoners' recklessness toward each other, but also their nearly infinite readiness to help each other, were impressions one could not avoid observing and registering with all one's capacities. For every thinking person, not only for a psychiatrist, there was one problem that was nearly always considered when it was possible to raise oneself over the daily worries and over the despair: What will the future be—if there will be one—how will we and all those people who have suffered so incredibly, who were humili-ated to a degree never heard of before, how will we be able to adjust ourselves again in the new world to come? That it would be a *new and better* world—there was no doubt about this in our hearts.

After the war was over, many former prisoners felt a deep urge to tell the world what really had been going on in the camps. I have read many of the reports and accounts, but most of them have been of little value to me. Nearly all were egocentric and only very few had a wider horizon. The two main questions of the camp remained unanswered and unsolved. How could these people live again under "normal cir-cumstances," and what actually was the meaning of this holocaust we had been through?

As a psychiatrist I considered it my duty to find an answer to the first question. The second was too overwhelming. But in reality I felt neither strong nor objective enough to tackle even the question of re-adjustment immediately after the war. Obviously, I was not readjusted myself. Who could have been? I tried to find out how less dramatic and traumatizing surroundings affect the mental health of human beings. I thus started an investigation on the influence of military life on the psychic life of young Norwegian males, and later one on the adaptation difficulties of refugees in Norway (3, 4, 5).

In 1957 it was my good fortune to become a member of a medical-psychiatric-psychological team of university teachers, whose task it was to investigate ex-prisoners thoroughly. We were asked to judge as objectively as we could the possibility of a connection between war experiences and actual disability in each case, and to decide on what action was to be taken in order to assure ex-prisoners the necessary medical help and social relief. Since then I have not been able to abandon the question of concentration camp survivors. I have interviewed and investigated survivors from nearly all the European countries living in Norway and Israel; I have been in all the mental hospitals of Israel and found all the survivors living there; I have followed the morbidity and mortality of all the Norwegians who had been in concentration camps outside Norway during the war; I have kept track of the few Norwegian Jewish survivors, practically from the day of their arrest until thirty years after the liberation. We have published three monographs (7, 11, 21) on the different aspects of the topic and dozens of articles (6, 8, 9, 10, 12, 13, 19). But all this knowledge did not offer a deeper understanding of the meaning of the Holocaust. This I did not learn before my encounter with Elie Wiesel.

It is not possible to give here a detailed account of all our findings, and only a few conclusions can be reported. When we investigated selected cases, be it in Norway or in Israel, be it refugees who had been in camps or people born and bred in Norway, arrested there, and returned to their families after having been exposed to the various forms of excessive stress in the different Nazi camps, we found that the persons concerned were suffering from many different diseases and disturbances. These disorders can be divided into two main groups. The first were somatic findings, which include, besides tuberculosis and other infectious diseases, the so-called concentration camp syndrome, characterized by premature aging, disturbances of memory, and other signs of organic brain damage. It was correlated to the degree of torture, head injuries, weight loss, and other physical aspects of captivity. The other group, psychological disturbances, mainly anxiety, sleep disturbances, and nightmares, were very frequent and correlated with psychic difficulties during captivity. The results of these studies showed beyond any doubt that a widespread morbidity and disability existed among the investigated ex-prisoners, and that the pathology was connected with the stay in the camps (6, 18, 21, 22).

The general validity of these results was, however, hampered by the fact that the persons who were included in our studies represented only a selected small group of the total ex-prisoner population, i.e., people who had fallen ill, who were not able to work, who needed medical help and care, who applied for pension, etc. A study of the mortality and morbidity of the *total* survivor population was therefore carried out (11). A total of 6,193 Norwegians were deported during World War II to concentration camps, prisons, and penitentiaries in Germany or German-occupied territory in Central Europe. Of the deported prisoners, 762 were Jews. Most were arrested during the razzias in October–November 1942 and sent to extermination camps. The ages of the Jewish prisoners varied from under one year to over eighty, with an average of forty-one years. Non-Jewish prisoners totalled 5,431; 597 of these were sent to NN camps (*Nacht- und Nebellager* = extermination camps). Most of the non-Jewish prisoners were fairly young men, with an average age of thirty-three; only 7% were fifty or more.

Of the 762 Jewish prisoners, 739 died during imprisonment, i.e., 97%. Of the 5,431 non-Jewish prisoners, 649 died in prison, i.e., 12% (44.9% of the NN prisoners and 7.9% of the "ordinary" prisoners).

After the liberation, the mortality of the Norwegian ex-prisoners was much higher than that of the general Norwegian population. In the observation period, i.e., 1945–66, the "expected number of deaths" (E) was 608.9, while the diagnosed number (D) was 719, the ratio D:E being 1.18.

The ex-prisoners also had a higher morbidity than a matched control group. For each ex-prisoner investigated, a control person of the same sex and the same age, the same branch of the insurance organization, the same socioeconomic status and the same occupational category was found. In many cases, mostly in the small places, the controls were also treated by the same doctor and, in some cases, the brother of the ex-prisoner was the control. The ex-prisoners—as a group—have been sick more often than the controls. (Among the ex-prisoners 57% had less than five registered sick periods against 78% among the controls. On the other hand, 8.5% of the ex-prisoners had sixteen or more sick periods against 1.2% of the controls.)

The number of registered sick days in the observation period was higher for the ex-prisoners than for the controls. (16% of the ex-prisoners had up to fourteen registered sick days against 33% of the controls. On the other hand, 64% of the ex-prisoners against 29% of the controls had more than ninety registered sick days.) Furthermore, the ex-prisoners had more hospitalization periods than the controls and the number of days spent in hospitals was much higher for ex-prisoners than for controls. (40% of the ex-prisoners were not hospitalized in the observation period, against 61% of the controls, and 20% of the ex-prisoners spent more than ninety days in hospitals against 3% of the controls.)

Accepting the view that health is not merely the absence of disease, we were also interested in the general adjustment of the ex-prisoners in the postwar period. As parameters, we used the number of professions, the number of residences, the changes in the occupational status, and the stability of work. The ex-prisoners were compelled to change their professions more often than the controls. The stability of the general Norwegian population is demonstrated by the fact that nearly 98% of the controls had one residence only. The ex-prisoners moved much more, either because of their restlessness or in order to find new jobs. The ex-prisoners were also less able to succeed in their occupational life. One out of four was characterized by an obvious professional decline, while in the controls this can be seen in only one out of twenty-five. The ex-prisoners were to an even lesser degree able to stick to their specific jobs. One out of three had to find four or more jobs during the observation period in order to remain in some sort of occupational life.

The greater morbidity among ex-prisoners is not restricted to any special diagnosis. The differences between the ex-prisoners and the controls varied somewhat from diagnostic group to diagnostic group, but there were *always* more ex-prisoners than controls suffering from the various illnesses. The question of whether there is a causal connection between the sojourn in concentration camps, or, more correctly, between the excessive stress situations experienced by the ex-prisoners, and the pathological findings, cannot be answered by a simple yes or no. For certain diseases the connection with the imprisonment is clear, for others it is less explicit. The most natural explanation of the ex-prisoners' higher mortality and morbidity is that the excessive stress they experienced during imprisonment lowered their resistance to infections and lessened their ability to adjust to environmental changes.

When a subject has undergone excessively traumatizing experiences such as those of the concentration camps, we must focus not on a monocausal mechanistic etiology but on the total change of the general resistance or vulnerability of the personalities involved. If we accept this holistic view it is easier to understand that the ex-prisoners present a group of people changed completely in their reactions and powers of resistance.

Of the twenty-four Jewish survivors (13), thirteen were refugees to Norway from Central Europe. At the end of 1975 no less than six of these thirteen were dead, two were untraced, and five were living in Norway (I happen to be one of them). The eleven Norwegian-born Jews managed somewhat better, and also better than the average non-Jewish concentration camp survivors in spite of the excessive stress they were exposed to during their stay in the camp. When comparing this little group with the total Norwegian survivor population, one cannot find any striking differences in their personal backgrounds, upbringing, family backgrounds, or occupations. Detailed medical examinations have shown that they suffer from injuries and chronic diseases to about the same extent as other survivors, and the diseases can thus be assumed to be the result of their stay in concentration camps. Only three of them are dead, the others more or less actively working.

Unlike the case of many of the other survivors, however, their reduced capacity for work has had little influence on their social adjustment, which seems to be good. They appear to be accepted, socially active members of their local communities, with families, friends, and other social contacts. Most were able to manage without war pensions for twenty to twenty-five years. Part of the explanation for their impressive achievement lies in their physical and mental powers of resistance, but I think an equally large part was played by their immediate families and friends. The sheltered environment and the support and protection so generously offered them since their return cushioned the impact of their reduced working capacity, and since the demands made on them were relatively modest, they were able to a large extent to compensate for their physical and mental injuries.

All this knowledge is of course to a certain degree rewarding; it was also satisfying to be able to do some therapeutic work. My past helped me to understand many problems of these patients better than other psychiatrists, who sometimes could not understand what the ex-prisoners were referring to when they mentioned different details from the camp. It was particularly gratifying that the Norwegian law of compensation was changed in response to the results of our investigations. Originally it was necessary for an ex-prisoner who was unable to work to establish with medical certainty or at least with high probability that the disease in question was caused *directly* by the stay in the camp. Now that the law has been changed, an ex-prisoner is eligible for pension even if the connection between the imprisonment and the reduction in work capacity is not evident. Only when the National Insurance Institute can prove that the incapacity is caused by an accident after the war is the ex-prisoner not entitled to war pension.

All these results were interesting, satisfying, and gratifying, but they did not solve my own problem as a survivor. It is here where Elie Wiesel came in. His books immediately gave one the impression of a wider perspective. The scenes were familiar, the transports, the selections, the beating and killing of prisoners, the filth and the hunger. We knew all that very well, but here it was not the individual young boy who was suffering; he was representing his whole people, and we were all suffering with him. What is more, Wiesel was coping with the sufferings in a new way. He tried to find a meaning by challenging God. But he never gave up his basic ethical values, never became a victim of the main and most devastating disease of all the camps, a complete anomy, loss of the original value system, and acceptance of the perverted values of the SS. Elie Wiesel's high personal ethos was the force and the strength that saved him from the abyss of anomy. It is also worth noting the fact that Elie Wiesel has stressed so many times, namely, the survivors as a group never really accepted identification with aggression as their leading principle. After the liberation, in a time of virtual anarchy, when the survivors in fact dominated vast areas of Germany and no resistance arose from the frightened civilian population, almost all the survivors were law-abiding people who by no means identified with the aggressor. Only in rare cases did they take revenge by treating the captured SS men in the same way as they had been treated by them during the dark years of captivity.

Among the survivors, there were substantial differences influenced not only by their individuality but also their nationality. The Norwegian survivors, for example, who had been arrested for a variety of activities—they had fought for their king, their country, their liberty, or generally for the noble cause of resistance against occupants—returned to their homes, where they were received as heroes. In most cases, they also returned to their previous occupations. They were met by the nation's gratitude and enthusiasm. The Jewish survivors were in quite a different situation. Most had no one left; there was nowhere to go; they were completely through with their old lives and had not the faintest idea of what they could or should do with the new life that had been given back to them so unexpectedly. A few figures from my investigations (7) are perhaps appropriate. Between 80 and 90% of those investigated in Israel had lost the majority of their close relatives, i.e., parents, siblings, spouse, and children. There was not a single person among them who had not lost at least one close relative. Between 75 and 80% of my interviewees were totally isolated at the end of the war and were the sole survivors of their families. We find practically the same conditions among the few Norwegian Jewish survivors, in spite of the fact that half of the small Jewish community in Norway was saved. This was possible only because of the attitude prevailing there during the war. Ragnar Ullstein (23), a Norwegian author and historian, describes the arrest of the Norwegian Jews as "a confrontation between the Norwegian State Police and the Gestapo on the one hand and a long series of scattered groups of resistance workers on the other." Thanks to those Norwegians who risked their lives by helping Norwegian Jews over the border to Sweden, the survivors could return to an established community. They were welcomed back by the other members of their circle with all the unusual warmth and kindness typical of this emotional and highly tense time. Their personal fate and their family relationships were, however, nearly as difficult as those of the other Jewish survivors all over Europe. Six of the eleven were the only surviving members of their families; the most extreme case is that of a man who lost his parents, four brothers, and three sisters in Auschwitz. Some of the family members of the other five had survived, but there was not one among them who had not lost at least two close relatives. Two surviving brothers in the latter group, for example, had lost both their parents and four siblings.

It is more than understandable that many a survivor was tormented by the question: why me, and not my brother? Though many rational reasons could be found, irrational feelings prevailed and were called—mainly by American psychiatrists—survivor guilt (20).

Here again Elie Wiesel and his work are of the greatest importance. Being a psychiatrist and a survivor, I was trying to solve not only the mystery of my own survival but also that of my investigated survivors. During the interviews one of the questions asked was why some people managed to survive the hell of the camps and others did not. And after having established an adequate interpersonal contact, the question was—always very cautiously—applied to the interviewed survivor himself.

First of all it is necessary to stress that a certain minimum of survival possibilities must have been present in order for anyone to survive. The first theory of coping with aggression in concentration camps was set forth by Bettelheim (1) in 1943. He was of the opinion that most of the long-term prisoners tried to cope with the violence and aggression that they met in the camps by identifying themselves with the aggressors. Bettelheim does not define coping in detail, and I would like to do it tentatively, considering as a positive form of coping mechanism a reaction of the individual that not only helped him to survive but also to maintain his mental health as undisturbed as possible, both during the stay in the camp and in the postcamp life. This definition alone would characterize the coping mechanism described by Bettelheim as a negative one. Furthermore, Bettelheim's description is based on a camp experience that has nothing to do with the realities of the wartime concentration camps. I cannot elaborate on this topic in detail, but would like to mention only the crucial points. In the prewar period the accepted aim of the camps was the "reeducation" of the inmates. During the war the aim was their annihilation. In the prewar camps it often happened that Jewish prisoners were released, especially when they had the possibility of emigrating—as proved by the fate of Bettelheim himself. During the war there was only one way out of the camp—through the chimney of the crematoria. The Jewish prisoners especially were in actual fact all sentenced to death, their stay in the camps being only the drawn-out execution of the death sentence.

There is no doubt that identification with the aggressor did occur in some prisoners, a fact that was sometimes made possible because the SS guards delegated some of their unlimited power to certain well-selected prisoners. But any shift of the regime in the camp, any transport to another camp or subcamp resulted in the dethronement of these "superprisoners," often in a drastic way and with fatal results for those involved. Both those experiences and my interviews proved that identification with the aggressor, as far as it occurred, was a negative coping mechanism, leading to the destruction of those involved and—in the few cases where they survived—to deep pathological changes in personality.

In contrast to Bettelheim's viewpoint, we have Frankl (14), who rightly stresses the fact that if you have something to live for, the amount of suffering you can endure is practically without limits. Frankl's description of a "contract with fate," which presumed that every misfortune, every traumatization that a prisoner was subjected to would spare his beloved in another camp from the same sort of misfortune, is very moving and deeply human; however, according to the experiences I have learned of in my interviews, it was an extremely rare form of coping mechanism, or rather maybe self-deception. How far this contract with fate can help a person when he is finally confronted with hard reality is difficult to say. The fact that none of my interviewed survivors referred to this sort of coping mechanism would indicate that it was not among the most prevalent or positive ones.

The group of people who were able to mobilize the most adequate coping mechanism were those who, for one reason or another, could retain their personality and system of values more or less intact even under conditions of nearly complete social anomy. Those who were most fortunate in this respect were the persons who, thanks to their profession, could both show and practice interest in others, who could retain their values inside the camp at the same level as outside the camp. The few fortunate ones were some doctors, nurses, even social workers and priests, as described by Kral (16) in Theresienstadt (Terezin). They were more preoccupied with the problems of their fellow prisoners than with their own and came through their trials in better mental condition than the average inmate of the camp. Only a tiny minority, however, had this good fortune. The greater part had to find other ways of surviving.

Prisoners who were completely isolated from their families, deprived of all contact with groups to whom they were related before the war, people who very quickly abandoned themselves and their innermost values, people who were completely overwhelmed by the notion that they had nobody and nothing to struggle or to live for, who felt completely passive and had lost their ability to retain some sort of self-activity were those who most easily succumbed. The symptoms of the feelings of hopelessness and submission could be seen by experienced observers rather early.

On the other hand, my interviews have shown that prisoners who had been able to stay together with some members of their family, to remain in contact with some of their prewar peers, to help others and to get help, as shown in Luchterhand (17) among others, were those who resisted best. They were not completely deprived of all feelings of personal and human dignity and values in their own eyes or in the eyes of their fellow inmates. These findings are to a certain degree the same for ex-prisoners interviewed in Norway and in Israel. When asking the Norwegian ones what helped them most to survive, the answers were nearly stereotyped: "Being together with other Norwegians." The answers of the Israelis were much more varied because of the complex family and group relations they had during imprisonment.

There were other means to survival as well. One—also described by Bettelheim—was the attitude of a detached observer. There were a few who really managed to tell themselves that life in the camps was "actually" no concern of theirs. They were not the ones who slaved and were ill-treated. They were just spectators of a terrible drama in which by chance their own bodies were also the actors. Or as Bettelheim put it: "This torture is happening to my body and not to me." Less than 1% of those interviewed, however, referred to this coping mechanism. A person who regarded his surroundings as unreal became unavoidably isolated and slowly lost contact with others and with reality.

The conservation of one's own ability to make some of one's own decisions was most important. In some cases it was only the decision about how to deal with the daily portion of bread, in other cases the question of keeping up personal hygiene. The decisive factor was always that the prisoners did not consider themselves completely passive. They did not lose their reasoning power, their ability to plan and to put their plans into action. They proved this by being capable of administering the diminutive remains of their right to decide for themselves, by showing that they were not willing to be overwhelmed completely by circumstances. They continued to be individuals and individualists.

For completeness it is important to mention that there are of course quite a number of survivors who readily admit that they survived by mere chance or by luck only, without any personal influence over themselves whatsoever.

When comparing the groups of survivors who mobilized their resources more or less consciously and actively with those who ascribed their survival to mere luck or chance, it appears, on a statistically significant level, that the former have less psychiatric complications than the latter. In other words, coping mechanisms that enhanced the individual's contact with a group, that were based on uninjured and positive value systems, on retaining self-respect as a human being in the best and truest sense of the word, coping where attachment to others was of central concern, proved to be not only of importance in relation to the capacity of immediate survival, but also a way of survival without too many psychological disturbances and with one's personality intact—when experiences like those in the concentration camps allow it at all.

Here it is perhaps worth mentioning a little study from Tasmania (15). The seven survivors of a shipwreck involving ten men were interviewed within a few days of their rescue. They had been floating in a rubber raft for nine days and had thereafter been on an isolated rocky beach for four days. Three of the men walked through dense brush to obtain help. Rescue came on the thirteenth day. The purpose of the authors' examination was to identify those behaviors that the survivors reported as helping them during their ordeal. The most prominent of these were attachment ideation (preoccupation with principal attachment figures such as wives, mothers, close peers, girl friends, etc.), the drive to survive, prayer, and hope.

Comparing the incomparable, we find nevertheless some of the same coping mechanisms. For an author of a scientific investigation it is valuable to get such information from another part of the world. But the greatest satisfaction I had was to hear Elie Wiesel elaborate on this topic. He was able to express precisely the ideas that mutual help and the enhancement of the individual's contact with other members of his group were the best ways to survive. Elie Wiesel portrayed the idea of retaining self-respect, of keeping human values intact—the same ideas I had found independently of him in my interviews. I must confess that at that time I did not grasp the full impact of my findings. It was in actual fact Elie Wiesel who opened my eyes. What can be a greater experience for a psychiatrist than a poet's expressing the same views and findings made in his intuitive and spiritual way?

There is, however, also a second, a general point. One could put it in the following way: Before Elie Wiesel, the survivors were afflicted with feelings of guilt because they had survived their stay in camp and because they had not sacrificed their life by "marching against the SS" (2). After Elie Wiesel published his works, the survivors' position changed completely. Elie Wiesel has placed the guilt and the guilt feelings where they really belong. He was—again in his sovereign form and with his boundless knowledge of Jewish history and lore—able to show how being a survivor relates to Jewish destiny. From Isaac, whom Elie Wiesel has called "the first survivor," to all the individual and collective survivors of pogroms and persecutions throughout our history, the survivor forms an unbroken chain. He is part of a tradition that passes from generation to generation, fulfilling his task as the bearer of the message of our people: "One can suffer and despair an entire lifetime and still not give up the art of laughter—and so defy death and assert life." This is the deepest meaning of our life, the meaning that will help us to live on, and that Elie Wiesel, his work, and his message have enabled us to see and to understand.

# Elie Wiesel

# Why I Write

Why do I write? Perhaps in order not to go mad. Or, on the contrary, to touch the bottom of madness.

Like Samuel Beckett, the survivor expresses himself "en désespoir de cause," because there is no other way.

Speaking of the solitude of the survivor, the great Yiddish and Hebrew poet and thinker Aaron Zeitlin addresses those who have left him: his father, dead; his brother, dead; his friends, dead: "You have abandoned me," he says to them. "You are together, without me. I am here. Alone. And I make words."

So do I, just like him. I also say words, write words, reluctantly.

There are easier occupations, far more pleasant ones. But for the survivor, writing is not a profession, but an occupation, a duty. Camus calls it "an honor." As he puts it: "I entered literature through worship." Other writers said: "Through anger, through love." Speaking for myself, I would say: "Through silence."

It was by seeking, by probing, silence that I began to discover the perils and power of the word.

I never intended to be a philosopher, or a theologian. The only role I sought was that of witness. I believed that, having survived by chance, I was duty-bound to give meaning to my survival, to justify each moment of my life. I knew the story had to be told. Not to transmit an experience is to betray it; this is what Jewish tradition teaches us. But how to do this? "When Israel is in exile, so is the word," says the Zohar. The word has deserted the meaning it was intended to convey—impossible to make them coincide. The displacement, the shift, is irrevocable. This was never more true than right after the upheaval. We all knew that we could never, never say what had to be said, that we could never express in words, coherent, intelligible words, our experience of madness on an absolute scale. The walk through flaming night, the silence before and after the selection, the monotonous praying of the condemned, the Kaddish of the dying, the fear and hunger of the sick, the shame and suffering, the haunted eyes, the demented stares. I thought that I would never be able to speak of them. All words seemed inadequate, worn, foolish, lifeless, whereas I wanted them to be searing. Where was I to discover a fresh vocabulary, a primeval language? The language of night was not human; it was primitive, almost animal—hoarse shouting, screams, muffled moaning, savage howling, the sound of beating. . . . A brute striking wildly, a body falling; an officer raises his arm and a whole community walks toward a common grave; a soldier shrugs his shoulders, and a thousand families are torn apart, to be reunited only by death. This is the concentration camp language. It negated all other language and took its place. Rather than link, it became wall. Could it be surmounted? Could the reader be brought to the other side? I knew the answer to be negative, and yet I also knew that "no" had to become "yes." It was the wish, the last will of the dead. One had to break the shell enclosing the dark truth, and give it a name. One had to force man to look.

The fear of forgetting: the main obsession of all those who have passed through the universe of the damned. The enemy counted on people's disbelief and forgetfulness. How could one foil this plot? And if memory grew hollow, empty of substance, what would happen to all we had accumulated along the way?

Remember, said the father to his son, and the son to his friend.

Gather the names, the faces, the tears. If, by a miracle, you come out of it alive, try to reveal everything, omitting nothing, forgetting nothing. Such was the oath we had all taken: "If, by some miracle, I emerge alive, I will devote my life to testifying on behalf of those whose shadow will fall on mine forever and ever."

This is why I write certain things rather than others: to remain faithful.

Of course, there are times of doubt for the survivor, times when one would give in to weakness, or long for comfort. I hear a voice within me telling me to stop mourning the past. I too want to sing of love and of its magic. I too want to celebrate the sun, and the dawn that heralds the sun. I would like to shout, and shout loudly: "Listen, listen well! I too am capable of victory, do you hear? I too am open to laughter and joy! I want to stride, head high, my face unguarded, without having to point to the ashes over there on the horizon, without having to tamper with facts to hide their tragic ugliness. For a man born blind, God himself is blind, but look, I see, I am not blind." One feels like shouting this, but the shout changes to a murmur. One must make a choice; one must remain faithful. A big word, I know. Nevertheless I use it, it suits me. Having written the things I have written, I feel I can afford no longer to play with words. If I say that the writer in me wants to remain loyal, it is because it is true. This sentiment moves all survivors; they owe nothing to anyone, but everything to the dead.

I owe them my roots and memory. I am duty-bound to serve as their emissary, transmitting the history of their disappearance, even if it disturbs, even if it brings pain. Not to do so would be to betray them, and thus myself. And since I feel incapable of communicating their cry by shouting, I simply look at them. I see them and I write.

While writing, I question them as I question myself. I believe I said it before, elsewhere: I write to understand as much as to be understood. Will I succeed one day? Wherever one starts from one reaches darkness. God? He remains the God of darkness. Man? Source of darkness. The killers' sneers, their victims' tears, the onlookers' indifference, their complicity and complacency, the divine role in all that: I do not understand. A million children massacred: I shall never understand.

Jewish children: they haunt my writings. I see them again and again. I shall always see them. Hounded, humiliated, bent like the old men who surround them as though to protect them, unable to do so. They are thirsty, the children, and there is no one to give them water. They are hungry, the children, but there is no one to give them a crust of bread. They are afraid, and there is no one to reassure them.

They walk in the middle of the road, like vagabonds. They are on the way to the station, and they will never return. In sealed cars, without air or food, they travel toward another world; they guess where they are going, they know it, and they keep silent. Tense, thoughtful, they listen to the wind, the call of death in the distance.

All these children, these old people, I see them. I never stop seeing them. I belong to them.

But they, to whom do they belong?

People tend to think that a murderer weakens when facing a child. The child reawakens the killer's lost humanity. The killer can no longer kill the child before him, the child inside him.

Not this time. With us, it happened differently. Our Jewish children had no effect upon the killers. Nor upon the world. Nor upon God.

I think of them, I think of their childhood. Their childhood is a small Jewish town, and this town is no more. They frighten me; they reflect an image of myself, one that I pursue and run from at the same time—the image of a Jewish adolescent who knew no fear, except the fear of God, whose faith was whole, comforting, and not marked by anxiety.

No, I do not understand. And if I write, it is to warn the reader that he will not understand either. "You will not understand, you will never understand," were the words heard everywhere during the reign of night. I can only echo them. You, who never lived under a sky of blood, will never know what it was like. Even if you read all the books ever written, even if you listen to all the testimonies ever given, you will remain on this side of the wall, you will view the agony and death of a people from afar, through the screen of a memory that is not your own.

An admission of impotence and guilt? I do not know. All I know is that Treblinka and Auschwitz cannot be told. And yet I have tried. God knows I have tried.

Did I attempt too much or not enough? Out of some fifteen volumes, only three or four penetrate the phantasmagoric realm of the dead. In my other books, through my other books, I try to follow other roads. For it is dangerous to linger among the dead; they hold on to you, and you run the risk of speaking only to them. And so, I forced myself to turn away from them and study other periods, explore other destinies and teach other tales: the Bible and the Talmud, Hasidism and its fervor, the *Shtetl* and its songs, Jerusalem and its echoes; the Russian Jews and their anguish, their awakening, their courage. At times, it seems to me that I am speaking of other things with the sole purpose of keeping the essential—the personal experience—unspoken. At times I wonder: And what if I were wrong? Perhaps I should not have heeded my own advice and stayed in my own world with the dead.

But then, I have not forgotten the dead. They have their rightful place even in the works about Rizhin and Koretz, Jerusalem and Kol-villàg. Even in my biblical and Midrashic tales, I pursue their presence, mute and motionless. The presence of the dead then beckons in such tangible ways that it affects even the most removed characters. Thus, they appear on Mount Moriah, where Abraham is about to sacrifice his son, a holocaust offering to their common God. They appear on Mount Nebo, where Moses enters solitude and death. And again in the Pardés, where a certain Elisha ben Abuya, seething with anger and pain, decided to repudiate his faith. They appear in Hasidic and Talmudic legends in which victims forever need defending against forces that would crush them. Technically, so to speak, they are of course elsewhere, in time and space, but on a deeper, truer plane, the dead are part of every story, of every scene. They die with Isaac, lament with Jeremiah, they sing with the *Besht*, and, like him, they wait for miracles —but alas, they will not come to pass.

"But what is the connection?" you will ask. Believe there is one.

After Auschwitz everything brings us back to Auschwitz. When I speak of Abraham, Isaac, and Jacob, when I evoke Rabbi Yohanan ben Zakkai and Rabbi Akiba, it is the better to understand them in the light of Auschwitz. As for the Maggid of Mezeritch and his disciples, it is to encounter the followers of their followers, that I attempt to reconstruct their spellbound, spellbinding universe. I like to imagine them alive, exuberant, celebrating life and hope. Their happiness is as necessary to me as it was once to themselves. And yet.

How did they manage to keep their faith intact? How did they manage to sing as they went to meet the Angel of Death? I know Hasidim who never vacillated; I respect their strength. I know others who chose rebellion, protest, rage; I respect their courage. For there comes a time when only those who do not believe in God will not cry out to him in wrath and anguish.

Do not judge either. Even the heroes perished as martyrs, even the martyrs died as heroes. Who would dare oppose knives to prayers? The faith of some matters as much as the strength of others. It is not ours to judge; it is only ours to tell the tale.

But where is one to begin? Whom is one to include? One meets a Hasid in all my novels. And a child. And an old man. And a beggar. And a madman. They are all part of my inner landscape. The reason why? Pursued and persecuted by the killers, I offer them shelter. The enemy wanted to create a society purged of their presence, and I have brought some of them back. The world denied them, repudiated them, so let them live at least within the feverish dreams of my characters.

It is for them that I write.

And yet, the survivor may experience remorse. He has tried to bear witness; it was all in vain.

After the liberation, illusions shaped one's hopes. We were convinced that a new world would be built upon the ruins of Europe. A new civilization was to see the light. No more wars, no more hate, no more intolerance, no fanaticism anywhere. And all this because the witnesses would speak. And speak they did, to no avail.

They will continue, for they cannot do otherwise. When man, in his grief, falls silent, Goethe says, then God gives him the strength to sing of his sorrows. From that moment on, he may no longer choose not to sing, whether his song is heard or not. What matters is to struggle against silence with words, or through another form of silence. What matters is to gather a smile here and there, a tear here and there, a word here and there, and thus justify the faith placed in you, a long time ago, by so many victims.

Why I write? To wrench those victims from oblivion. To help the dead vanquish death.

*Translated by Rosette C. Lamont*

Irving Abrahamson

# Elie Wiesel:
# A Selected Bibliography

The following bibliography of Elie Wiesel's writings is intended to assist those who wish to investigate this work primarily in relation to the Holocaust. In a sense all of Wiesel's work is related to the Holocaust Universe, but the items listed here are among the most directly useful. The lists of hardbound and paperbound books enumerate the most readily available texts of Wiesel's work. These and the other lists given here are arranged in a chronological order.

Absolutely indispensable is *Elie Wiesel: A Bibliography*, compiled by Molly Abramowitz (Metuchen, N.J.: The Scarecrow Press, Inc., 1974), an annotated bibliography listing works by and about Wiesel. It is especially useful for works on Wiesel in English.

I. The following is a working bibliography of Elie Wiesel's books. Unless otherwise indicated the edition listed here has been translated from the French original:

*Night*. Trans. Stella Rodway; Foreword by François Mauriac. New York: Hill and Wang, 1960.

*Dawn*. Trans. Frances Frenaye. London: MacGibbon and Kee, 1961.

*Dawn*. Trans. Anne Borchardt. New York: Hill and Wang, 1961.

*The Accident*. Trans. Anne Borchardt. New York: Hill and Wang, 1962.

*The Town Beyond the Wall*. Trans. Stephen Becker. New York: Holt, Rinehart and Winston, 1967.

*The Gates of the Forest*. Trans. Frances Frenaye. New York: Holt, Rinehart and Winston, 1966.

*The Jews of Silence*: *A Personal Report on Soviet Jewry*. Translated from the Hebrew by Neal Kozodoy. New York: Holt, Rinehart and Winston, 1966.

*Legends of Our Time*. Trans. Steven Donadio. New York: Holt, Rinehart and Winston, 1968.

*A Beggar in Jerusalem*. Trans. Lily Edelman and Elie Wiesel. New York: Random House, 1970.

*One Generation After*. Trans. Lily Edelman and Elie Wiesel. New York: Random House, 1970.

*Souls on Fire*: *Portraits and Legends of Hasidic Masters*. Trans. Marion Wiesel. New York: Random House, 1972.

*The Oath*. Trans. Marion Wiesel. New York: Random House, 1973.

*Ani Maamin*: *A Song Lost and Found Again*. Trans. Marion Wiesel. New York: Random House, 1973.

*Zalmen, or the Madness of God*. Based on a translation by Nathan Edelman, adapted for the stage by Marion Wiesel. New York: Random House, 1974.

*Messengers of God*: *Biblical Portraits and Legends*. Trans. Marion Wiesel. New York: Random House, 1976.

*Four Hasidic Masters and Their Struggle against Melancholy*. Notre Dame, Indiana: University of Notre Dame Press, 1978.

*A Jew Today*. Trans. Marion Wiesel. New York: Random House, 1978.

II. The following is a working bibliography of current paperbound editions of Elie Wiesel's books:

*Night*. Trans. Stella Rodway; Foreword by François Mauriac. New York: Avon, 1969.

*Dawn*. Trans. Frances Frenaye. New York: Avon, 1970.

*The Accident*. Trans. Anne Borchardt. New York: Avon, 1970.

*The Town Beyond the Wall*. Trans. Stephen Becker. New York: Avon, 1969.

*The Gates of the Forest*. Trans. Frances Frenaye. New York: Avon, 1967.

*The Jews of Silence*: *A Personal Report on Soviet Jewry*. Translated from the Hebrew by Neal Kozodoy. New York. New American Library (Signet), 1967.

*Legends of Our Time*. New York: Avon, 1970.

*A Beggar in Jerusalem*. Trans. Lily Edelman and Elie Wiesel. New York: Avon, 1971.

*One Generation After.* Trans. Lily Edelman and Elie Wiesel. New York: Avon, 1972.

*Souls on Fire: Portraits and Legends of Hasidic Masters.* Trans. Marion Wiesel. New York: Random House (Vintage), 1973.

*The Oath.* Trans. Marion Wiesel. New York: Avon, 1974.

*Messengers of God: Biblical Portraits and Legends.* Trans. Marion Wiesel. New York: Pocket Books, 1977.

III. Elie Wiesel has spoken frequently at various symposia. The following are addresses relevant to the Holocaust Universe and collected in the books that have resulted from those conferences:

"Talking and Writing and Keeping Silent," in *The German Church Struggle and the Holocaust,* ed. Franklin H. Littell and Hubert G. Locke. Detroit: Wayne State University Press, 1974. Wiesel challenges certain positions stated by Richard Rubenstein in "Some Perspectives on Religious Faith after Auschwitz," contained in this volume. He emphasizes that at the core of Jewishness is the obligation to reject silence and tell the tale of the Holocaust.

"On Revolutions in Culture and the Arts," in *Revolutionary Directions in Intellectual and Cultural Production: Their Consequences for the Higher Learning.* New York: Research Foundation of City University of New York, 1975. (Address delivered May 4, 1973, at Tenth Anniversary Convocation of Graduate School of City University of New York.) Wiesel discusses revolutions past and present, political and cultural, their justifications and their betrayals. Seen from the essential perspective of the Holocaust, the most vital of all revolutions is to maintain a belief in language and literature and "a faith . . . in man, despite man," a faith in his survival and in his capacity to change.

"Art and Culture after the Holocaust," in *Auschwitz: Beginning of a New Era? Reflections on the Holocaust,* ed. Eva Fleischner. [New York:] The Cathedral Church of St. John the Divine; KTAV Publishing House, Inc.; Anti-Defamation League of B'nai B'rith, 1977. (Introductory Lecture to International Symposium on the Holocaust held at the Cathedral of Saint John the Divine, June 3–6, 1974, in New York City.) Despite the fundamental impossibility of ever telling the tale of the Holocaust adequately, the poems, documents, chronicles, and personal testimonies of the witnesses—victims and survivors— succeed better than imaginative literature in bringing the past back to life and thus in frustrating the executioner and his accomplices in their attempt to erase the Holocaust from memory.

"The Holocaust and the Future," in *The Holocaust: Its Meaning for*

*Christians and Jews.* St. Louis: National Conference of Christians and Jews, Inc., 1977. (Introductory address delivered November 3, 1976.) Wiesel examines the various forms of madness exhibited by executioners, victims, bystanders, and survivors, as well as the madness that has characterized the post-Holocaust years. He develops the responsibility of Christianity for the Holocaust and argues that the world's survival depends upon telling the tale of the Holocaust.

"The Holocaust as Literary Inspiration," in *Dimensions of the Holocaust.* Evanston: Northwestern University, 1977. Originating as a response to Prof. Arthur Butz of Northwestern University, who (like others) has challenged the factual reality of the Holocaust, this essay examines the impossibility for fiction to treat of the event. Wiesel stresses that a new literary form has grown out of the Holocaust—the literature of testimony—and he offers numerous telling quotations that illustrate this new genre and authenticate the event.

"Freedom of Conscience and the Jewish Holocaust," in *Religious Liberty in the Crossfire of Creeds,* ed. Franklin H. Littell. Philadelphia: Ecumenical Press, 1978. Wiesel deals here with problems of conscience and freedom in the Jewish tradition, with special emphasis on post-Holocaust experiences.

IV. Elie Wiesel has given numerous interviews and participated in many formal discussions. The following list includes much material relevant to the Holocaust Universe:

"Jewish Values in the Post-Holocaust Future—A Symposium." *Judaism,* XVI (Summer, 1967), 266–99. (The other participants were Emil L. Fackenheim, George Steiner, Richard Popkin.) Before Jewish values for the post-Holocaust future can even be defined, the Jew must confront the full, unparalleled, largely untold story of the Holocaust. Only then can he use the Holocaust as a standard for values for a new era.

Flender, Harold. "Conversation with: Elie Wiesel." *Women's American ORT Reporter,* XX (March/April, 1970), 4–6. Wiesel discusses such matters as solitude, questions and answers, the Talmud, contemporary novelists (Schwartz-Bart, Bellow, Malamud, Roth, Nabokov), and some of his own works (*Night, One Generation After, Zalmen, or the Madness of God, A Beggar in Jerusalem, The Jews of Silence, The Town Beyond the Wall*); contains much useful biographical information.

Goulston, Michael, and Rudolf, Anthony. "Beyond Survival." *European Judaism,* VI, 1 (Winter, 1971–72), 4–10. (The participants were Elie Wiesel, Eugene Heimler, Goulston, and Rudolf.) Wiesel discusses the direct connection of the Holocaust experience to *Night* and its indirect connection to *A Beggar in Jerusalem, Souls on Fire, The Gates of the Forest,* and *Legends of Our Time*. With respect to these connections he considers such matters as the guilt of the survivor, the joy of Hasidism, the corruption of language, and the guilty conscience of the world.

Koppel, Gene, and Kaufmann, Henry. *Elie Wiesel: A Small Measure of Victory*. Tucson: University of Arizona, 1974. (Koppel and Kaufmann interviewed Wiesel November 25, 1973. 28 pp.) Wiesel discusses his personal background, offers opinions on contemporary affairs, religion, and literature. Brief but valuable.

Edelman, Lily. "A Conversation with Elie Wiesel." *The National Jewish Monthly*, LXXXVIII (November, 1973), 5–18. While the interview concentrates on the genesis, themes, characters, and message of *The Oath*, it also contains an especially good brief introduction to Wiesel's theory of literature—emphasizing the writer's responsibilities to himself, his subject, his words, and his audience.

Cargas, Harry James. *Harry James Cargas in Conversation with Elie Wiesel*. New York: Paulist Press, 1976. Cargas presents a book length series of wide-ranging and in-depth interviews with Wiesel. The overwhelming theme of the Holocaust dominates Wiesel's ideas about the function of the author, his material, his audience, and his craft.

V.  The following items are a representative selection of addresses, articles, and pamphlets relevant to the Holocaust Universe:

"Remembrance at Bergen Belsen." *Hadassah Magazine*, XLVII (Sept., 1965), 9, 16.

"Words from a Witness." *Conservative Judaism*, XXI (Spring, 1967), 40–48.

"On Being a Jew." *Jewish Heritage*, X (Summer, 1967), 51–55.

"Telling the Tale." *Dimensions in American Judaism*, II, 3 (Spring, 1968), 9–12. (Excerpt from address delivered November, 1967, at 49th General Assembly of Union of American Hebrew Congregations.)

"Conversation with Nelly Sachs." *Jewish Heritage*, X (Spring, 1968), 30–33.

*From Holocaust to Rebirth*. New York: The Council of Jewish Federations and Welfare Funds, 1970. (Address delivered November 14, 1970, at 39th General Assembly of Jewish Federations and Welfare Funds, Kansas City, Missouri. 12 pp.)

"To a Young Rebel." *Washington Post*, February 18, 1971, pp. Cl, C10.

"Golda at 75: An Interview with Elie Wiesel." *Hadassah Magazine*, LIV (January, 1973), 6–7, 25–26.

"Faces of a Slaughtered People: Captions for an Exhibit on the Holocaust." *The National Jewish Monthly*, LXXVIII (January, 1973), 6–8.

"Warsaw '43." *Hadassah Magazine*, LIV (April, 1973), 10, 46.

"Between Hope and Fear." *City College Alumnus*, October, 1973, pp. 6-8. (Commencement address delivered June 11, 1973, at City College of New York.)

*Against Despair*. New York: United Jewish Appeal, 1974. (The First Annual Louis A. Pincus Memorial Lecture, delivered December 8, 1973, at United Jewish Appeal 1974 National Conference. 15 pp.)

*Two Images, One Destiny*. New York: United Jewish Appeal, 1974. (Address delivered June, 1974, at Jewish Agency Assembly in Jerusalem. 14 pp.)

"Where Solzhenitsyn Troubles Me." *The National Jewish Monthly*, LXXXIX (November, 1974), 16, 18, 20.

"Ominous Signs and Unthinkable Thoughts." *New York Times*, December 28, 1974, p. C23.

"Remembering." *Moment*, I (May/June, 1975), 97.

"For Some Measure of Humility." *Sh'ma*, October 31, 1975, pp. 314–15.

*Our Jewish Solitude*. New York: United Jewish Appeal, 1976. (Address delivered December 11, 1975, on receiving First David Ben Gurion Award. 12 pp.)

# Notes

### Rosenfeld: The Problematics of Holocaust Literature

1. T. W. Adorno, "Engagement," in *Noten zur Literatur III* (Frankfurt am Main: Suhrkamp Verlag, 1965), pp. 109–35.

2. Reinhard Baumgart, "Unmenschlichkeit beschreiben," in *Literatur für Zeitgenossen: Essays* (Frankfurt am Main: Suhrkamp Verlag, 1966), pp. 12–36.

3. Michael Wyschogrod, "Some Theological Reflections on the Holocaust," *Response* 25 (Spring 1975), 68.

4. Elie Wiesel, "For Some Measure of Humility," *Sh'ma* 5/100 (October 31, 1975), 314.

5. Abraham I. Katsh, ed., *The Warsaw Diary of Chaim Kaplan* (New York: Collier Books, 1973), p. 400.

6. Ernst Schnabel, *Anne Frank: A Portrait in Courage* (New York: Harbace Paperback Library, 1958).

7. Emil Fackenheim, "Sachsenhausen 1938: Groundwork for Auschwitz," *Midstream* XXI (April 1975), 27–31.

8. See George Steiner, *Language and Silence* (New York: Atheneum, 1967), p. 67.

9. Two critical studies are in print: Irving Halperin's *Messengers from the Dead* (Philadelphia: The Westminster Press, 1970) and Lawrence Langer's *The Holocaust and the Literary Imagination* (New Haven: Yale University Press, 1976).

10. A. J. P. Taylor, *The Second World War* (New York: G. P. Putnam's Sons, 1975), p. 149. By distinguishing "the war against the Jews" from the Second World War, I do not want to imply, of course, any approval of avoidance of the Holocaust in texts on the war period. My intention is quite the opposite: to see the Holocaust for what it was so as to afford it a greater emphasis in historical writings.

11. Elie Wiesel, *Night* (New York: Avon, 1969), p. 44.

12. Wiesel, "Snapshots," in *One Generation After* (New York: Random House, 1970), pp. 46–47.

13. Uri Zvi Greenberg, "We Were Not Likened to Dogs among the

213

Gentiles," in Ruth Finer Mintz, *Modern Hebrew Poetry* (Berkeley: University of California Press, 1968), p. 126.

14. Wiesel, "The Death of My Father," in *Legends of Our Time* (New York: Holt, Rinehart and Winston, 1968), p. 7.

15. "One Generation After," in *One Generation After*, p.*10.

16. *Night*, p. 42.

17. Jacob Glatstein, "Smoke," in I. Howe and E. Greenberg, *A Treasury of Yiddish Poetry* (New York: Holt, Rinehart and Winston, 1969), p. 331; the translation is by Chana Faerstein. Reprinted by permission.

18. Rolf Hochhuth, *The Deputy* (New York: Grove Press, Inc., 1964), p. 72.

19. "A Plea for the Dead," in *Legends of Our Time*, p. 190.

20. "My Teachers," in *Legends of Our Time*, p. 8.

21. *The Warsaw Diary of Chaim Kaplan*, pp. 27, 34, 377.

22. Primo Levi, *Survival in Auschwitz* (New York: Collier Books, 1973), p. 94.

23. George Steiner, *In Bluebeard's Castle* (New Haven: Yale University Press, 1971), pp. 53–56. The landscape of hell is referred to repeatedly throughout the literature; the moral conditions that obtain, however, are altogether absent. My interest here is only in the endless tortures of the place, not at all in the ethical system that governs it in Christian religious writings.

24. *The Holocaust and the Literary Imagination*, pp. 82, 84.

25. "A Plea for the Dead," in *Legends of Our Time*, p. 190.

26. Jerry Glenn, *Paul Celan* (New York: Twayne Publishers, Inc., 1973).

27. Götz Wienold, "Paul Celan's Hölderlin-Widerruf," *Poetica* 2 (1968), 216–28.

28. *The Warsaw Diary of Chaim Kaplan*, p. 208.

29. Ibid., pp. 36, 209, 207, 213. As conditions in the ghetto changed, Kaplan vacillated between moments of religious despair and moments of faith; the attitude illustrated by the quotation cited in these passages, while prevalent, was not constant.

30. *Survival in Auschwitz*, p. 113.

31. Ibid., p. 59.

32. Nelly Sachs, *The Seeker and Other Poems* (New York: Farrar, Straus and Giroux, 1970), p. 387; the translation is by Michael Hamburger.

33. Saul Bellow, *Mr. Sammler's Planet* (New York: Viking, 1970), p. 4.

34. Wiesel, *Zalmen, or the Madness of God* (New York: Random House, 1974), p. 79.

35. Ibid., p. 169: "Poor hero, poor dreamer. You have lost. . . . How could you have been so naive? Did you really—really—believe that your gesture would shake the earth? Mankind has other worries. . . . Life goes on. And those who don't suffer refuse to hear about suffering—and particularly about Jewish suffering."

36. Ibid., p. 96.

37. Scholars have excavated several layers of madness in the writings of Elie Wiesel, but the one that I am stressing here—the nonmystical layer—has gone virtually ignored. Yet it is precisely madness in the common or clinical sense that requires attention. Wiesel himself has indicated its presence all along, as in this passage from *The Accident* (New York: Hill and Wang, 1962), p. 104: "We cannot forget. The images are there in front of our eyes. Even if our eyes were no longer there, the images would remain. I think if I were able to forget I would hate myself. Our stay there planted time bombs within us. From time to time one of them explodes. . . . One of these bombs . . . will undoubtedly bring about madness."

### Langer: The Divided Voice

1. Albert Camus, *The Rebel: An Essay on Man in Revolt*, trans. Anthony Bower (New York: Vintage Books, 1958), p. 5.

2. Reprinted in Sigmund Freud, *Civilization, War and Death*, trans. E. Colburn Mayne, rev. Joan Riviere, ed. John Rickman, new and enlarged edition (London: The Hogarth Press, 1953), pp. 17–18.

3. Elie Wiesel, *The Accident*, trans. Anne Borchardt (New York: Hill and Wang, 1962), p. 107.

4. Wiesel, *Dawn*, trans. Frances Frenaye (New York: Hill and Wang, 1961), p. 65.

5. Wiesel, *The Town Beyond the Wall*, trans. Stephen Becker (New York: Atheneum, 1964), p. 78.

6. Wiesel, *The Gates of the Forest*, trans. Frances Frenaye (New York: Holt, Rinehart and Winston, 1966), p. 172.

7. Wiesel, *Legends of Our Time* (New York: Holt, Rinehart and Winston, 1968), p. 181.

8. Wiesel, *One Generation After*, trans. Lily Edelman and Elie Wiesel (New York: Random House, 1970), p. 11.

9. Wiesel, *A Beggar in Jerusalem*, trans. Lily Edelman and Elie Wiesel (New York: Random House, 1970), p. 133.

10. *Legends of Our Time*, p. 173.

11. Ibid., pp. 183, 189, 182.

12. Ibid., p. 191.

13. Ibid., pp. 194, 197.

14. Wiesel, *Messengers of God: Biblical Portraits and Legends*, trans. Marion Wiesel (New York: Random House, 1976), p. 52.

15. *Legends of Our Time*, p. 180.

16. *Gates of the Forest*, p. 33.

17. *One Generation After*, p. 8.

18. *Dawn*, p. 86.

19. Ibid., p. 30.

20. *One Generation After*, p. 162.

21. Ibid., p. 43.

22. Wiesel, *The Oath*, trans. Marion Wiesel (New York: Random House, 1973), p. 41.

23. *One Generation After*, p. 174.

24. *The Oath*, pp. 237, 238.

25. Ibid., p. 239.

26. *Legends of Our Time*, p. 182.

27. Wiesel, *Souls on Fire: Portraits and Legends of Hasidic Masters*, trans. Marion Wiesel (New York: Random House, 1972), p. 240.

28. *Messengers of God*, p. 228.

29. *A Beggar in Jerusalem*, pp. 135, 208.

### Des Pres: The Authority of Silence in Elie Wiesel's Art

1. Elie Wiesel, *Legends of Our Time* (New York: Holt, Rinehart and Winston, 1968), p. 6.

2. Wiesel, *One Generation After* (New York: Random House, 1970), p. 40.

3. Wiesel, *Legends of Our Time*, p. 181.

4. Wiesel, *One Generation After*, p. 72.

5. Wiesel, *Legends of Our Time*, p. 6.

### Roth: Telling a Tale That Cannot Be Told

1. Elie Wiesel, *One Generation After*, trans. Lily Edelman and the author (New York: Avon Books, 1972), p. 213.

2. The dates in parentheses after the titles refer to the publication dates for the first American editions of Wiesel's books.

3. Wiesel, *Messengers of God*, trans. Marion Wiesel (New York: Random House, 1976), p. 181.

4. *One Generation After*, p. 214.

5. Wiesel, *Night*, trans. Stella Rodway (New York: Avon Books, 1972), p. 127.

6. Ibid., p. 76.

7. Ibid., p. 43.

8. Ibid., p. 75.

9. Deut. 30:20 (Revised Standard Version).

10. *Night*, p. 43.

11. Wiesel, *Dawn*, trans. Frances Frenaye (New York: Avon Books, 1970), p. 42.

12. Ibid., p. 126.

13. Wiesel, *The Accident*, trans. Anne Borchardt (New York: Avon Books, 1970), pp. 22–23.

14. Ibid., p. 81.

15. Wiesel, *The Gates of the Forest*, trans. Frances Frenaye (New York: Avon Books, 1972), Introduction.

16. Ibid., p. 57.

17. Ibid., p. 180.

18. Ibid., p. 178.

19. Wiesel, *The Town Beyond the Wall*, trans. Stephen Becker (New York: Avon Books, 1970), p. 101.

20. Ibid., p. 159.

21. Ibid., pp. 53, 49.

22. Wiesel, *A Beggar in Jerusalem*, trans. Lily Edelman and the author (New York: Avon Books, 1971), pp. 87–88.

23. Ibid., p. 16.

24. Ibid., p. 172.

25. Wiesel, *The Oath*, trans. Marion Wiesel (New York: Random House, 1973), p. 32.

26. Ibid., p. 16.

27. Ibid., p. 189.

28. Wiesel expressed such feelings to me in a conversation on November 28, 1975.

29. Wiesel, *The Jews of Silence*, trans. Neal Kozodoy (New York: Signet Books, 1967), p. vii.

30. Ibid., p. 14.

31. Ibid., p. 97.

32. Wiesel, *Legends of Our Time*, trans. Steven Donadio (New York: Avon Books, 1972), p. 82.

33. Ibid.

34. Ibid., p. 230.

35. *One Generation After*, p. 215.

36. Wiesel, *Zalmen, or the Madness of God*, trans. Nathan Edelman (New York: Random House, 1974), p. 53.

37. Wiesel, *Souls on Fire*, trans. Marion Wiesel (New York: Random House, 1972), p. 38.

38. Wiesel, *Ani Maamin*, trans. Marion Wiesel (New York: Random House, 1973), p. 105.

39. *Messengers of God*, p. 235.

40. Num. 6:23-27 (Revised Standard Version).

### Lamont: Elie Wiesel: In Search of a Tongue

1. Elie Wiesel, *Entre deux soleils* (Paris: Editions du Seuil, 1970), p. 128. All the works of Elie Wiesel in this essay are newly translated from the original French edition. The same will hold for all the French texts by other authors quoted in the body of this essay.

2. Lucy S. Dawidowicz, *The War Against the Jews 1933–1945* (New York: Bantam Books, 1976), p. xxv.

3. Lawrence L. Langer, *The Holocaust and the Literary Imagination* (New Haven: Yale University Press, 1975), p. 252.

4. *Entre deux soleils*, pp. 35–36.

5. Gershom G. Scholem, *On the Kabbalah and its Symbolism* (New York: Schocken Books, 1969), p. 13.

6. *Entre deux soleils*, pp. 37–38.

7. Ibid., p. 171.

8. Ibid., p. 173.

9. Ibid., p. 11.

10. Ibid.

11. André Malraux, *Romans, La Condition Humaine* (Paris: NRF, Bibliothèque de la Pléiade, 1960), p. 227.

12. Pierre-Henri Simon, *L'Homme en procès* (Paris: Petite Bibliothèque Payot, 1965), p. 27.

13. André Malraux, *Les chênes qu'on abat* (Paris: Gallimard, 1971), pp. 41–42.

14. Malraux, *Romans, L'Espoir*, p. 569.

15. Morvan Lebesque, *Camus par lui-même* (Paris: Editions du Seuil, 1963), p. 63.

16. Albert Camus, *La Chair*, p. 299.

17. Wiesel, *Le Mendiant de Jérusalem* (Paris: Editions du Seuil, 1968), p. 25.

18. Wiesel, *La Nuit* (Paris: Editions de Minuit, 1958), p. 178.

19. *La Chair*, p. 304.

20. *Entre deux soleils*, p. 105.

21. Camus, *Essais, Lettres à un ami allemand*, p. 242.

22. Camus, *Essais*, Préface à "L'Allemagne vue par les écrivains de la Résistance Français" de Konrad Bieber, p. 1489.

23. Camus, *Carnets, Mai 1935–Février 1942* (Paris: Gallimard, 1962), p. 239.

24. Wiesel, *Le Jour* (Paris: Editions du Seuil, 1961), pp. 127–28.

25. Ibid., p. 56.

26. Ibid., p. 137.

27. Ibid., p. 16.

28. Camus, *Théâtre, Récits, Nouvelles; La Peste* (Paris: NRF, Bibliothèque de la Pléiade, I, 1963), p. 1321.

29. *Le Jour*, p. 83.

30. *La Peste*, p. 1394.

31. *Le Jour*, p. 79.

32. *Entre deux soleils*, p. 170.

33. Ibid., p. 107.

34. Andrei Siniavsky, *A Voice from the Chorus* (New York: Farrar, Straus and Giroux, 1976), p. 59.

### Fackenheim: Midrashic Existence after the Holocaust

1. In a sense more so: Sinai gave the singled-out Jews the choice between life and death. Treblinka only gave the choice—and this only in the best of cases—between ways of meeting death.

2. Reinhard Baumgard, "Unmenschlichkeit Beschrieben: Weltkrieg und Faschismus in der Literatur," in *Merkur*, XIX (Jan. 1965), no. 1, p. 46.

3. Raul Hilberg, *The Destruction of the European Jews* (Chicago: Quadrangle, 1961), p. 657.

4. "Preface to the English Edition of *Spinoza's Critique of Religion*," in *The Jewish Expression*, Judah Goldin, ed. (New York: Bantam, 1970), p. 345.

5. *The Destruction of the European Jews*, p. 669.

6. The presence of a social Darwinist element in Nazism and its antecedents is evident. (See, e.g., H. G. Zmarzlik, "Social Darwinism in Germany," in *Republic to Reich*, H. Holborn, ed. [New York: Vintage, 1973], pp. 436ff.) However, a quantum leap is necessary if the "right" or even "duty" of the strong to exterminate the weak is to become a criminal prosecution in which the weak suffer extermination as a just punishment. This difference was fully revealed in the *Götterdämmerung*, when Hitler declared that the mighty Russians had, after all, historical right on their side, even as he wrote a last will and testament obligating future gen-

erations to complete the "Final Solution"—the extermination of a people that, in his view, fully matched the Russians in might.

7. The present writer was able to observe in 1938 that S.S. men, too, could land in a concentration camp and that if they did, they were punished as brutally as the other inmates. But their punishment was, of course, for acts of disobedience.

8. In his classic "The Devil and Yom Kippur" (*Midstream*, Aug./Sept. 1974) Eckardt deals with the monotonous repetition by anti-Semites, in ever new code words, of the same false accusations and mendacious arguments. However, he does not deal with Nazism in this article.

9. In Plato's *Republic*, *thymos*, or the emotional part of the soul that is capable of enthusiasm, is merely chaotic, not a possibility of the demonic; and the worst state is not hell but merely a tyranny governed by cynicism.

10. Hell is related to purgatory. But filth does not purge. See Terrence Des Pres, *The Survivor*, ch. III, "Excremental Assault" (New York: Oxford, 1976).

11. See Rudolf Hoess, *Commandant of Auschwitz* (London: Pan, 1974), p. 145. In this autobiography, written in prison, the Auschwitz *Kommandant* writes:

> I was opposed to *Der Stürmer*, Streicher's anti-Semitic weekly, because of the disgusting sensationalism with which it played on people's basest instincts. Then, too, there was its perpetual and often savagely pornographic emphasis on sex. This paper caused a lot of mischief and, far from serving serious anti-Semitism, it did a great deal of harm. It is small wonder that after the collapse it was learnt that a Jew edited the paper and that he also wrote the worst of the inflammatory articles it contained.

The last sentence is, of course, quite untrue, but all the more significant when it is remembered that Hoess was in *total* command of *all* the actions at Auschwitz, the Streicher-type included. In his introduction to the German edition of the Hoess memoirs, Martin Broszat rightly notes how, even after, Hoess fancies himself a decent person deeply moved by the murder of children—as if he had not himself ordered the murders! Broszat can find no better adjective than the obviously inadequate "schizophrenic" to describe this consciousness. (*Kommandant in Auschwitz*, M. Broszat, ed. [Stuttgart: Deutsche Verlags-Anstalt, 1958], pp. 17–18.)

12. The previous account is in no way opposed to the numerous investigations to the effect that not all Germans were Nazis, not all Nazis S.S. men, not all S.S. men murderers, and that the whole Reich contained within itself different and even conflicting fiefdoms. However, if anything ever was, the Reich was a whole that was more than the sum of the parts.

If historical investigators lose sight of this truth they lose the whole.

13. See the prayer in the traditional High Holiday service: "May the righteous see and rejoice, the upright exult, and the godly thrill with delight. Iniquity shall shut its mouth, wickedness shall vanish like smoke, when Thou wilt abolish the rule of tyranny on earth."

14. Elie Wiesel, *Night* (New York: Avon, 1969), p. 44.

15. This question will dominate the remainder of this essay. Except for the epilogue, the essay does not consider possibilities that may be found ouside Jewish existence, or those that may be found within Jewish existence for religious Jews who never committed themselves to words such as those just quoted, for those who, having done so, remained silent thereafter, or for those who live outside the sphere of Jewish religiosity.

16. My view of Midrash is summarized in a rather doctrinaire fashion because I have stated and defended it in many places over the years; see my *Quest For Past And Future* (Boston: Beacon, 1970), *passim*, and especially *God's Presence in History* (New York: Harper Torchbook, 1973), ch. 1.

17. *Night*, pp. 75 ff.

18. The above two judgments are made with a view to guilt and innocence in the context of social structures. The issue "individual vs. collective guilt (or innocence)" becomes spurious when it is abused in order to ignore these structures and their moral implications.

19. Wiesel, *The Gates of the Forest* (New York: Holt, Rinehart & Winston, 1966), p. 225.

20. Ibid.

21. See my *God's Presence in History*, ch. 3.

22. *The Gates of the Forest*, p. 225.

23. Perhaps the foremost aim of Kierkegaard's literary production is to wrestle with this last temptation. Still more instructive is Hegel's critique (in his *Phenomenology*) of the "beautiful soul's" withdrawal into inwardness, for in Hegel's account it is unambiguous that the withdrawal is from political action, and that its unadmitted purpose is to avoid the necessity of dirtying its hands.

24. Wiesel, *A Beggar in Jerusalem* (New York: Random House, 1970), pp. 61 ff.

25. *The Gay Science* #125.

26. Friedrich Nietzsche, *Zarathustra*, end of part I. While significantly the earlier passage speaks of the death of God, the present one asserts the death of "all gods." Hegel—who preceded Nietzsche in both assertions— let the death of all gods happen in the Roman pantheon, with the consequence that the event did not encompass God, while asserting the death

of God within the Christian realm, where it was followed by a resurrection. Hegel was unable to place Jewish existence into either of these contexts.

27. *Zarathustra*, part I, section 5.

28. See my *God's Presence in History*, chapter 3. The reader who wonders why this writer's second set of reflections on the work of Elie Wiesel, like his first, implicates thoughts by Nietzsche may be assured that this is not accidental. In both cases there is a shared anguish—in the first, concerning the fate of God, in the second, concerning the fate of man. And in both cases there is a need to confront Nietzsche's post-Protestant view of the anguish with a Jewish view—a need that after the Holocaust brooks no compromise.

29. See Konrad Kellen, "Seven Beauties: Auschwitz—The Ultimate Joke?" *Midstream*, Oct. 1976, pp. 59–66. This brilliant essay is a review not only of Lena Wertmuller's movie *Seven Beauties* but also of the reception it has received by the critics. Kellen writes:

> Wertmuller uses the agony of Auschwitz not just as backdrop for some depraved and ridiculous sexual fantasy, but as a joke. This is something new, surpassing in intellectual and moral depravity all that "entertainers" have done so far. Even the Nazis did not treat the extermination camps as a joke. On visiting Auschwitz, Heinrich Himmler, inhuman though he was, became ill; but not Wertmuller or her giggling, guffawing audiences throughout the Western civilized world. (p. 59)

30. Kellen's article gives numerous examples of critics, Jewish as well as non-Jewish, who found (or pretended to have found) the Wertmuller Auschwitz-as-fun "liberating." Why liberating? Because, Kellen replies, the people in question never rejected Nazism viscerally, as a "blemish on the entire human race." One need hardly add that this answer only begins a much-needed inquiry into this kind of "liberation."

### Sherwin: Wiesel's Midrash

References to Wiesel's work have been abbreviated to conserve space and repetition. These abbreviations are as follows (only hard-cover edition references are offered):

N—*Night* (New York: Hill and Wang, 1970).

D—*Dawn* (New York: Hill and Wang, 1961).

A—*The Accident* (New York: Hill and Wang, 1962).

T—*The Town Beyond the Wall* (New York: Holt, Rinehart, Winston, 1964).

G—*The Gates of the Forest* (New York: Holt, Rinehart, Winston, 1966).

J—*The Jews of Silence* (New York: Holt, Rinehart, Winston, 1966).

L—*Legends of Our Time* (New York: Holt, Rinehart, Winston, 1968).
B—A *Beggar in Jerusalem* (New York: Random House, 1970).
OGA—*One Generation After* (New York: Random House, 1970).
S—*Souls on Fire* (New York: Random House, 1972).
O—*The Oath* (New York: Random House, 1973).
AM—*Ani Maamin* (New York: Random House, 1973).
M—*Zalmen, or the Madness of God* (New York: Random House, 1974).
MG—*Messengers of God* (New York: Random House, 1976).

1. Emil Fackenheim, *God's Presence in History* (New York: New York University Press, 1970), p. 20.
2. Abraham J. Heschel, *The Insecurity of Freedom* (New York: Farrar, Straus, 1966), pp. 115–27.
3. On Wiesel's "story" in particular, see Robert McAfee Brown, "My Story and 'The Story,' " *Theology Today*, Fall 1975, pp. 166–73, esp. 168–73. See also Sam Keen, *To a Dancing God* (New York: Harper and Row, 1970), pp. 82–106; Sallie M. TeSelle, "Parable, Metaphor and Theology," *Journal of the American Academy of Religion* (1974) 42: 630–46.
4. MG, xi, xii, xiii.
5. O, 186.
6. AM, 17.
7. MG, 6.
8. MG, 95; also see O, 117, AM, 33.
9. MG, 197; 211, 234; 112; 138; xiv.
10. *Berahot* 7a.
11. "Useless Prayers, useless tears. The intercession has done no good. God has closed his eyes and let it all happen." Wiesel, "The Last Return," *Commentary*, March 1965.
12. *Taanit* 19a, 23a.
13. *Hullin* 7b, *Sanhedrin* 47a, *II Kings* 13.
14. *Hagiga* 14b–15a. Milton Steinberg, in his novel, *As a Driven Leaf* (New York: Behrmann House, 1939), a fictional biography of Aher, suggests the apparently meaningless death of R. Meir's sons as the impetus for Aher's apostasy. The source for this account of the deaths seems to be *Midrash Mishle* 3:10 (Buber ed. 496–50a) in Steinberg, pp. 130–34.
15. S, 111.
16. *Midrash on Psalms* 77:1.
17. *Moed Kattan* 16b.
18. *Mekhilta de Rabbi Ishmael*, ed. Horowitz and Rabin, p. 142.
19. G, 33.

20. Cf. Eliezer Berkovits, Emil Fackenheim, etc.
21. *Sabbath* 55a.
22. *Sabbath* 88a.
23. In Glatstein's poem "The Dead do Not Praise God"; B, 200.
24. O, 145; B, 116.
25. AM, 35.
26. In Wiesel, see S, 230; B, 73. For the idea that God is a person in the law, see Moshe Silberg, "Law and Morals in Jewish Jurisprudence," *Harvard Law Review* (1961) 75: 309–11; *Talmudic Law and the Modern State*, trans. B. Z. Bokser (New York: Burning Bush Press, 1973), pp. 1–2.
27. S, 47; AM, 55–56; G, 197; man as witness for God: O, 188.
28. *Genesis Rabbah* 6:3; see Abraham Heschel, *Theology of Ancient Judaism* (Hebrew) (London: Soncino, 1962), Vol. I, pp. 87–92.
29. The entire present discussion of Wiesel's relationship to Jewish tradition, specifically to the covenant, implicitly challenges Michael Berenbaum's interpretation of Wiesel in general and specifically with regard to Wiesel's notion of the covenant. In Berenbaum's view Wiesel's works may be considered a Midrash on the Holocaust, pregnant with theological meaning, but one that "demonstrates the incompatibility of previous Midrashic traditions with the post-Holocaust world." The present discussion rejects this notion by attempting to demonstrate that Wiesel's Midrash is closely akin to the more "radical" Midrashim, written in response to past tragedies and traumas. See Berenbaum, "Elie Wiesel and Contemporary Jewish Theology," *Conservative Judaism* (1976) 30:3, pp. 19–39. For further elucidation regarding my views on Wiesel's relationship to Jewish tradition, see my articles: "Elie Wiesel and Jewish Theology," *Judaism* (1969) 18: 39–53. "Elie Wiesel On Madness," *Central Conference of American Rabbis Journal* (1972) 19:3, pp. 24–33. "Jewish Messianism and Elie Wiesel," in B. Sherwin, ed., *Perspectives in Jewish Learning—Volume Five* (Chicago: Spertus College Press, 1973), pp. 48–60.
30. *Midrash on Psalms* 10:3.
31. Rashi to Psalms 44:10; probably quoting *Midrash on Psalms* 78:7.
32. *Genesis Rabbah* 54:1.
33. T, 47–48, 149; D, 66; N, 73.
34. A, 72; N, 16.
35. See *Hagiga* 14b.
36. A, 11; T, "motto"; N, 73; A, 116.
37. G, 134, 190; N, 73; T, 165.

38. See OGA, 68.

39. *Menahot* 29b; MG, 175.

40. André Neher, "A Reflection on the Silence of God," *Judaism* (1967) 16:436.

41. *Midrash on Psalms* 14:6, 121:3; see also 29:1.

42. *Pesikta Rabbati* 28:1.

43. *Midrash on Psalms* 121:3.

44. AM, 103. At the very end of *Ani Maamin*, God speaks two words—*Nitzhuni Banai*—my children have defeated me. (AM, 105; see also MG, 93). The patriarchs have broken the divine silence. They have aroused divine compassion. They have brought the creator closer to his creation. Wiesel's obvious reference is to a famous talmudic story where these words appear. (*Baba Metzia* 59b.) But Wiesel may be making reference to a later Midrash that is more relevant to confronting tragedy and trauma. According to this Midrash, God's victories are His defeats: "The Holy One, blessed be He, says—when I win I lose, and when I lose I win. I won out over the destruction during the Flood and I lost, for I had to destroy that generation . . ." (*Pesikta Rabbati* 40:1).

45. Sidney Hook, *From Hegel to Marx* (Ann Arbor, Michigan: University of Michigan paperbacks, 1962), p. 36.

46. Zeev Eshkoli, *Tenuath Ha Meshihiyuth B'Yisrael* (Hebrew) (Jerusalem: Mosad Bialik, 1952), p. 280; Abraham Heschel, *Israel: Echo of Eternity* (New York: Farrar, Straus, 1969), p. 159.

47. See, for example, *Shaar Maamarey Rashbi*, "Pekuday," 34:71; *Shaar Ha Pesukim*, "Genesis," 3:4.

48. See Meir ibn Gabbai. *Avodath Ha Kodesh*, "Helek Ha Avodah," Chapter 38; see *Numbers Rabbah* 13:12.

49. Gershom Scholem, *The Messianic Idea in Judaism* (New York: Schocken, 1971), p. 47; *Shabbtai Zevi* (Hebrew) (Jerusalem: Am Oved), Volume I, p. 37; Isaiah Tishbi, *Torath Ha Ra v' ha Klipoth b' Kabalath Ha Ari* (Hebrew) (Jerusalem, 1963), pp. 134 ff.

50. Scholem, *The Messianic Idea*, pp. 186ff.; *Major Trends in Jewish Mysticism* (New York: Schocken, 1941), chapter six.

51. T, 41; S, 33, 198. See Louis Jacobs, "The Doctrine of the 'Divine Spark in Man' in Jewish Sources," in *Studies in Rationalism, Judaism and Universalism*, ed. R. Loewe (London: Routledge and Kegan Paul, 1966), pp. 98ff.

Wiesel's lack of a careful distinction between the divine and the human sparks is also expressed in the fact that the Hebrew word for God—*El*—forms part of the names of each of his major figures—*Eliezer, Elisha,*

Gabriel, Kathriel, Michael. Man's redemptive capabilities draw from the divine element within him. The Kabbalists, beginning with the sixteenth century, stressed the divine element in man. No longer intimidated by Christian polemics, they asserted the possibility of a divine "part" within man. The great Jewish mystic of sixteenth-century Prague, Judah Loew (Maharal), even asserted the possibility of the incarnation of God and man in the personage of Moses, the redeemer of Israel from Egypt. Loew calls Moses the man-God; see his *Tiferet Yisrael*, chapter 21. Hence, Wiesel's messianism is not humanistic but Kabbalistic. One should read Wiesel's work, specifically *Beggar*, in Kabbalistic terms.

In Kabbalistic parlance, certain personalities symbolize various *sefirot* or divine emanations. References to these personalities are to be read on two levels: literal and symbolic. In *Beggar* Kathriel represents the upper emanation *Kether*, David the emanation *Tiferet*, and Malkah the lowest emanation, the female aspect of God—*Malkut* or the *Shekinah*. Thus, Kathriel and David's relationship with Malkah has not only a human but also a divine referrent. When union occurs between the human couple, it effects a union in the divine realm of the *sefirot*. Redemptive acts below—on the human sphere—reflect above into the divine realm. *Beggar* is therefore not only a novel but a modern attempt at Kabbalistic discourse.

52. T, 10, 135.

53. J, 4, 94; G, 225.

54. A, 42.

55. T, 49. Despite Wiesel's restatement of notions rooted in Jewish mystical messianism, some commentators on Wiesel's Midrash claim that his story has eliminated the Messianic hope from the Jewish story. Some critics claim that Wiesel "asserts that it is too late for the Messiah," that he rejects the Messianic advent. (Fackenheim, *God's Presence in History*, pp. 88, 78.) Yet Wiesel does not reject the Messianic idea. While he does not eliminate the idea of the individual Messiah, he stresses the Lurianic notion of a collective Messiah over the role of an individual Messiah. The same text that has been used to illustrate Wiesel's rejection of the Messiah can be used to validate his opting for a collective Messiah. Wiesel writes: "The Messiah is not coming. He's not coming because he has already come. This is unknown, but he is neither at the gates of Rome nor in heaven. Everybody is wrong. The Messiah is everywhere. . . . The Messiah, he used to say, is that which makes man more human, which takes the element of pride out of generosity, which stretches his soul toward others. . . . We shall be honest and humble and strong, and then he will come, he will come every day, thousands of times every day. He will have no face, because he will have a thousand faces. The Messiah isn't one man,

Clara, he's all men. As long as there are men there will be a Messiah."
(G, 32–33, 42–43; G, 225; S, 189).
Prophetic literature contains both notions, an individual as well as
a collective Messiah. Rabbinic literature strongly opts for an individual
Messiah. See sources noted in Joseph Klausner, trans. W. R. Stinespring,
*The Messianic Idea in Israel* (New York: Macmillan, 1955), pp. 214,
217; Solomon Schechter, *Some Aspects of Rabbinic Theology* (New
York: Schocken, 1961), p. 101, n. 2; Steven Schwarzschild, "The Personal Messiah," *Judaism* 5:2, pp. 123–35. On the question of Wiesel's
relationship to classical Jewish messianism, see my aforementioned essay
(n. 29) "Jewish Messianism and Elie Wiesel."

56. See OGA, 165–75.
57. John Hick, *Evil and the God of Love* (New York: Harper and
Row, 1966), p. 371.
58. L, 6; see OGA, 43.
59. OGA, 67; see OGA 11, 257.
60. *Avodah Zara* 18a.
61. *Taanit* 29a; see also *Avot d'R. Nathan* ch. 4; II Barukh 10:18;
*Leviticus Rabbah* 19:6. Compare OGA, 44.
62. S, 259.

### Ezrahi: The Holocaust Writer and the Lamentation Tradition

1. See the novels of Ilona Karmel, Anna Langfus, Zdena Berger,
Elżbieta Ettinger, Michel del Castillo, Ladislav Fuks, and Arnošt Lustig
for examples of the struggle to maintain the integrity of the self as part of
the struggle for survival, and the fiction of Edgar Hilsenrath and Tadeusz
Borowski for explorations of degrees of disintegration of the self and
submission to the concentrationary system.
2. Adolf Rudnicki, "Ascent to Heaven," in *Ascent to Heaven*, trans.
H. C. Stevens (London: Dennis Dobson Ltd., 1951), p. 23.
3. Maurice Samuel, "The Story that Must Build Itself," in *Mid-
Century*, ed. Harold U. Ribalow (New York: The Beechhurst Press,
1955), p. 233.
4. W. Rabi, "Vingt Ans de Littérature," in *D'Auschwitz à Israel*:
*Vingt Ans Après la Libération*, ed. Isaac Schneersohn (Paris, 1968), p.
361.
5. Elie Wiesel, *One Generation After*, trans. from the French by
Lily Edelman and the author (London: Weidenfeld and Nicolson, 1970),
p. 82.

6. Manès Sperber, . . .*Than a Tear in the Sea,* trans. from the French by Constantine Fitzgibbon (New York: Bergen Belsen Memorial Press, 1967), p. 9.

7. Sachs's play *Eli* is subtitled "Ein Mysterienspiel vom Leiden Israels." In *O the Chimneys* (New York: Farrar, Straus and Giroux, 1967).

8. The "selihoth" are prayers recited during the month of Elul and variations on the dirge "El Maleh Rahamim." The "kinah" was originally recited when an important person had died (Jer. 22:18, Gen. 23:2); later it was recited over a whole community that had suffered catastrophe. The Book of Lamentations is referred to in rabbinic literature as "kinoth." The Talmud preserved many of the early kinoth. The first collection of kinoth, in the Ashkenazic tradition, was published in 1585. Since then many versions have been published. In 1923 Shimeon Bernfeld published the three-volume Hebrew anthology *Sefer HaDemaoth* (The Book of Tears), which included representative stories and poems generated by the major catastrophes that Jews had endured since the days of Antiochus Epiphanes. As an aside, one may note the rather intense interest in martyrology among German Jewish scholars in the 1920s and 1930s, especially when compared to the relative lack of interest by American Jewish scholars in the subject. Bernfeld strikes an ominous note when he writes, in the introduction to his work, "we are fearful that what will come after us will be more terrible than that which we have witnessed" (*Sefer HaDemaoth,* Vol. I [Berlin: Eschkol Publishers, 1923], p. 77).

9. The historiographical function of the Midrash as well as of the kinah can be discerned even in the etymology of the word "Midrash," which, as translated in the Septuagint, suggests "an account," "the result of inquiry . . . of the events of the time" (Moshe D. Herr, "Midrash," *Encyclopedia Judaica,* Vol. 11, p. 1508).

10. Simon Dubnow, in his monumental *History of the Jewish People,* attests to the fact that "the Middle Ages have bequeathed us no systematic chronography; our horrifying tragedies have found no competent annalists" (quoted in Jacob Lestschinsky, "For a Survey of the Jewish Tragedy," *The Chicago Forum,* Vol. 4, No. 3 [Spring, 1946], p. 151). A few fledgling historians did overcome this resistance to historiography. But for the most part they too shared the poet's vocabulary and sacred perspective on history (see, for example, *Shevet Yehuda, Emek HaBachah,* and *Yeven Metzulah,* accounts of Jewish persecution written in the sixteenth and seventeenth centuries). It was not until the pogroms of 1903–1905 in Russia that thorough documentation provided reliable sources for secular historical evaluation of collective Jewish catastrophe.

11. A glance at some of the discussions among medieval rabbis and scholars on the subject reveals the extent to which the aversion toward historiography was a matter of principle, not of oversight. Chronicles of the deeds of men may, it is argued, be enlightening for the Gentiles, "who have not seen the light of Torah and must stumble through the darkness of human records" to find some sparks of virtue after which they may pattern their lives (Azaria Min HaAdumim, *Meor Einayim*, ed. Yitzhak Ben-Ya'acov, Vol. I [Vilna: n.p., 1863], p. 254).

12. This structure and formulaic phrases like "shever bat-ami" ("disaster [has befallen] my people"–Jer. 14:17 and Lam. 2:14) appear in a representative poem lamenting the auto-da-fé of twenty-four Marranos in the Papal city of Ancona in 1556 ("The Heavens are Desolate," by Shlomo Hazan Yatzav, in Bernfeld, *Sefer HaDemaoth*, Vol. II, pp. 347–50; see also "There is No King and No Governor in Israel," Ibid., Vol. III, pp. 169–72).

13. "The Heavens are Desolate," Ibid., Vol. II, p. 347.

14. "Listen All Ye Nations, to my Grief," poem by David Yehuda ben David ibn Yechiah lamenting the massacre of Spanish and Portuguese Jews, Bernfeld, Vol. II, p. 219.

15. Selihah prayer by R. Shabbetai Cohen Ba'al Hashah commemorating the victims of Chmielnicki, in Bernfeld, Vol. III, p. 172.

16. In devising forms of desecration of Scriptures, the Nazis, it turns out, were not always original; a seventeenth-century Italian poet, recounting the brutal acts committed by Chmielnicki's Cossacks, describes how "the Torah came into their hands / They made of it shoes for the soles of their feet" ("May the Heart of Man be Sickened . . ." by R. Ya'acov Bar Moshe Halevi, in Bernfeld, Vol. III, p. 167). The desecration of the Holy Scrolls was a recurrent theme in the most impassioned lamentations of the Middle Ages.

17. One example of the priority of "documentation" over artistic quality is a kinah on the destruction of Spanish Jewry; "Adat kodesh Barzelona / Harugei herev shmena" (a liberal English equivalent might be: "The holy community of Barcelona / Its dying let out a great moan–ah!"). ("I will Keen and Wail Bitterly," anonymous, in Bernfeld, Vol. II, p. 224.)

18. A. M. Haberman, ed., *Sefer Gezeroth Ashkenaz V'Tzarefat* (Jerusalem: Tarshish Books, 1946), p. x.

19. The Spanish paytanim were among the most distinguished; as Israel Zinberg has put it, whereas "in other lands . . . it was the muses of terror and misfortune that inspired lamentations and religious poems," in Spain the paytanim were often also blessed with considerable poetic

talent (A *History of Jewish Literature*, trans. and ed. Bernard Martin [Cleveland: The Press of Case Western Reserve, 1972], Vol. II, p. 24).

20. In this respect, as in others, the so-called historical chronicles served the same purpose in prose. Nathan Hanover elucidates this in his introduction to *Yeven Metzulah* (The Abyss of Despair), which was perhaps the most significant history of Jewish persecution, published in 1652: "I recorded all the major and minor decrees and persecutions; also the days on which those cruelties occurred, so that everyone might be able to calculate the day on which his kin died, and observe the memorial properly" (trans. from the Hebrew by Abraham J. Mesch [New York: Bloch Publishing Company, 1950], p. 25).

21. Selihah prayer by R. Shabbetai Cohen Ba'al Hashah, in Bernfeld, Vol. III, p. 172. The same was true of the kinoth written in commemoration of the martyrs of Ancona, which were recited for generations thereafter as part of the Tisha B'Av service in the local community.

22. See Second Book of Maccabees, 6:21-7:41; Lamentations Rabbah, I:16; and a Sephardic kinah for Tisha B'av in Bernfeld, Vol. I, pp. 91–95. For a discussion of the versions of this legend in the contemporary martyrological literature, see Gershon David Cohen, "Ma'aseh Hanna v'Shivat Baneha b'Sifrut HaIvrit," in the *Mordecai Kaplan Jubilee Volume*, Hebrew section (New York: Jewish Theological Seminary of America, 1953), pp. 109–22.

23. For a discussion of the general climate of consensus out of which the paytan wrote, see Itzhak Be'er's introduction to Haberman, ed., *Sefer Gezerot Ashkenaz V'Tzarefat*, pp. 1-7.

24. "Israel neglected the good; her enemies will pursue her until the debt is paid" ("There is no King or Governor in Israel," in Bernfeld, Vol. III, p. 101). In repeated Midrashim on the destruction of the Temple the disaster is attributed to the unworthiness of and the fraternal strife among the Jews themselves: "Had you been worthy, you would be dwelling in Jerusalem, uttering songs and praises to the Holy One, Blessed be He; but now that you are unworthy, you are exiled to Babylon where you utter lamentations. Alas!" (Proem XIX to *Midrash Rabbah: Lamentations*, trans. and ed. H. Freedman and Maurice Simon [London: Soncino Press, 1939], p. 24.)

25. See again "The Heavens are Desolate," a lamentation by Shlomo Hazan Yatzav on the burning of twenty-four Marranos in Ancona in the sixteenth century:

> "Oh God, Lord of mercy and compassion,
> Have mercy on the remnant of Israel

Through the merit of these martyrs we plead
. . . that you will build the House of Ariel"

(Bernfeld, Vol. II, p. 350).

26. See, for example, the phrase, "who is like unto Thee among the speechless, O God, / Who can be compared with Thee in Thy silence?" in the twelfth-century kinah by Menahem ben Jacob ("Allelai Li," published in *Kovetz Al Yad* and quoted in Zinberg, *A History of Jewish Literature*, Vol. II, p. 26). The antecedents of this inversion ("who is like unto Thee among the *mighty*"—*elim*—into "who is like unto Thee among the *speechless*"—*ilmim*) are Tannaitic (see Mechilta de-Reb Ishmael). For a further elaboration of this theme in Midrashic literature, see the essay by Byron Sherwin, "Wiesel's Midrash: The Writings of Elie Wiesel and Their Relationship to Jewish Tradition," in this volume.

27. Haberman, intro. to *Sefer Gezeroth Ashkenaz V'Tzarefat*, p. x.

28. Bialik's struggle is reflected in numerous poems such as the following:

"My soul bowed down to the dust
Under the burden of your love . . .
Not a poet, nor a prophet,
But a hewer of wood am I"

("Shaha Nafshi" [My Soul Bowed Down], in *Kol Kitvei Bialik* [Tel Aviv: Dvir Publishers, 1971], p. 61).

29. See "HaMatmid" (the Scholar) and "B'Ir Haharegah" (In the City of the Slaughter) in Ibid., pp. 89, 98.

30. See "Achen Hatzir Ha'Am" (Surely the People is Grass) and "Lifnei Aron HaSefarim" (In Front of the Bookcase) as well as "Al HaShehitah" (On the Slaughter) in Ibid., pp. 17–18, 54–55, 41.

31. See "B'Ir Haharegah," especially the scene in which the women are raped while their men cower in dark corners, watching, and then run to the rabbi to inquire whether they are allowed to sleep with their defiled wives (Ibid., pp. 95 ff.).

32. See, for example, his invocation of the ritual act of animal slaughter in the context of human massacre—an inversion that is an indictment of the divine powers that would countenance such slaughter ("Al Hashehitah," in Ibid., p. 41).

33. *The Warsaw Diary of Chaim Kaplan* (originally published as *The Scroll of Agony*), trans. and ed. Abraham I. Katsh (New York: Collier Books, 1973), p. 79.

34. Quoted by Leon Poliakov in *Harvest of Hate* (London: Elek Books, 1956), pp. 232–33.

35. See Louis Ginzberg, *Legends of the Jews*, for a recounting of this Midrash (Philadelphia: Jewish Publication Society, 1946), Vol. IV, pp. 303 ff.

36. Yitzhak Katzenelson, "Lieder fun Kelt," from *Dos Lied fun Oisgehargetn Yiddishn Folk*, in *Lieder fun Hurbn*, ed. Kadia Maladowska (Tel Aviv: I. L. Peretz, 1962), p. 40.

37. Aharon Zeitlin, "Ani Ma'amin," in *Lieder fun Hurbn*, p. 190.

38. Ya'acov Glatstein, "Ohn Yiddn," in Ibid., p. 96.

39. Quoted by Hillel Barzel in his introduction to *HaShoah B'shira Halvrit*, ed. Natan Gross (Tel Aviv: HaKibbutz Hameuhad, 1974), p. 7.

40. Robert Alter, "A Poet of the Holocaust," *Commentary*, November 1973, p. 57; see also Alter's "Confronting the Holocaust," in *After the Tradition: Essays in Modern Jewish Writing* (New York: E. P. Dutton & Co., Inc., 1971), p. 164.

41. From a speech delivered in San Francisco, January 20, 1972. See, for example, "Ahoti K'tana" (My Little Sister), trans. Shirley Kaufman and Nurit Orchan, in *Abba Kovner and Nelly Sachs: Selected Poems* (Middlesex: Penguin Books, 1971). Even in the fiction of a writer like Aharon Appelfeld, an unexpected dialectic emerges between traditional and alternative forms of confronting the Holocaust; see his story, "K'Ishon Ha'Ayin" (The Apple of his Eye) in the collection of his short stories, *K'Meah Eydim* (Tel Aviv: HaKibbutz HaMeuhad, 1974).

42. *Un di Velt Hot Geshvign*, 1956.

43. On stylistic grounds, Wiesel's occasional lapses into a kind of staccato, journalistic realism are startlingly intrusive (see, for example, *The Town Beyond the Wall*, trans. from the French by Stephen Becker [New York: Avon Books, 1964], p. 73; *The Oath*, trans. from the French by Marion Wiesel [New York: Random House, 1973], p. 11; and *A Beggar in Jerusalem*, trans. from the French by Lily Edelman and the author [New York: Random House, 1970], p. 170). On the other hand, his attempts to embrace and commemorate a world that was lost by typologizing and duplicating its characters, often divested of specificity, occasionally lead him to sacrifice the "histoire" to the legend. And just as an overdose of realism can dispel the aura of legend, so an attenuation of realism can betray the *ground* of legend (see, for example, "Dialogues I" in *One Generation After*, pp. 31–32).

44. *One Generation After*, p. 166.

45. See, for example, the concluding stanza of U. Z. Greenberg's "Keter Kinah l'Chol Beit Yisrael," which places Israel's martyrdom within

a normative framework in which those who follow the "laws" attain the "kingdom"; it is "because of them," the martyrs, that their heirs have inherited the "Land" (p. 62).

46. See *Lamentations Rabbah*, Proem XXIV.

47. Wiesel, *Ani Maamin: A Song Lost and Found Again*, trans. from the French by Marion Wiesel (New York: Random House, 1973), pp. 93, 97, 103, 105.

48. Wiesel, *Night*, trans. from the French by Stella Rodway (New York: Hill and Wang, 1960), p. 47.

49. *Ani Maamin*, p. 33.

50. Rabbi Isaac Nissenbaum, one of the leaders of Polish Jewry, is reported to have told his people: "This is a time of *kiddush ha-hayyim*, the sanctification of life, and not for *kiddush ha-Shem*, the holiness of martyrdom. Previously the Jew's enemy sought his soul and the Jew sacrificed his body in martyrdom; now the oppressor demands the Jew's body and the Jew is obliged therefore to defend it, to preserve his life." (Quoted by Shaul Esh, "The Dignity of the Destroyed," *Judaism*, Vol. XI, No. 2, pp. 106–107.)

51. Sperber, . . . *Than a Tear in the Sea*, p. 89.

52. Sachs, *Eli*, in *O the Chimneys*, pp. 368–70.

53. Sachs, "O the Chimneys," in Ibid., p. 3.

54. *Lamentations Rabbah*, proem XXXIV, p. 64.

55. Sachs, "Landscape of Screams," in *O the Chimneys*, pp. 127, 129.

56. Sachs, "Numbers," in Ibid., p. 71.

57. Sachs, "But Who Emptied Your Shoes of Sand," in Ibid., p. 9.

58. Paul Celan, "There was Earth in Them," in *Speech-Grille and Selected Poems*, trans. from the German by Joachim Neugrochel (New York: E. P. Dutton & Co., Inc., 1971), p. 173.

59. Celan, "Psalm," in Ibid., p. 183.

60. Celan, "Zürich, Zum Storchen," in Ibid., p. 179.

61. Celan, "Todesfuge," trans. Karl S. Weimar, in "Paul Celan's 'Todesfuge,' Translation and Interpretation," *PMLA*, Vol. 89, No. 1 (Jan., 1974), p. 85.

62. André Schwarz-Bart, *The Last of the Just*, trans. Stephen Becker (London: Secker & Warburg, 1961).

## Neher: Shaddai: The God of the Broken Arch

1. See André Neher, "Job, the Biblical Man," *Judaism*, Winter 1964; "The Motif of Job in Modern Literature," *Dor-le-Dor*, Fall 1974; *L'Exil de la Parole, du silence biblique au silence d'Auschwitz* (Paris: Ed.

du Seuil, 1970), with special reference to the meaning of silence in Elie Wiesel's Holocaust writings.

## Eckardt: The Recantation of the Covenant?

1. Elie Wiesel, A *Beggar in Jerusalem*, translated from the French by Lily Edelman and the author (New York: Random House, 1970), p. 200.

2. At the end of the novel Wiesel dates the work "Jerusalem 1967—Christiansted 1968."

3. A. Roy Eckardt, *Your People, My People: The Meeting of Jews and Christians* (New York: Quadrangle/The New York Times Book Company, 1974), p. 228. This wording is closer to Jacob Glatstein's affirmation in a poem "The Dead Do Not Praise God," but Wiesel's phrasing appears to echo Glatstein.

4. *A Beggar in Jerusalem*, p. 30.

5. In attendance at our conference was a good friend who is a Christian. After hearing my paper, she observed to me that the absence in it of any real reference to the terrible Christian treatment of Jews as a possible basis for the recantation of the covenant of demand could be received by Jewish hearers in the following way: We are confronted here by one more typical Christian case of a readiness to find evil everywhere but within the Christian community. My friend's comment points up a substantial moral fault in my presentation. But had I acted to remedy this fault in revising the paper for publication, I would have hidden, culpably, the unfortunate truth about the original presentation. I can only point now to the element of irony in the situation. Having assailed Christian responsibility for anti-Semitism and the Holocaust over a period of years, I had early decided to omit this element from my paper. My intent was—doubtless with gratuitous pridefulness—to forestall the reaction, "Here is that Eckardt playing his same old tune once again." Perhaps the lesson here is that an ostensibly ingenuous resistance to repetitiveness and boredom can contain evil seeds within itself.

6. Jürgen Moltmann, *The Crucified God* (New York: Harper & Row, 1974), pp. 148, 151.

7. This account is adapted, with some changes, from a representation in an unpublished paper by Irving Greenberg at the International Conference on the Church Struggle and the Holocaust, Haus Rissen, Hamburg, BRD, 8-11 June 1975.

8. *A Beggar in Jerusalem*, p. 28.

9. Wiesel, *Ani Maamin: A Song Lost and Found Again*, translated by Marion Wiesel (New York: Random House, 1973), pp. 89-103.

10. A. Roy Eckardt, "Is the Holocaust Unique?" *Worldview*, XVII, 9 (September 1974), 34–35.

11. Yehuda Bauer, *They Chose Life: Jewish Resistance in the Holocaust* (New York: Institute of Human Relations, American Jewish Committee; Jerusalem: Institute of Contemporary Jewry, The Hebrew University, 1973); Yuri Suhl, editor and translator, *They Fought Back: The Story of the Jewish Resistance in Nazi Europe* (London: MacGibbon & Kee, 1968); Reuben Ainsztein, *Jewish Resistance in Nazi-Occupied Eastern Europe* (London: P. Elek, 1974).

12. Following upon our conference, the Jewish Telegraphic Agency and Herbert J. Farber Associates alleged in a news release that in my paper I personally opposed the teaching of Jewish election as a dangerous one that has led to attacks upon Jews. This was the only point they reported on my presentation. Anyone reading the foregoing phenomenological and pluralistic discussion will note the false and misrepresentative character of this published report.

13. Reinhold Niebuhr, frontispiece to *Justice and Mercy*, edited by Ursula M. Niebuhr (New York: Harper & Row, 1974).

### Berenbaum: The Additional Covenant

1. R. J. Werblowsky, "Faith, Hope, and Trust—An Analysis of the Concept of Bittachon," *Annual of Jewish Studies*, Vol. 2 (1964).

2. Unless otherwise signified, the word "Israel" refers to the people Israel rather than the state of Israel.

3. Lurianic Kabbalism dates roughly from the late sixteenth century onward. Rabbi Isaac Luria was born in 1534 in Jerusalem. At his death in 1572, he was head of the famous mystical circle of Safed. His doctrines were made known by his disciple, Rabbi Hayyim Vital.

4. Gershom Scholem, *Major Trends in Jewish Mysticism* (New York: Schocken, 1946), pp. 29–30.

5. Rabbi Scheneor Zalman of Liadi was the founder of HABAD Hasidism. He was born in 1747 and died in 1812. For a critical discussion of Scheneor Zalman's psychology, see Louis Jacobs, *Seeker of Unity* (New York: Basic Books, 1966), pp. 64–73, and specifically pp. 67–68.

6. Revealing biographical passages are found in *Souls on Fire*, *Legends of Our Time*, and *One Generation After*.

7. Elie Wiesel, "Jewish Values in the Post Holocaust Future,"

*Judaism*, Vol. 16, No. 3 (Summer 1967), pp. 281–82.

8. Emil Fackenheim, *God's Presence in History* (New York: New York University Press, 1969), pp. 3–14.

9. "Jewish Values in the Post-Holocaust Future," pp. 281, 282, 285. Italics mine.

10. This attitude of acceptance of the historical reality as God ordained is seen very clearly in Irving Rosenbaum's work *The Holocaust and Halachah* (New York: KTAV Books, 1976). Two comments of Rosenbaum are striking. He writes that the Jews who observed the Halachah were "able to face life with dignity, death with serenity—and sometimes ecstasy" (p. 8). He also writes:

> Indeed in almost all the halachik literature of the Holocaust there is hardly any attempt at questioning, let alone vindicating the justice of the Almighty. To some extent this avoidance of theodicy may be explained by the apothegm attributed to the great spiritual leader of East European Jewry, Rabbi Israel Meir Hacohen, the *Hafetz Hayyim* (d. 1933): "For the believer there are no questions; and for the unbeliever there are no answers."

Since Wiesel has emphasized the centrality of questions in Judaism and continually challenges God, it is important to remember that he is as much creating a tradition as he is reflecting one. The normative stance of the covenantal Jew was much closer to what Irving Rosenbaum described than to the Hasidic masters of *Souls on Fire*. The latter were the exception rather than the rule. See also Peter Schindler, *Responses of Hasidic Leaders and Hasidism During the Holocaust* (Ph.D. Diss., N.Y.U., 1972) for a specific understanding of the Hasidic tradition during the war.

11. For a textual analysis of *Dawn*, see Michael Berenbaum's *Elie Wiesel: Theologian of the Void* (Ph. D. Diss., Florida State University, 1975), pp. 14–22.

12. Wiesel, *Dawn* (New York: Hill and Wang, 1961), p. 19.

13. Ibid., p. 21.

14. Wiesel, *Legends of Our Time* (New York: Holt, Rinehart and Winston, 1968), pp. 181–97. In this short story entitled "Moscow Revisited," Wiesel's mood and tone differ sharply from *The Jews of Silence* (New York: Holt, Rinehart and Winston, 1966).

15. He captures this mood particularly in *A Beggar in Jerusalem* but also in two short stories in *One Generation After*, one entitled "Motta Gur" and the other "Postwar 1967."

16. "Prayer for the New Moon" in the traditional liturgy.

17. Shevuot 39a, see also *Leviticus Rabbah* 1:10 and *Song of Songs Rabbah* 2:3.

18. Wiesel, *Souls on Fire* (New York: Random House, 1972), p. 20.

19. This is the language with which the additional service for the three pilgrimage festivals begins.

20. As I rewrite this paper in the state of Israel, I am acutely aware of the fact that the future of the state may be determined by its ability to combat some of the demands of one strain of Jewish mythic consciousness as well as by its ability to create a new Jewish mythic consciousness.

21. Wiesel, *One Generation After* (New York: Random House, 1970), p. 25.

22. *Souls on Fire*, p. 111. A similar quote is found in *One Generation After*, p. 215.

23. Albert Camus, *The Rebel* (New York: Vintage, 1956), p. 33.

24. Wiesel, *The Oath* (New York: Random House, 1973), p. 69.

25. Ibid., p. 138.

26. Viktor Frankl, *Man's Search for Meaning* (Boston: Beacon Press, 1959), pp. 70-79. See also Ezrahi, this volume.

27. Wiesel, *Night* (New York: Hill and Wang, 1960), pp. 117–24.

28. Wiesel, "A Plea for the Survivors," in *Shma*, No. 100 (Feb. 1976), p. 2.

29. *One Generation After*, pp. 3–4.

30. Morris Silverman, trans., *Passover Haggadah* (Hartford: Prayer Book Press, 1959), p. 28.

31. Wiesel, *The Jews of Silence* (New York: Holt, Rinehart, and Winston, 1966), p. 28.

32. The response of life was also one of the earliest and most basic responses of the Israeli Jews to the Holocaust. The final line in so many memorial prayers for the victims of the Holocaust reads "in their death they command us to live."

33. Wiesel, *The Jews of Silence*, p. 28.

34. Wiesel, *Messengers of God* (New York: Random House, 1976), p. 201.

35. Wiesel, *Zalmen, or the Madness of God* (New York: Random House, 1974), p. 53.

36. "Jewish Values in the Post-Holocaust Future," p. 299.

37. Ibid., p. 299.

38. *Souls on Fire*, p. 31.

39. *One Generation After*, p. 170.

40. *Souls on Fire*, p. 143.

41. Ronald Sanders, "Israel at 25," *Midstream*, Vol. XIX, No. 6 (June/July 1973), p. 68.

42. *Ethics of the Fathers*, 2: 6.

### Eitinger: On Being a Psychiatrist and a Survivor

1. Bettelheim, B. (1943): Individual and mass behaviour in extreme situations. J. Abnorm. (soc.) Psychol. 38, 417–52.
2. Bettelheim, B. (1960): The Informed Heart, The Free Press, Chicago.
3. Eitinger, L. (1958): Psykiatriske undersøkelser blant flyktninger i Norge. Universitetsforlaget, Oslo.
4. Eitinger, L. (1960a): The symptomatology of mental disease among refugees in Norway. J. Ment. Sc. 106, 947–66.
5. Eitinger, L. (1960b): A clinical and social psychiatric investigation of a "hard-core" refugee transport in Norway. Internat. J. Soc. Psychiat. 5, 261-275.
6. Eitinger, L. (1961): Pathology of the concentration camp syndrome. Arch. Gen. Psychiat. 5, 371–79.
7. Eitinger, L. (1964): Concentration camp survivors in Norway and Israel. Oslo University Press, Oslo. (Martinus Nijhoff, The Hague, 1972.)
8. Eitinger, L. & Askevold, F. (1968): In Strøm: Norwegian concentration camp survivors. Oslo University Press, Oslo.
9. Eitinger, L. (1971): Organic and psychosomatic aftereffects of concentration camp survivors. Internat. Psychiat. Clinics, 8: 205–15.
10. Eitinger, L. (1973): A follow-up study of the Norwegian concentration camp survivors' mortality and morbidity. Israel Annals Psychiat. 11, 199–208.
11. Eitinger, L. & Strøm, A. (1973): Mortality and morbidity after excessive stress. Universitetsforlaget, Oslo.
12. Eitinger, L. (1974): Coping with aggression. Mental Health Soc. 1, 297-301.
13. Eitinger, L. (1975): Jewish concentration camp survivors in Norway. Israel Annals Psychiat. 13, 321-334.
14. Frankl, V. E. (1959): From Death-Camp to Existentialism. Beacon Press, Boston.
15. Henderson, A. S. & Bostock, F. T. (1975): Coping behaviour: correlates of survival on a raft. Austral. New Zeal. J. Psychiat. 9, 221–23.
16. Kral, V. A. (1951): Psychiatric observations under severe chronic stress. Am. J. Psychiat. 108, 185–92.
17. Luchterhand, E. (1967): Prisoner behaviour and social system in the Nazi concentration camps. Int. J. Soc. Psychiat. 13, 245–64.
18. Lonnum, A. (1961): An analytical survey of the literature published on delayed effects of internment in concentration camps and their

possible relation to the nervous system. In: Experts' Meeting on the later effects of imprisonment and departation. Oslo 1960. W.V.F., pp. 21–53, Paris.

19. Nathan, T. S., Eitinger, L. & Winnik, H. Z. (1963): The psychiatric pathology of survivors of the Nazi-holocaust. Israel Annals Psychiat. 1, 113.

20. Niederland, W. G. (1961): The problem of the survivor. J. Hillside Hospital, 10, 233–47.

21. Strøm, A., et al. (1962): Examination of Norwegian ex-concentration-camp prisoners. J. Neuropsychiat. 4, 43–62.

22. Strøm, A. (ed.) (1968): Norwegian Concentration Camp Survivors. Universitetsforlaget, Oslo.

23. Ulstein, R. (1974): Svensketrafikken (The Traffic to Sweden). Det norske samlaget, Oslo.